The Undivided Heart

The Western Monastic Approach to Contemplation

Michael Casey

ST. BEDE'S PUBLICATIONS
Petersham, Massachusetts

Some articles in this book have been published previously and permission to reprint is gratefully acknowledged. Complete bibliographic
data is given in the Introductory Note of each article.

"Paul's Response to Corinthian Enthusiasm" appeared in *The Bible Today*,
copyright © 1977 by The Order of St. Benedict, Inc. Published by The
Liturgical Press, Collegeville, Minnesota. Used with permission.

"St. Benedict's Approach to Prayer," "Mindfulness of God in the
Monastic Tradition," "Spiritual Desire in the Gospel Homilies of St.
Gregory the Great," "The Prayer of Psalmody," "The Virtue of Patience
in Western Monastic Tradition," all appeared in *Cistercian Studies*. Used
with permission.

"Seven Principles of Lectio Divina," "Cardiomimesis," "Solitariness,"
"Consecrated Chastity," all previously published in *Tjurunga*. Used with
permission.

LIBRARY OF CONGRESS CATALOGING IN PUBLICATION DATA

Casey, Michael, monk of Tarrawarra.
    The undivided heart : the Western monastic approach to contem-
plation / Michael Casey.
        p.   cm.
    ISBN 1-879007-04-5
    1. Contemplation.   2. Monastic and religious life.   3. Spiritual
formation. I. Title.
BV5091.C7C375   1994
248.3'4--dc20   94-6259
                                                                 CIP

Published by: St. Bede's Publications
              P.O. Box 545
              Petersham, Massachusetts 01366-0545

Contents

For

Dom Kevin O'Farrell, OCSO

In gratitude

Foreword

The desire to have some experience of God is widespread. Many persons of all ages have a genuine yearning for communion with the spiritual world. The trouble is that we are never quite certain how we should invest our energies to ensure that we are moving closer to the truth and not deeper into delusion. It seems prudent, therefore, to look for guidance from those who have actually made the journey and are skilled in initiating others.

This is why we approach the great contemplative traditions: to find out something about prayer and the sort of life that facilitates its growth. We cannot always generate our own solutions because our horizons are limited. The first thing we need to learn is to look at life from a different perspective. Here the ancient spiritual masters can serve us well.

The West had a very long tradition of contemplation until it was dissipated by the onset of rationalism and the effects of the Industrial Revolution. The names of Augustine, John Cassian, Benedict, Gregory and Bernard may not be household words today, but they were well known to many generations who dedicated their lives to the search for God and found inspiration in the writings of these men. It is the tradition built around these spiritual giants that is explored in this book.

The key idea that is common to these teachers is that contemplation is possible only for those who have *puritas cordis*: an undivided heart. The act of communion with God is one which engages the whole person and calls upon all the interior energies. It can occur only when these energies are working together, when inner disharmony has been overcome and unity reigns within. Such a state is not achieved quickly but only by the grace of God and the labor of decades. It involves a radical conversion of life and a persevering will to live in accordance with the Gospel. Spiritual growth is thus seen as a matter of progressively purifying the personal center of will and knowledge, eliminating inner division and becoming more intent on seeking the one thing necessary.

It is a challenging approach which places great emphasis, in the early stages, on renewal at the level of behavior motivated by a personal sense of discipleship of Christ. It is a long-term project, less concerned with techniques for altering consciousness than with self-forgetfulness and generosity towards others. It may not be a dramatic or esoteric approach, but it continues to be effective in helping people to find God.

This is a collection of a dozen articles, written over as many years, chiefly concerned with aspects of Christian prayer as it has been understood in this western monastic tradition. Earlier I published a book which attempts to synthesize the various lines of development represented in this collection (*Towards God: The Western Tradition of Contemplation*, Melbourne: Collins Dove, 1989). Here the elements of that approach are presented as they first appeared.

There is an inherent danger of obsolescence in such a project. I have been conscious of this and tried to select articles which would have an ongoing interest. In reviewing the various pieces, I have become aware that in the past decade inclusive language has become more usual. In this and in other matters which I would today approach differently, I have left the articles as they appeared in their own time. To keep the chronological reference intact the various texts are here presented in publication sequence, although the gap between composition and printing was sometimes as much as three years. Likewise, I have resisted the temptation to update the bibliographic references. I have contented myself with correcting a number of minor errors which managed to slip unnoticed onto the printed page, and have lightly retouched a few sentences where the meaning is less clear than I had hoped.

In the introductory notes I have attempted to give some indication of the context in which each article was written, giving what I recall was my purpose in writing and mentioning similar pieces I may have done at about the same time.

The last two articles came together in 1988 and are published here for the first time. Except for one which appeared in *The Bible Today*, the other articles were first published either in *Tjurunga: An Australasian Benedictine Review* or in *Cistercian Studies*. I am grateful to the editors of these periodicals for their encouragement over the years and for their permission to reprint.

The collection is dedicated to my former abbot, Dom Kevin O'Farrell, who for nearly three decades provided me with the training, leisure and support which made writing possible.

Michael Casey, OCSO

THE UNDIVIDED HEART

Abbreviations

ASOC	Analecta Sacri Ordinis Cisterciensis
CChr	Corpus Christianorum
CChrM	Corpus Christianorum: Continuatio Mediaevalis
Coll	Conferences [of John Cassian]
COCR	Collectanea OCR, subsequently Collectanea Cisterciensia
CS	Cistercian Studies
DSp	Dictionnaire de Spiritualité
PG	Patrologia Graeca
PL	Patrologia Latina
RB	Rule of St. Benedict
RBS	Regulae Benedicti Studia
RM	Rule of the Master
SBO	Sancti Bernardi Opera
SC	Bernard of Clairvaux's Sermons on the Song of Songs
SChr	Sources Chrétiennes
ThLL	Thesaurus Linguae Latinae

Introductory Note

"Seven Principles of Lectio Divina" was first printed in *Tjurunga* 12 (1976), pp. 69-74. It was intended to highlight the distinctive nature of the monastic method of approaching the Scriptures as something more than "spiritual reading." On the one hand it aimed to present *lectio divina* as a technique of prayer, that is to say, as a means of making contact with the heart and with the God who dwells there. On the other, it implied that this practice is a necessary complement for those who spend time in quiet "objectless" meditation; it serves as a bridge between this imageless prayer and the other elements of Christian living: liturgy, the sacraments and the practice of virtue.

In the same issue of *Tjurunga* (pp. 75-84), there was a companion piece entitled "Eleven Difficulties in Reading the Fathers." This article explored the possibility of using the writings of the Church Fathers for *lectio divina*. It is somewhat less relevent today since there are considerably more resources available now than then.

Seven Principles of Lectio Divina

Experience confirms that the most ordinary cause of "dryness" or "staleness" in prayer is a defect in genuine spiritual reading. Without consistent intake of the Word of God, prayer never comes naturally and interest in prayer declines. On the other hand, the first step in any program to revitalize the practice of prayer is always a renewed contact with God's Word.

However, many people continue to experience such dryness even though they do devote regular periods to spiritual reading. This is usually due to the fact that the reading is not done in such a way as to provoke prayer. If no distinction is made between the manner in which one approaches *lectio divina* and the way in which one's ordinary professional or leisure reading is done, then prayer will not easily follow. *Lectio divina* is not simply a matter of reading books about the spiritual life, theology or the Bible. *Lectio divina* is chiefly distinguished from other reading by the way in which it is done. Even the most suitable material can fail to yield results if approached in the wrong way.

This article is intended to recall the most fundamental differences between genuine *lectio divina* and other forms of reading.

Principle 1. *Lectio divina is aimed not at confirming and reinforcing our individual approach to life, but at breaking into our subjective world and enriching it from the outside, delivering us from the prejudices and limitations of closed convictions and ideology and exposing our lives to the fullness of revelation and not simply to that part which presently appeals to us.*

Historically, the expression "lectio divina" was first used in connection with the proclamation of the Scriptures in the liturgy. When people were less literate and books were rarer, more reliance was placed on public reading as the means of daily renewal. The drawbacks of such a system are obvious, but there was one advantage. The reading was outside the individual's choice; there was always an element of unpredictability. This meant that the Christian was forced to adapt his thinking to suit the reading, rather than model his choice of reading on his personal preference at a given moment. In this way there was a possibility of real dialogue between the Word and the person. In opening his life to such reading the person was giving God *carte blanche*. On the one hand, this meant that any comfort or consolation received in the course of such reading was the stronger for being unsolicited. On the other hand, the possibility was left open for one's life and values to be subjected to the saving judgment of God's Word.

In all our *lectio divina* we must be prepared to be surprised. This is why it is important that our intake be somewhat fluid. Reading only familiar passages from the Scriptures and other "old favorites" is like owning a tape-recorder but having no radio. It has the convenience of being able to provide something to suit each mood as it comes along, but it has no power to cater for our developing range of moods and needs. The danger is that we grow weary of what used to be so apt and have nothing with which to replace it. Our reading should always have some element of adventure about it; it should not be static or stale.

Insofar as *lectio divina* is a means by which we progress toward the fullness of revealed truth and leave behind the narrow limits of our subjective world, it is a significant factor in our communion with the Church. Since most disunity is a result of partial views of the truth rather than from positive untruth, it follows that harmony among Christians is powerfully helped by a search for the whole truth. This is why it is important for us to expose ourselves to something broader than the type of reading dictated by our immediate needs. There is much to be said of a certain objectivity in our choice of reading.

Ecclesial writings form the best basis of genuine *lectio divina*. The Bible has first claim on our attention. But it is a great mistake for us to limit ourselves to the Scriptures. Throughout the centuries there have been many other works which have been of considerable assistance to Christians in their efforts to put the Scriptures into practice. Having rediscovered the Bible it is time for our generation to renew contact with the great spiritual masters of antiquity. Notwithstanding the cultural difficulties inherent in understanding these ancient authors, almost any effort we make in this direction is a source of ample enrichment for our lives as Christians. Finally must be mentioned among ecclesial writings, the official documents of the Church, conciliar decrees, encyclicals and so forth.

Principle 2. *Lectio divina is a long-term activity. It is not a source of immediate gratification as much as general provisioning for life. Fidelity and constancy are most valuable adjuncts to such reading.*

It is wrong to think of *lectio divina* as being like a quick trip to the refrigerator for a snack when one feels a little hungry. It is more like the regular meals which constitute life's basic source of energy. It is quite important that we are convinced that it is impossible for us to remain genuine followers of Christ without continued contact with his Word. Our own feelings of need are not always an accurate gauge in this respect; our effectiveness in conveying Christ to others is voided long before we ourselves begin to decay. The fact is that to the extent that we are involved in apostolic activity we must be prepared to carry excess baggage. We cannot transmit to others what we ourselves have never learned.

Lectio divina is not always thrilling; sometimes it severely taxes our sense of dedication. But it is always obligatory. If we find ourselves regularly spending less than two or three hours per week in free, personal contact with God's Word we can, in most cases, expect trouble. To excuse ourselves from this minimum is to step off the common way and it would be prudent for us to consult with a plain-speaking director.

Principle 3. *Lectio divina is connected with our personal sense of vocation. The aim of our reading is to hear the call of God clearly and concretely in our present situation.*

Lectio divina is never part of a program of self-improvement. It is a response to an invitation. The first fidelity required of a disciple is that he be open to accept guidance and concrete directives from his master. By exposing himself fully to his master's influence the disciple becomes imbued with his attitudes and values and is progressively aware of how to shape his life. In *lectio divina* we give God a chance to get at us, to guide us, to teach us, maybe to call into question some of our bright ideas and pet projects. Turning aside, for the moment, from our own beliefs and plans we concentrate on being responsive to God's call. We go to our reading in a spirit of submission, prepared patiently to cede the initiative to Christ.

The trust, reverence and submission necessary for true *lectio divina* points to the necessity of care in our choice of readings. It is imprudent to credit everything that is published with total reliability. The books we use for *lectio divina* must be substantial enough to sustain our reverence. They must be for us an opening out into the whole truth, not a closing in on part of that truth. If we have books we can trust, we can afford to relax our critical faculties and allow God's Word to speak to our hearts.

Principle 4. *Lectio divina applies the Word of God to our own life-situation, allowing revelation and experience to overlap.*

The Holy Spirit, who sustains faith in the Church, is active not only in the expression and recording of revealed truth. He makes his presence felt also in the reading and reception of what has been written. Through our reading, the Spirit intends to renew our lives, to reshape them according to God's plan. Because this is so, it is important that our *lectio divina* be done not in isolation from real life, from our past and present, our joys and sorrows, our pluses and minuses. The Word of God speaks to us in the here-and-now, as we are. It has now no interest in what we used to be or what we might have been.

We do not read in order to garner information. Most of us have probably already acquired sufficient brute facts to last us through several lifetimes. The purpose of *lectio divina* is to allow us to interpret our experience of life with all its ups and downs in the light of God's Word in the faith of the Church. It is not a question of opting out of life, for example, by pretending that our problems do not exist. *Lectio divina* involves accepting the incredible truth that God speaks to me only as I am. It is most important that in my reading I leave aside all fantasy and play-acting and be myself. It is only the discovery of our native neediness that motivates us to seek from God power to rise above it. It is only when our search for light and strength in the Scriptures is imbued with a certain urgency that success is in sight. If our reading lacks seriousness and depth and is merely a dabbler's hobby, nothing permanent will result from it.

Principle 5. *There is a certain purposelessness or gratuity about lectio divina which is reflected in the leisure and peace which surround it. Lectio divina is done in such a way that it may be punctuated by prayer.*

Central to the very notion of *lectio divina* is its lack of utilitarian value or purpose. It is possessed of a certain freedom or *vacatio* which comes from having nothing particular to achieve. There is a place for useful spiritual activities which include reading about the spiritual life, studying theology and working with the Sacred Books. Sermons have to be prepared and religious instructions planned. None of these useful activities, however, is *lectio divina*. Beyond the religious tasks imposed on an individual which may involve activity in the same area as *lectio divina*, time must be left for a leisurely reading which leaves room for God's grace to impact and which is more like prayer than work.

Quiet and stillness invest reading with an atmosphere of mellowness. Prayer thrives in such a climate. When, during *lectio divina*, prayer comes naturally, it should not be elbowed aside but allowed to spread. When one's heart is inflamed or one's interest captivated, no pressure should be felt to keep moving. In *lectio divina* the "interruptions" are habitually more important than the reading itself. Having allowed God's Word entrance into our hearts we should extend to it also the possibility of moving without restriction and of exercising its influence over us without stoppage or hindrance. For this to happen, any form of pressure must be eschewed.

Principle 6. *Reading is not merely an "inner" exercise. As far as possible our whole body should participate in our lectio divina.*

When we are engaged in *lectio divina* our whole person should be involved in this quiet opening to God's Word. Some attention to posture is necessary to ensure that we are at once relaxed and disciplined. It often helps, if we are the sort of people who are professionally involved in much reading, to have a particular posture for our *lectio divina* (e.g., away from our desk or even on the floor) that we do not employ for other activities. If we are alone we should begin our reading with a deliberate Sign of the Cross or something similar to remind ourselves what we are about.

In antiquity, reading always meant reading aloud; it was far from the rapid eye-scanning that we associate with the term. Even for us moderns there is a certain value in mouthing the words as we read. It has the effect of slowing down the reading and of rendering it more deliberate. By more completely involving ourselves in what we are reading, the text becomes richer for us and, to the extent that such bodily participation keeps us busier, it acts as an effective block to distractions. So long as we avoid turning our *lectio divina* into an exercise in amateur dramatics, reading aloud can be a valuable aid in giving more impact and feeling to our contact with the Word of God. And it will certainly slow us down.

Principle 7. *When something is encountered in our lectio divina which particularly speaks to us we should endeavor to retain it in our memory lest any of its savor escape us.*

From time to time in our reading we come across something which specially appeals to us or which seems to apply very aptly to our particular situation at a given moment. We should make the most of such opportunities and spend as much time with the text in question as we can. If it helps we can write it out and keep it before us for a few days, allowing ourselves the leisure to ruminate upon it and really let it become part of us. If it is something particularly attractive to us and is fairly short we can use it as the basis of our prayer. When occasion presents itself for brief or even momentary prayer during the day, we should take this as our starting point. In this way we are trying to give full scope to a text which the attraction of grace has signalled to us as being of special relevance. When the attraction fades we should pass on to something else without regret.

Our *lectio divina* should be conducted in such a way that we develop a sensitivity to the call of grace. In the beginning the texts which cause us to come alive will usually be of a confirmatory nature. As our sensitivity increases other texts will begin to clamor for our attention, texts which offer challenge rather than comfort. To these also we must learn to submit, knowing that it is in this way that God renews our life.

Introductory Note

"Paul's Approach to Corinthian Enthusiasm" appeared in *The Bible Today* of February 1977, pp. 1075-1081. It was occasioned by a concern that a popular emphasis on spiritual manifestations was crowding out the traditional monastic approach which favors sober, undramatic prayer. In the mid-1970s, the quiet way of the desert seemed to be losing ground to the boisterous euphoria of charismatics.

Using the device of commenting on First Corinthians, I tried in the article to place a question mark alongside some of the presuppositions of charismatic spirituality and, in particular, to query the use made by it of First Corinthians. In the process, I became convinced that there is a clear message in this epistle for everyone interested in spirituality. Fidelity to the Cross and to non-achievement is a very difficult task in contemporary western society. We are all so pleased when "something happens" during prayer that we need to be reminded that a spiritual experience is not self-accrediting. It needs to be evaluated by its fruits. Only that which binds us to the Church and opens us to love can be regarded as coming from God. In the last analysis our prayer can be regarded as genuine only to the extent that it leads us closer to the Cross of Jesus Christ.

Paul's Response to Corinthian Enthusiasm

One of the most persistent difficulties encountered by the Apostle Paul in his work among the Gentiles was the formulation of Christian faith in terms that did not presuppose a previous formation in the religion of the Old Testament. It seems to have taken Paul some time to realize that the Good News he preached to the Gentiles took for granted some basic assumptions that were specifically Jewish and not, as he supposed, universal. His cunningly contrived speech in the Areopagus failed simply because he had not appreciated how impossible it was, in speaking to educated Athenians, to gloss over the problem of resurrection.

Paul's teaching about the Christian emancipation from the Law was readily intelligible only in a climate of Jewish piety and practice. Elsewhere Paul was seen to be advocating licentiousness. This led to a certain polarization among Gentiles. Some gladly pushed Christian liberty to its extremes, retaining in their life and worship many favored elements of paganism. In reaction to such abuse, others turned with relief to the stronger, safer, and more demanding teaching of the Judaizing parties. We know from the various letters of Paul that much guidance was necessary to ensure that Gentile Christians avoided both these extremes.

The Church at Corinth was, from all accounts, an enthusiastic and "pneumatic" community. The Corinthians were brought to the faith, not by means of skillful argumentation concerning the fulfillment of Old Testament prophecies, but through the dramatic manifestations associated with the outpouring of the Spirit (1 Cor. 2:4). There was no rigorism at Corinth but, on the contrary, liberty and exaltation to the point of abandon. The Corinthian community, lacking both Paul's personal supervision and sound local leadership, had become fixated at the most external and dramatic level of Christianity and had stopped growing.

It was not the enthusiasm of the Corinthian community as such that caused Paul concern. He recognized the important role played by spiritual exhilaration in the first stages of the acceptance of the Christian faith.

His anxiety was occasioned by the fact that the Corinthians had become so dependent on spiritual gifts that the various manifestations of the Spirit became detached from their source. The community was becoming disoriented, and disintegration had set into its common life.

Enthusiasm in History

Some understanding of the random issues raised by Paul in his Corinthian correspondence can be gained by viewing the situation at Corinth in terms of religious enthusiasm. "Enthusiasm" is a term applied in the study of religions to a type of religious response that flows from an overemphasis on the immediacy of the relation between God and man.

Some Gnostic sects, Montanism, Albigensianism are some of the better known examples of enthusiastic and "pneumatic" movements within Christianity. Since the seventeenth century there has been a pro-liferation of enthusiastic sects, the most readable description of which can be found in Ronald Knox's book *Enthusiasm*.

Although there are considerable differences among the various enthusiastic sects, it is possible to formulate some general qualities that occur repeatedly in the history of enthusiasm. There is a strong convic-tion of immediacy of God and an emphasis on inner experience. This results in a certain pluralism in beliefs, attitudes, and practices which can degenerate into individualism and divisiveness. There is a preference for spontaneous and uninhibited worship, which caused Aldous Huxley to apply to enthusiasm the nickname "Corybantic Christianity." There are often strong sexual motifs just beneath the surface. Sometimes a rigorous repression is enforced, sometimes complete license is allowed, and occa-sionally spiritual purity happily cohabits with practical permissiveness. Finally, on a social level, it seems that enthusiasm flourishes best outside the establishment. C. Y. Glock's theory that sect behavior is a form of strategic withdrawal in the face of felt economic deprivation may offer a partial explanation of this fact.

Enthusiasm at Corinth

There is a lot of evidence to indicate that it was the enthusiasm of the Corinthian community that was the object of Paul's concern. Division and individualism were becoming evident there; their assemblies were disorderly, and their prevailing sexual attitudes were ambivalent. There was an immaturity and selfishness that Paul felt would be finally destructive if not remedied.

Corinth was a crowded working-class city with a life of its own that resisted the designs of its political overlords to change. The Christian community was drawn from these rough, port-side people and included few of the rich and powerful (1 Cor. 1:26). There were slaves in the

Church (1 Cor. 7:21), and women (socially inferior in those days) exercised a disproportionate influence there (1 Cor. 11:2-16; 14:33-36).

Written in the late 50s, less than ten years after the Council of Jerusalem (Acts 15:1-29), First Corinthians is addressed to a predominantly non-Jewish group (1 Cor. 12:2; 7:18), far enough removed both geographically and culturally from the Jerusalem élite to feel like second-class Christians. Perhaps we do not appreciate sufficiently how difficult it was for Gentiles to win acceptance in the primitive Church and how this made the Corinthians all the more eager to demonstrate their equality by displaying so eagerly their range of spiritual gifts.

The truth is that Corinth could never have been regarded, in Jewish eyes, as a religious city. And the easygoing morals for which this city was famous found some difficulty in accepting the developing Christian consensus regarding sexual behavior. While there is no evidence that the Christians continued to assist in pagan orgies (1 Corithians 10:14 probably refers to more civic and social occasions), we do find evidence of a certain ambivalence in the community. Paul is aghast at their nonchalance in the face of incest (1 Cor. 5:1-2) and has to reiterate the condemnation of fornication (1 Cor. 6:12-20). Likewise, his listing of sins in 1 Corinthians 6:9-10 seems more concerned with specifically sexual sins than the lists in Galatians 5:19, Romans 1:29-31 and Colossians 3:5 (cf. Eph. 5:3-5). On the other hand, Paul has to intervene against too rigoristic attitudes and to insist on moderation in the practice of abstinence (1 Cor. 7:1-10). Second Corinthians 12:21 reminds us that those who, throughout history, have tried to be too spiritual have been brought to their ruin by the flesh, whose importance they had so long overlooked.

The behavior of the Corinthians at their assemblies had become so boisterous and disorderly that Paul remarks that an observer would think them mad (1 Cor. 14:23). Paul devotes most of chapter 14 to a discussion of the issues raised by the Corinthians' preoccupation with speaking in tongues, a phenomenon apparently concentrated in Gentile communities (Acts 10:46; 19:6) and culturally akin to the ecstatic languages evidenced in many sectors of the contemporary religious scene. Paul's concern is not to suppress such ecstatic outbursts, but to channel them so that the community is helped.

Nowhere does Paul denigrate spiritual gifts. In fact, he commends the Corinthians for the presence of these in their community (1 Cor. 1:5-7). He is not asking them to give up what they have, but to enrich their faith further by accepting the full range of spiritual endowment (1 Cor.

12:4-11), by appreciating the relative value of the different manifestations of the Spirit (1 Cor. 12:31), and by restoring orderliness and intelligibility to their assemblies (1 Cor. 14:40). Paul is calling, above all, for a growth in maturity and for the relinquishing of childish ways (1 Cor. 3:1-4; 14:20).

Disorder and selfishness at community gatherings (1 Cor. 11:21) were a reflection of the divided state of the Corinthian Church. Much of the first four chapters of First Corinthians is devoted to the problem of dissensions and factions among believers at Corinth, and the theme is not far below the surface throughout the letter (cf. 1 Cor. 1:10-16; 3:1-4). Not only is Paul concerned about such blatant ruptures of unity as involving brother Christians in litigation before pagan judges (1 Cor. 6:1-8), but he seems convinced that a much more cohesive doctrinal basis is needed. It is interesting, moreover that the word hekastos ("each one") occurs more often in First Corinthians than in the rest of the Pauline corpus. Granted that the situation envisaged in First Corinthians is not doctrinal aberration nor schismatic tendencies but misplaced enthusiasm, it is interesting to note what Paul suggests to remedy matters.

Paul's Response

Paul's direct response to the situation at Corinth may be summarized under three headings: discernment, a sense of the Church, and love.

One of the most persistent themes in First Corinthians is that a certain critical reserve is called for when it comes to evaluating spiritual gifts. The various words used in the New Testament for discernment occur more often in this letter than in any other New Testament book, as does the term syneidesis, "conscience." For Paul, such discrimination was the necessary adjunct of every spiritual man (1 Cor. 2:15), since even spiritual gifts are subject to careful scrutiny (1 Cor. 12:10). It is on this note precisely that the whole correspondence ends: "Continue to test yourselves on whether you are established in the faith; continue your self-examination" (2 Cor. 13:5).

Secondly, Paul calls for a renewed awareness of the Church, both on the local and universal level. First he locates the spiritual gifts (pneumatika) within the broader sphere of the charisms (charismata), assigning importance according to the profit effected by the different gifts to the Church (1 Cor. 12:12-31) and strives to bring the community at Corinth in line with the universal Church (1 Cor. 11:23-26; 14:17; 14:36). One may be permitted to wonder whether the collection for the saints in Jerusalem (1 Cor. 15:4; 2 Cor. 9:1-15) was not used by Paul as a practical device for broadening the Corinthians' vision and interest.

Above the gifts, above all purely external service to the community, is love. Chapter 13 of First Corinthians must be among the most-quoted parts of the Bible, yet its fullest significance is yielded only through a consideration of its context. Paul sees love as the primary dynamism in Christian growth, weaning the believer from a narcissistic concentration on his own inner experience, opening the way for his Christianity to find expression in practical everyday life, and ensuring that harmony and mutual service which can alone build up the Church. Without love, Christian life lacks substance; with it, problems of disunity, discord, and mutual offense disappear.

Eschatology and the Cross

Paul's solution to the problems at Corinth presupposed a vision of Christian life that the Corinthians had to learn to appreciate. The basic malaise at Corinth was the opposite of that at Thessalonica: at Corinth there was too little appreciation of eschatology.

It was because the Corinthians were so convinced that they possessed the fullness of the Spirit, as Paul ironically notes in 1 Corinthians 4:8, that they seek to distance themselves from the Cross of Christ. They had come to doubt that any further resurrection was possible (1 Cor. 15:12). So sure were they in their possession of the Spirit that they became complacent (1 Cor. 10:12), arrogant regarding Paul's right to teach them (1 Cor. 4:18), and insensitive to the needs of others (1 Cor. 11:21). Leaving no room for further development, growth ceased and disintegration began to manifest itself.

Paul has to insist that the "preaching of the Cross" is not merely elementary doctrine, but the true and essential wisdom of Christian faith. It is a touchstone by which faith is evaluated. Acceptance of the Cross belongs only to those on the way to salvation (1 Cor. 1:18) and is their guarantee of access to the "secret and hidden wisdom of God" (1 Cor. 2:7). It is only through this wisdom that spiritual gifts can be appropriately assessed (1 Cor. 2:12). Those who consider the Cross outrageous or foolish are on the way to damnation, and match in their lack of understanding those who crucified the Lord of Glory (1 Cor. 2:8).

Paul's own life accords with his teaching (1 Cor. 4:9-13; 2 Cor. 4:9-13; 5:3-10; 9:24; 12:7-10), a fact that makes him contemptible in the eyes of many. For Paul, however, it is supportable, even desirable, because it was balanced by the hope of an unimaginable reward (1 Cor. 2:9). "For if in this life only we have hope in Christ, then of all men we are the most to be pitied" (1 Cor. 15:19). The definitive transformation of man is not something that has already taken place; it still awaits us (1 Cor. 15:12-47). It is this hope of resurrection that makes present hardships tolerable (1 Cor. 15:32) and at the same time renders foolish the Corinthians' concentration on the present (1 Cor. 3:13). The Christian's life is a training for the future (1 Cor. 9:24-27); to think that one has received it all is to reveal a very limited conception of the goal.

Conclusion

The fundamental flaw at Corinth was a faulty eschatology. Failing to appreciate the role of suffering and death in Christian life, the Corinthians had allowed themselves to become obsessed with pneumatic gifts, which caused them to undervalue the role of the Church and to become blind in assessing their own everyday conduct. To counter the disintegration apparent in this community, Paul insists on a stronger eschatological vision that will provide motivation for a renewed discernment, greater communion, and a more practical exercise of love.

Introductory Note

"Saint Benedict's Approach to Prayer" (CS 15 [1980], pp. 327-343), was written for the 1500th anniversary of the birth of the Patriarch of the West. It represents an attempt to answer the question posed in the first paragraph: Why is there so little about "prayer" (as we know it) in the Rule of Benedict? The answer given is that, in the Benedictine tradition, deep prayer is seen as the quasi-automatic effect of a life lived according to Gospel priorities. On the one hand the Liturgy of the Hours was not considered as less a prayer because it was structured, communal and "objective." On the other hand there was far less drama involved in personal prayer; it was taken for granted. "Let him simply go in and pray." For St. Benedict, spiritual experience is not to be sought in itself but is the natural consequence of investing effort and energy in purifying the heart and simplifying one's goals. A life so lived leads to fervent prayer as witnessed by the strong affective language current in this tradition. An example of this, *intentio cordis* (RB 52.4), was the subject of an article written about the same time which appeared in RBS 6/7 (1981), pp. 105-120.

Saint Benedict's Approach to Prayer

Considering the fact that Benedictinism is a major factor in the contemplative and mystical tradition of the western Church, it is surprising to find so little about prayer, as it is generally understood today, in the Rule of Benedict. A modern searcher after truth who approaches the RB for guidance in prayer may well find that it has no answers to his questions and feel compelled to continue his research elsewhere. Even when it is read with good will and some understanding, Benedict's Rule does not seem to convey the sort of teaching for which many persons are looking in these times.

There are two things to be said in this regard. Firstly, it is impossible to understand the full meaning of the RB unless it is viewed within the context of its own tradition—both antecedent and subsequent. The Rule of Benedict claims to be no more than a practical compendium for beginners (73.8); much of its meaning emerges only through contact with its sources. Furthermore, the rich streams of tradition emanating from the RB are a constant reminder that beneath the surface of the Rule there is an abundant underground well of inspiration which becomes visible only through subsequent surfacings. The integral meaning of the Benedictine Rule yields itself only to one who is conversant with and, to some extent, immersed in the entire monastic tradition. The casual reader can miss much.

In the second place, the fact that a reading of the RB leaves many a modern questioner unsatisfied, need not be an indication that it is deficient in its capacity to offer guidance for a life of prayer. It may, on the contrary, signify that the person is asking the wrong questions, that he is approaching prayer with the wrong presuppositions. In other words, contact with the Benedictine tradition can have the effect of subjecting to criticism our modern ideology of prayer and the expectations which derive from it.[1] St. Benedict is, perhaps, calling us to reconsider the dominant contemporary view of contemplative life and reassess some of its priorities.

Benedict, along with most of the monastic masters of prayer, tends to speak more about the quality of daily life than about performance during periods of prayer. There are few practical directives given about how to pray and almost no theology of prayer. The general presupposition seems to be that prayer comes readily and unselfconsciously to one who does his best to implement the teachings of the Gospel in concrete behavior. The monk seeks God, not "experiences"; he lives in the luminous twilight of faith and is content with the unpredictability of Providence. He instinctively accepts the famous saying of St. Antony, "That prayer is not perfect in which a monk is conscious either of himself or of the content of his prayer."[2] Prayer, for Benedict, is not an end sought in itself, but a dimension of a life progressively lived for God.

1. A Life Characterized by Prayerfulness

The life envisaged by St. Benedict in his Rule was a restructuration and adaptation of the style of living exemplified in the careers of the archetypal figures of the monastic tradition. Benedict duly regrets the inability of his contemporaries to live up to the standards set by their forebears, but he does not hesitate to propose the same fundamental priorities. The monk lives a life of disciplined fidelity to the divine call. Progress in that life is signaled by a growing awareness of the will of God in every situation and by a willingness to respond to it. What Benedict describes is the unrestricted admittance of the divine into human life, even at the price of alternative self-gratification and apparent independence.

The chapter on humility details some aspects of the phenomenology of growth in prayerfulness. The steps of the ladder are signs, *indicia*, that mere material renunciation is in the process of being transformed into a love which embraces the whole of the monk's being.[3] The means by which such divinization is effected is the monk's attention to the diverse forms under which God presents himself to men, and his progressive self-distancing from alternative objects of affection. It is a matter of the monk consenting to be transfigured by the *memoria Dei*, transmitting this awareness to all his members (7.12), until his entire being is possessed and impressed by the evangelical spirit of prayer (7.62-66). Prayer saturates his existence, wherever he is, whatever he does. The monk who, in the course of a lifetime, submits himself to the divine pedagogy, becomes a living prayer.

A degree of caution is necessary in describing this state as one of continual prayer, although that is what it is, and it was in such a manner that the ancient monks often referred to it. The state of prayer is not so much the culmination of a lifetime of *saying prayers* or of giving oneself to the practice of meditation. It is rather the natural outcome of a life dedicated to receptivity to grace. The monk who arrives at the pinnacle of contemplation does so only by reason of his having walked the arduous path of fear of the Lord, obedience and self-forgetfulness. A particular state of prayer is not sought directly; paradoxically it is the one who labors conscious of his unworthiness whom God exalts beyond expectation.

St. Benedict differs from the Master in his confidence that the process of exaltation is not completely deferred until the future life. A life lived in fidelity to Gospel teaching begins to be suffused by the outshining of eternal light; the final realities are already in the process of being realized.[4]

Benedict places little emphasis on the idea of experiences in prayer serving as a lure to entice men toward greater general fidelity. He did not hide from the prospective monk that the way to God passed through difficult and arduous regions.[5] For him, a monk was one who committed himself to persevere in his attempts to live according to the teaching of the Gospel irrespective of where such a commitment led. What counted was the monk's voluntary gift of himself "for love of Christ," not the enjoyment of spiritual gifts.

The key determinant of the experience of prayer according to the monastic tradition is the quality of daily life. "Your prayer will show you what condition you are in. Theologians say that prayer is the monk's mirror."[6] Energy is expended primarily in deepening one's responsiveness to the call of grace in every circumstance; "improvement" in prayer follows naturally in normal circumstances.

Benedict views prayer as a dimension of a monk's whole life, realized differently in the different occupations in which he is engaged. Prayer is not, in the monastic tradition, an activity which exists in competition with other activities so that growth in prayer is facilitated by withdrawal from other works. The injunction of 1 Cor. 10:31 is important: every action is to be directed toward God, even such mundane tasks as the fixing of prices on monastery produce (57.9). Admittedly, there are moments of disengagement in which prayer *seems* less diffuse and more intense, but there is a question of difference in degree rather than a case of two distinct activities. What happens when prayer is pure or unmixed is simply a more explicit form of what is more latent at other times.

The unity of prayer and life means that any attempt to upgrade the experience of prayer without simultaneously attending to lived values is liable to result in distortion. A monk who is dissatisfied with his prayer needs to make use of that feeling to motivate himself to greater daily fidelity to grace rather than to attempt to alleviate his pain by techniques for altering consciousness. To banish contrition, compunction and fear of the Lord by such opiates is not spiritual progress but the concession of defeat. Monastic tradition and ordinary common sense remind us that any stage of growth is heralded by initial negative experience. Growing *into* something new necessarily involves growing *out of* what is familiar, and that is always hard. Mysterious "failure" in prayer is often a call to give grace more scope in daily living; it can be an invitation to greater divinization—it must be accepted and attended to, not blotted out by techniques of mental manipulation.

Prayer is to be assessed, therefore, by the evangelical character of life as a whole rather than by its capacity to afford to the individual the sort of spiritual "experiences" he expects and desires. *Iudicium fidei sequere, et non experimentum tuum* ("Follow the judgment of faith and not your own experience").[7] The psychocentric approach to prayer which has dominated spirituality over the last four centuries tends, like any analysis of consciousness, to highlight individual problems in prayer at the expense of objective criteria. While this emphasis has been of some service in answering the specific questions of these times, it has often resulted in an unbalanced degree of introversion in spiritual matters. The monastic emphasis on the unity of prayer and daily life and on the *personal* (as distinct from the emotional and conceptual) content of prayer is a useful counterbalance. The monk prays from the same basis as he lives—what is revealed in prayer is the personal stance he embodies in all his responses to life.

2. Structures of Prayerful Living

Notwithstanding the potential for sanctity in everyday tasks, St. Benedict is aware that the memory of God will be eroded during the day unless it is specifically cultivated on a fairly regular basis. Far from asserting that "work is prayer," Benedict realizes that the prayerfulness of work is largely dependent on the monk's continual re-focusing of his life on God. Thus he suggests that the beginnings of projects be seasoned by earnest prayer, so that God may bring the work to its completion.[8] Guests are received with prayer (53.4-8), those performing routine duties begin with prayer (35.15, 38.3) and meals begin and end with prayer (43.13). Benedict, although he showed little tendency to ritualize and formalize monastic living, nevertheless appreciated the value of pausing before tasks to solicit the blessing of God on what is about to be done.

The mindfulness of God which is the goal of all monastic living is especially required during worship.[9] The liturgy is, for Benedictines, not a service to be performed at fixed hours and then forgotten, but a framework around which a life of sustained prayerfulness is built.[10] The day begins and ends with communal prayer and its course is marked off by further assemblies. The night itself is sanctified by a vigil. There is question here, not of times for prayer, but of the sanctification of time itself. During the Office the convenant with God which governs the whole of life is recalled and renewed.[11] The experience of many ordinary monks confirms that the most potent factor in assuring a prayerful liturgy is the quality of responsiveness to grace in daily life. The ability to derive prayer from the Word of God is an ordinary indication of co-operation with grace at other times. A person who works too frenetically or reads too little, who is selfish, rebellious and contentious will find these conflicts recurring during the Office, inhibiting its capacity to release prayer. This is why Benedict cites the ability to find prayer in the Office as an indication that a novice is seeking God.[12]

The Work of God is a structural means by which a prayerful life is supported rather than the injection of a predetermined amount of prayer into an otherwise prayerless life. It is a heightening of the prayer-quality of life as a whole and thus in necessary continuity with daily experience. It must be remembered, however, that what is paramount in the regimen of a Benedictine monastery is that *all* the details of its structure are responsive to the same spiritual priorities. The whole thrust of regulation and administration is directed to no other goal than the fostering, on both individual and communal levels, of a spirit of prayer.

Benedict is generally more interested in the personal content of what is done than its visible results. Much of the Rule is concerned with generating and supporting appropriate attitudes in the monks as they go about their daily round. The monks are to work at purifying their intention; their occupations will contribute to their sanctification only to the extent that they are undertaken with the right motivation. It is the quality of a monk's zeal which determines whether his monastic observance is a source of growth or an element in damnation.[13]

It is clear from a consideration of St. Benedict's teaching about obedience that what he has in mind is far more than mere compliance with organizational imperatives. The heart of Benedictine obedience transcends simply doing what is ordered. In the first place there is Benedict's insistence that the abbot take care that what he commands is, *in fact,* an expression of God's will in that situation—and repeatedly threatens him with hell if he does otherwise.[14] The monk, for his part, is able to take for granted that what he is asked to do is God's will and plan for him and to devote his energies not to deciding *what* is to be done but to giving himself fully and personally to the doing.

St. Benedict suggests two principal motives which should govern the monk's behavior. The first is his willingness to accept the teaching of Christ as this is mediated by the twin sources of rule or tradition and the personal pastorate of the abbot.[15] If a man becomes a monk in order to live a life which is in substantial conformity with the teachings of the

Gospel, it follows that a continuing willingness to be formed and influenced by evangelical principles constitutes the very heart of his fidelity. Entry into the Kingdom of God is reserved to those who accept the reign of Christ. By his obedience to that authority which concretely serves to embody the imperatives of the Kingdom, the monk demonstrates his acceptance of God's Word and his personal assent to God's plan in his regard.[16]

The monk's obedience is not only an expression of his status as disciple *vis-à-vis* a master, it is also an act of imitation of Christ.[17] He reproduces in his own life the submission and acceptance which Christ himself proposed as a pattern: "I have not come to do my own will, but the will of the One who sent me."[18] In imitation of the self-emptying of his Master, the disciple commits himself to be obedient until death.[19]

St. Benedict recognizes that this conscious following of the way proposed by Christ is constricting and painful.[20] There are many occasions in which the divine content of commands is not evident, in which human blindness, deviance and injustice are only too apparent. In such situations, if due representation does not effect a change,[21] the monk is to act purely for the love of God, trusting in His help and quieting his troubled thoughts with the memory of eternal life.[22]

It is often under the weight of such unfair treatment that the moral character of the monk is uncovered. This is why Benedict advises the senior to whom the novices have been committed to see how they perform in difficult circumstances.[23] Such reverses tend to polarize reactions. Either the monk makes use of the turmoil to refocus his attention on fundamental, spiritual priorities or he loses heart altogether. If he accepts the trial, it is usually the occasion for much heartfelt prayer; what is latent at other times is rarely far from the surface in such situations.[24] A monk who responds creatively to such negative experiences usually finds that his prayer is deepened and strengthened. On the other hand, one who rebels and rationalizes his way around such "undue interference" with his personal autonomy generally experiences that prayer eludes him more than ever—sometimes despite frantic efforts at compensation. Patience is not a trivial virtue for monks; it is their principal means of making contact with the saving Passion of Christ.[25] Those who refuse opportunities for patience consistently find themselves further from God.

The spiritual attitudes recommended by St. Benedict to his monks are particularly those found in the Psalms. This is why the Psalter has been not only the monk's prayer book, but also his favorite source of guidance in the formation of a practical philosophy of life. A monk who lives according to such values is therefore greatly confirmed in them by his repeated use of the Psalms in the liturgy. The Office is, for him, not time set apart from the daily round for prayer, but the deepening and evangelization of his experience of life in general. The monk's internalization of the Scriptures is the bond which unites his life and his prayer. *All* that he does is a positive response to God's self-revelation in Christ.

3. Reading, Meditation

It is impossible to live an evangelical life without a profound assimilation of the evangelical message. It is for this reason that Benedict makes provision for ample exposure to the Word of God. Many problems result from a loss of contact with the Scriptures, not the least of which is the monk's confusion concerning ultimate values and his over-concern with elements of his experience which matter less.

Benedict sets aside from two to three hours each day for the practice of *lectio divina*;[26] this is in addition to the readings of the liturgy and those accompanying communal exercises.[27] Sunday is reserved for *lectio*, except in the case of those for whom this is not feasible.[28] It is interesting that during the period of Lent, when he hopes for an improvement in the monk's response to grace, he makes provision for extra time for reading.[29]

The fidelity of Benedictines to the practice of reading has been of great service to mankind. It had been to secure suitable reading materials for the monks that monastic libraries were established and the skills of literacy preserved. Although Benedict did not envisage his monks as custodians of culture, as Cassiodorus did, nevertheless the devotion to reading which he infused into his followers was sufficiently strong to ensure that much was accomplished in securing the accumulated wisdom of the Greco-Roman World and of western Christianity from the erosion which accompanied the collapse of the western Roman Empire.[30]

Nor should the communal sacrifice demanded by such fidelity be underestimated. The building up of even a small library was an expensive project and the copying of manuscripts kept many workers away from more lucrative employments. When we consider that Clairvaux, during the forty years of Bernard's abbacy, acquired several hundred tomes, only some of which were gifts, we can form some idea of how many hours some of his monks spent at *scriptorium* tasks. To provide a library, an educational system and scope for personal reading demands the outlay of considerable resources and the corresponding acceptance of a lower standard of living and less capital-based influence than would otherwise have been possible. Dedication to reading is a guaranteed means of staying poor!

The expense of manuscript production was also a factor in the choice of what was copied and, by extension, what was available for the monks to read. Generally, the main body of work was done in the area of Scripture, the more important writings of the Fathers and in texts of special monastic interest, though this central core of work never excluded the copying of more peripheral or ephemeral texts, on occasion. An accidental effect of this policy was that monks had most access to the most important books; tomes of lesser value were less available.

This monastic reading was less like study, as we know it, and more like prayer. It was not an intellectual exercise aimed at gathering information or achieving some sort of personal synthesis at the level of theory, It was, rather, a full and voluntary immersion of the monk in the Word of God, allowing it to touch his awareness, to enflame his desire, to direct his understanding and eventually to serve as a guide and incentive to Gospel living. The monk prayed and reflected even as he read, allowing his situation to determine the blend of different elements in the exercise. But, above all, his reading was at the service of living; exposing himself to the evangelical teaching was the first and fundamental stage in implementing that teaching in life.[31]

Such reading was a more active exercise than that to which we are accustomed. The monk gave himself fully to the text; he did not approach it merely with a view to extracting from it a selection of ideas and items of information. The fact that he verbalized as he read meant that he became attuned to the subtle poetic rhythms in which revelation is couched; the text as a whole made a greater impact on him and he preserved more of its lingering flavor in his memory.

The ancient monks appreciated far more than we do the role which the memory can play in prayer. It was expected that every well-equipped monk would carry about with him a stock of favored scriptural texts from which he could select food for thought and forms of prayer, as occasion warranted. The Master set aside three hours each day for the memorizing of Psalms and Benedict was also familiar with this requirement.[32]

This memorization was not a technique of brainwashing, the overwhelming of rationality by massive exposure to disembodied verbal sequences such as are the techniques of rote learning employed in some modern cults. What was preserved in the memory was preserved precisely because it was a factor in the evangelization of the monk's life; it made sense, it mediated God's call and the monk desired to keep the text in his heart to serve as a reminder of God's intervention in his life.

Some part of your daily reading should, each day, be stored in the stomach (i.e., the memory) and be allowed to be digested. At times it should be brought up again for frequent rumination. You should select something that is in keeping with your calling and in line with your personal orientation, something that will seize hold of your mind and not allow it to think over alien matters.[33]

In this way the texts of Scripture carried in the memory and applied to the different circumstances of life became a means by which the monk kept in touch with the movements of grace in his own life and allowed God's Word to speak to each situation as it occurred.[34]

The custom of prayerfully reciting texts from the Scriptures during work and at other times was described as *meditatio*. This was not conceived as an intense mental exercise, but as an almost automatic repetition of the text with a view to assimilating its inner meaning. The favored image is that of a cow chewing the cud, *ruminatio*. The monk simply stays with a text which speaks to him—but easily and naturally, forcing nothing. When he wishes to pray, the words in which the movement of his heart is expressed are scriptural. There is no dissonance between inner grace and outward form; he is unable to discern where Scripture ends and his own prayer beings. This traditional approach to meditation protects the person praying from the paroxysms of self-expression which result from a misunderstanding of the nature of spontaneity. The monk's prayer is not less his own because he uses the words of Scripture. In the unlovely image dear to St. Bernard, he has fed so well on the Word of God that when he belches, the impetus is provided by what he has eaten: *eructavit cor meum verbum bonum!*

As a monk's life becomes simpler and his purpose single, his prayer tends toward fewer words but richer content. A short prayer from Scripture, or perhaps a small selection of such texts, may serve as sufficient support for sustained prayerfulness.[35] The repetition of such cardiomimetic texts is sufficient to allow the monk to make contact with his own inner source of prayer and to become identified with it easily and unselfconsciously. He has attained pure prayer, perhaps without noticing that he had done so.

The Word of God informs all phases of a monk's life and prayer. It is for this reason that contact with the Scriptures and with other texts which embody the faith of the Church is the first and fundamental practice in the monastic tradition of prayer. *Lectio divina* and the life-long *meditatio* which proceeds from it are the formative elements in any Benedictine community just as they are constitutive of the Church itself.

4. Prayer of the Heart

Although monastic spirituality seems—especially in legislative texts such as the RB—to be greatly concerned with organizational and disciplinary matters, its central concern is nearly always not with good order but with subjective dispositions. This is especially the case with the Rule of Benedict.[36] Because monastic life is not structured with a view to producing any result external to the spiritual growth of the monks, there is no subordination of personal vocation to organizational commitment, no system to be maintained beyond its own utility and no exaltation of the institution at the expense of the values of community. Monastic spirituality is, in fact, a spirituality of the heart; it is entirely directed to helping the monk discover his own inner source of spiritual vitality and living in substantial accord with it.

Monastic discipline is aimed at enhancing the monk's capability for living from the heart. Contrary to what many of our contemporaries believe, such fully personal involvement in living requires instruction, training, industry, application and perseverance. It is not the easy and immediate effect of the renunciation of all structures of thought and behavior. On the contrary, history shows that precipitate and unreflective self-expression is far more likely to be responsive to the urgings of instinct than to the promptings of the Spirit. A monkey at a keyboard is fully free to play whatever notes he wishes, whereas a great musician is inhibited by his knowledge of harmonics and by his desire to be faithful to the inspiration of the composer. Yet it is the "unfree" musician who can express ultimate truth in sound; the monkey produces only cacophony.

The monk has to learn how to live from his personal center and this means identifying and subjecting the sub-personal forces which tend to take over the control of behavior and preempt the interposition of personal choice. The monk seeks *apatheia*: freedom from such tendencies as would determine behavior without reference to the will. This includes not only emancipation from passions which lead to evil acts, but also liberation from those emotional states such as fear, depression and apathy, which prevent him from engaging in good. Such sub-personal forces are not purely biological—they are also historical, social and conceptual. They cannot be countered simply by repeated acts of will—a whole lifestyle revolution is needed.[37]

The distinctive features of monastic *conversatio*—*fuga mundi*, asceticism, self-knowledge, solitude and silence—are ordered to facilitating the monk's growth in freedom. The whole purpose of his rejecting secular behavior is the building up of a pre-disposition to act freely and from grace. Monastic tradition knows by experience that a prayerful existence is possible only for one who has found his heart, and to the extent that this discovery proceeds, prayer comes easily, though variously, throughout the day.

This tradition recognizes that a superficial *monotony* is imperative if the monk is to become attuned to spiritual realities. Masters of all generations have commented on the corrosive effects of the pursuit of novelties on monks' spirit of prayer. The whole purpose of stability is to make provision for an atmosphere of creative monotony in which there is nothing that unnecessarily binds the monk to transitory things or loosens the tenor of wholesome discipline. Restrictions in such matters as food, travel, entertainment and conversation are aimed at inhibiting the onset of *acedia*—the dreaded noonday devil which strikes at the heart of a monk's response as he relaxes after having overcome initial obstacles.

Within this context the practice of silence plays an important part. Silence or taciturnity (*taciturnitas*) is not primarily a phlegmatic quality.[38] It is rather the result of a well-ordered personality, quit of the compulsion to communicate, to express itself, to engage others in conversation or to terminate an awkward pause. It is the characteristic of one who speaks for a reason, rather than out of an inner need to give voice (7.60-61). Authentic silence results from wholeness and contentment; it comes from within, it cannot be imposed successfully from without.[39]

Silence enhances the reflective quality of life and allows prayer to pass easily into awareness. It also provides that element of free-time which allows practical matters to be processed mentally as they occur, instead of forcing them to wait until the time of prayer, where they reappear as distractions. When work ceases to be leisurely, attempts to pray are bedeviled by unrest.

The whole monastic structure is aimed, therefore, at allowing the monk to live a fully personal life, at some distance from whatever might enslave him or weaken his giving of himself to the service of Christ. The unexciting lifestyle is meant to give the monk scope to assimilate what he has read and to become sensitive to the workings of grace. The Word of God fills the vacuum left by the recession of alternative interests. This is why it is often possible to conclude that monks who get up to mischief or who are overwhelmed by boredom are those who have fallen away from reading, especially *lectio divina*.

A prayerful existence is the result of the monk's living from the heart. Complementary aspects of this state are described in four important terms found in the monastic tradition: a) *humilitas cordis*, b) *puritas cordis*, c) *compunctio cordis* and d) *intentio cordis*.

Humility's role in the development of prayerfulness has been mentioned above. Benedict views it in terms of a progressive awareness of the divine presence and a corresponding willingness to submit one's life to God's plan. The lowliness and awe, which are characteristic of genuine spiritual experience, generate in the monk vigilance, dedication, sobriety and a willingness to serve. By thus removing most of the obstacles to spiritual sensitivity, humility greatly advances growth in prayerfulness.

Purity of heart is understood in a number of ways in monastic tradition.[40] Initially, *puritas cordis* refers to that active renunciation by which a monk concretely rejects whatever in his life hinders progress toward the Kingdom of God. This involves the progressive elimination of sin and vice and their effects through energetic and disciplined measures. Furthermore, it leads to the renunciation of those sources of gratification which, though not overtly sinful, yet retard growth. Thus a man, in becoming a monk, concretely chooses to renounce the pleasure he derives from his family, his work, his possessions and his possibilities, not because they are evil, but because they are so good that there is a probability that they will minimize his commitment to his primary goal.

A second stage of purity of heart is attained when the habit of renunciation is so well established that the monk experiences some degree of freedom from the vices and desires which are the proximate causes of infidelity. Instead of being divided within himself and having to struggle to maintain direction, the monk finds that, progressively, life is simplified, integrated, harmonized with the bulk of his energies flowing in substantially the same direction.

A final stage is attained when the monk discovers himself gradually to be free even from contrary imaginations. His thoughts are less rebellious and the mind is no longer beset by the onrush of notions which disturb its concentration. In this state the monk is substantially free of distractions; prayer comes readily and often, but it is so in tune with the monk's entire subjectivity that he scarcely notices its presence. Pure prayer, mentioned three times in RB 20, is simply prayer which proceeds naturally from an undivided heart, fully possessed by charity.

Compunction of heart is another aspect of monastic teaching on prayerfulness, and one richly developed by both Cassian and Gregory the Great.[41] This experience of the shattering of one's deluded complacency and the discovery of one's true state before God is more than disgust at one's personal failure. It also includes an insight into one's heavenly vocation and a desire to be with God.

Fundamentally, *compunctio* is the experience of being pricked, pained, stung by the truth. It is a question of being abruptly shaken out of torpor and complacency and stimulated to action. It is the means by which one is motivated to amend one's life; the discomfiture it causes is so severe that even conversion is preferable.

Compunction is often associated with tears (20.3). The experience of one's vulnerability before God overwhelms the sensibilities. One's guilt before the Judge mingled with a feeling of the irresistibility of divine love touches one intimately. *Simul peccator et justus*, the person thus pierced can do no more than express his regret at his unresponsiveness to love and at the same time ardently yearn to be quit of compromise. Monastic prayer tends to alternate between these poles.

The term used in RB 52.4, *intentio cordis*, is a rich and evocative one in monastic tradition.[42] It is also reflected in the Middle English mystical writings.[43] It is unfortunate that its wealth of meaning is not always appreciated.

Intentio cordis refers to the single outward movement of the heart in the direction of God which becomes possible when outward clamor recedes. Because there are no alternative interests occupying the one praying, this movement is simple and intense, involving all aspects of being which at other times are dispersed. The one who prays thus is, in the Sanskrit expression, one-pointed, *ekagra*.

His concentration is complete, because he is absorbed, intent on God. It is not so much that he makes an effort actively to apply himself to the task (though this also is necessary); it is rather a question of his attention being seized and held by the object of his gaze.

Prayer, for Benedict, is a movement away from outward occupation and a responsiveness to the promptings of the Holy Spirit leading the heart to God. Such responsiveness is not initiated during prayer but is begun and consolidated by the effort to live a life based on Gospel priorities. It becomes more apparent in prayer when there is nothing to offset it.

Monasticism has a long and respected tradition of prayer. The practice of the Desert Fathers was expressed theoretically by Cassian and Evagrius and incorporated into a lifestyle by the monastic legislators. It drew depth and extension from the writings of Augustine and Gregory the Great and was restated in the Middle Ages in the words of John of Fécamp, Bernard and others. That it still has power to animate searchers for prayer today is clear from the words of Thomas Merton.[44] It is not a dead tradition awaiting resurrection; it flourishes yet. And perhaps its austere yet humane understanding of what is involved in a life of prayer may have something to offer modern man, which otherwise he might overlook.

NOTES

[1]Cf. M. Casey, "Principles of Interpretation and Application of RB," *Tjurunga* 14 (1977), pp. 33-38. Principle no. 5 is stated thus: "The capacity of RB to enhance the consciousness of the modern reader is grounded in the fact that it proposes an alternative perspective to that normally adopted by him."

[2]Quoted in John Cassian, *Coll.* 9.31; SChr 54, p. 66.

[3]Cassian, *Inst.* 4.39.1-2; SChr 109, pp. 178-180.

[4]Benedict modifies such eschatological texts as RM 3.78-94 and RM 10.92-122; perhaps they seemed to him to lack *gravitas*. He demonstrates his interest in the earthly goal of spiritual development in the famous additions at RB 7.67-70 and RB Prol. 46-49.

[5]Cf. RB 58.8

[6]John Climacus, *The Ladder of Divine Ascent*, (London: Faber, 1959); Step 28, 34, p. 255.

[7]Bernard of Clairvaux, Quad. 5.5; SBO 4.374.20-21.

[8]Prol. 4. This is not in RM. Benedict may have inserted this in an effort to counterbalance the semi-Pelagianism which some found in the ascetical writings of Cassian. RB was probably written some years after the Council of Orange (529) which drew attention to the existence of such opinions.

[9]RB 19.1-7. This chapter is strongly reminiscent of the first degree of humility (7.10-30) and makes the point that the avoidance of forgetfulness of God which always obliges the monk (7.10) is especially (*maxime*, 19.2) appropriate when he is engaged in the *opus divinum*.

[10]The monk's vocation is quite distinct from that of canons. "We should vainly seek in the Rule for a trace of the assertion that the Divine Office is the object of the monastic life," wrote Germain Morin in *The Ideal of the Monastic Life*, (London: Washbourne, 1914), p. 104. In fact, the early monks resisted any growth in liturgical prayer which would upset the organic balance of their lives. Cf. Eligius Dekkers, "Were the Early Monks Liturgical?," in COCR 22 (1960); pp. 120-137. *Idem.* "Moines et Liturgie," in COCR 22 (1960), pp. 329-340. The relationship between the *Opus Dei* and the monastic pursuit of constant prayer is well stated in A. de Vogüé, "Prayer in the Rule of Saint Benedict," in *Monastic Studies* 7 (1969), pp. 113-140. See also Nathan Mitchell, "Monks and the Future of Worship," in *Worship* 50 (1976), pp. 2-18. Cf. the articles in *La Maison-Dieu*, no. 64 (1960) under the general heading, "Priez sans cesse."

[11]RB 13.12-13 enjoins the public recitation of the Our Father at Lauds and Vespers as a reminder of and incentive to evangelical attitudes throughout the day.

[12]RB 58.7

[13]RB 72 recognizes the possibility that the perfect performance of the "right" actions can be a pathway to damnation if it is animated by the wrong dispositions.

[14]Cf. M. Casey, "Discerning the True Values of Monastic Life in a Time of Change," *Regulae Benedicti Studia* 34 (1974/1975), pp. 75-88; see p. 81.

[15]Cf. A. de Vogüé, "Sub Regula vel Abbate: The Theological Significance of the Ancient Monastic Rules," in *Rule and Life: An Interdisciplinary Symposium*, ed. B. Pennington, (Spencer, MA: Cistercian Publications, 1971), pp. 21-64.

[16]"The abbot is believed to act as Christ's representative" (RB 2.2, 63.14). On this see Berd Jaspert, " 'Stellvertrete Christi' bei Aponius, einem unbekannten 'Magister' und Benedikt von Nursia. Ein Beitrag zum altkirchlichen Amtsverständnis," ZThK 71 (1974), pp. 291-324. On the two streams of scriptural thought that coalesce to form Benedict's synthesis, see A. de Vogüé, *La communauté et l'abbé dans la règle de Saint Benoît*, (Bruges: Desclée de Brouwer, 1961), pp. 266-289.

[17]Three out of the four occurrences of *imitari* in RB have to do with the monk's attitude to obedience (5.13, 7.32, 7.34). This important theme perhaps deserves more attention than it has hitherto received. Cf. A. Heitmann, *'Imitatio Dei': Die ethicische Nachamung Gottes nach der Väterlehre der zwei ersten Jahrhunderts* (StA n. 10), (Rome: Herder, 1942); E.J. Tinsley, *The Imitation of God in Christ: An Essay in the Biblical Basis of Christian Spirituality*, (London: S.C.M. Press, 1960).

[18]RB 5.13, 7.32.

[19]RB 7.34.

[20]RB 5.11-12.

[21]RB 68.1-5.

[22]RB 7.35-39, 68.5.

[23]RB 58.7.

[24]This is clear from the number of scriptural texts which come to the surface in Benedict's treatment of the fourth degree of humility—patience when unfairly treated.

[25]RB Prol. 50. See below pp. 96-97.

[26]RB 48.4: the monks give themselves to reading (*lectioni vacent*) from the fourth hour to the sixth, more or less; Benedict thus reserves the cooler time of the day (RM 50.39-40) for reading rather than for work. There is also time available after Vigils (8.3) and after the meal in winter (48.10-13).

[27]There are readings at the Office of Vigils (9.5-8; 11.2-9), at meals (38.1-12) and in the evening before Compline (42.2-7). Benedict takes great care in legislating for these sessions, leaving nothing to chance—a sign that he considered it important that monks be happy to listen to holy readings (4.55). Chapter 73 gives his reading list.

[28]RB 48.22-23.

[29]RB 48.14-20; 49.4

[30]Cf. M. Casey, "St. Benedict and Civilisation," *Australasian Catholic Record* 57 (1980), pp. 359-365.

[31]Cf. M. Casey, "Seven Principles of Lectio Divina," *Tjurunga* 12 (1976), pp. 69-74. See above, pp. 3-9.

[32]Cf. RM 75.4, 50.14; RB 8.3, 58.5

[33]William of St Thierry, "Epistola Aurea" XXXI 120-124; trans. M. Casey, *Tjurunga* 12 (1976), p. 67.

[34]The cardiomimetic quality of Scripture reading (i.e., its capability of giving expression to what lies in the heart, hitherto undisclosed) is emphasized by St. Athanasius in his *Letter to Marcellinus* (newly translated by R. Gregg in the Classics of Western Spirituality Series, (New York: Paulist Press, 1980). "And it seems to me that these words become *like a mirror* to the person singing them, *so that he might perceive himself and the emotions of his soul*, and thus affected, he might recite them" (n. 12). Cf. M. Casey, "Cardiomimesis," in *Tjurunga* 20 (1980), pp. 118-122. See below, pp. 35-40.

[35]A short account of the role of short prayers in early monastic writings on prayer is given, with some documentation, in I. Hausherr, *The Name of Jesus*, (Kalamazoo: Cistercian Publications, 1978), pp. 203-214. For a rough outline of how this exercise might take shape practically, see M. Casey, "The Pilgrim's Lament," *Tjurunga* 13 (1977), pp. 297-398; the relevant section is pp. 363-375. The rudimentary nature of this contribution needs to be taken into account. See also S. Houédard, "One-Word and No-Word Prayer," in *Clergy Review* 64 (1979), pp. 173-176.

[36]Cf. A. de Vogüé, *La communauté*, p. 488.

[37]Cf. M. Casey, "The Monk in the Modern World," a double address given at the Benedictine Union Symposium, Arcadia, 9 July 1980, *Tjurunga* 21 (1981), pp. 5-24.

[38]This is clearly recognized in St. Gregory's *Pastoral Rule*, where virtue is clearly distinguished from temperament. Chapter 14 of the third part is entitled, "How to admonish the taciturn and the talkative"; trans. Henry Davis, (ACW no. 11), (London: Longmans, Green & Co., 1950), pp. 129-134.

[39]As monastic legislators, administrators and visitators attest. This is not to say that there is no point in structures of silence or that attempts to form monks in its values are not important.

[40]Cf. J. Raasch, "The Monastic Concept of Purity of Heart and Its Sources," StMon 8 (1966), 7-33, 183-213; 10 (1968), 7-55; 11 (1969), 269-314; 12 (1970), 1-41. See also G. Bekes, "Pura oratio apud Clementem Alexandrinum," in StA 1819 (1947), pp. 157-172, especially p. 162.

[41]Cf. M. Casey, "Spiritual Desire in the Gospel Homilies of Gregory the Great," *Cistercian Studies* 16 (1981), pp. 297-314. See below, pp. 41-60.

[42]Cf. M. Casey, "Intentio Cordis (RB 52.4)" in *Regulae Benedicti Studia* 67 (1981), pp. 105-120.

[43]Cf. J.P.H. Clark, "Intention in Walter Hilton," in *Downside Review* 97 (1979), pp. 69-80.

[44]Cf. M. Casey, "Thomas Merton Within a Tradition of Prayer," *Cistercian Studies* 13 (1978), pp. 372-378; 14 (1979), pp. 81-92.

Introductory Note

Years ago I came across the notion of sympathomimetic agents—drugs which mimic the effects resulting from stimulation of the sympathetic nervous system. In a moment of whimsy I coined the term "cardio-mimetic" to characterize that aspect of reality which has the capacity to set the heart aflame, to cause us to become conscious of our latent depths. At the back of my mind was the idea of finding a word that would be inclusive both of *lectio divina* and of the other human experiences which awaken the inner self and cause the heart to be disclosed.

Normal spiritual progression will result not only in a more fruitful experience of *lectio divina*, prayer and liturgy, but also in a deepening awareness of the presence of God elsewhere, in other people, in nature, in beauty, in crisis, in life and in death. In this way the whole of creation and all those whom we encounter become carriers of a spiritual message. Progressively the spiritual component of our sense of self becomes stronger and we begin to experience the world around us as deeply consonant with our most heartfelt aspirations.

This is the sort of horizon I had in mind in this inchoate essay which first appeared in *Tjurunga* 20 (1980), pp. 118-122.

Cardiomimesis

Monastic spirituality is a spirituality of the heart. It is not primarily concerned with the performance of particular actions or the adoption of determinate attitudes. Its major concentration is in the area of man's becoming aware of his own interior dynamics; it aims to have man live from his personal center, gradually becoming attuned to the inner promptings of grace and willing to cooperate with them. To find God, it is necessary to find one's heart.

Such a task is not as easy or as pleasant as it may appear. What man *is* only partially penetrates the realm of consciousness. Authentic self-knowledge is the outcome of a lifetime of learning; meanwhile man is subject to delusions about himself, partly inspired by wishful thinking and the desire to avoid effort, and partly implanted by misinformation and by the misinterpretation of reality communicated to him as a means of social control. To know himself and his potential beyond the arena of social roles and expectations, man has to be prepared to expend much effort.

The first steps to be taken in the pursuit of authentic existence are negative. There has to be some withdrawal from secular involvement. No Christian can allow himself to be defined by his relationship to a profoundly godless society nor permit his values and attitudes to be entirely formed by the prevailing climate of opinion.[1] On a personal level, the individual needs to subject to examination his patterns of interaction with other persons and to reject unhealthy dependencies as potential sources of delusion. True self-knowledge requires good psychological health and the ability to recognize and to counter neurotic tendencies as they appear. Finally, a person wishing to find the freedom to be himself must protect himself against instinctual autonomy. Instinctual tendencies or passions are sub-personal forces; to the extent that a person's life is ruled by them, it is out of control of the will and liable to lead away from the goals according to which the person desires to live.

This is to say that without discipline it is impossible to know oneself or to live from the heart. Easy "spontaneity" and glib "self-expression" are illusory unless the self has first been purified of the substitute elements which make up an inauthentic identity. It is only when one has found oneself and established the pattern of living authentically that real spontaneity and self-expression become possible. As the author of *The Cloud of Unknowing* cautions,

> Look that thy stirrings to silence or to speaking, to fasting or to eating, to onliness or to company, whether they come from within of abundance of love and devotion in spirit, and not from without by windows of thy bodily wits, thy ears and thine eyes.[2]

But there is more to Christian life than authentic existence. A Christian not only lives from conscience, but from a conscience positively formed according to Gospel values. This means that more than honesty and self-discipline is required. To live and act according to evangelical priorities presupposes that the individual has assimilated the beliefs and values specific to the Gospel. It is a matter of response to revelation more ✓ than the formulation of a personal program of life, and no response is possible unless one exposes oneself to that revelation and allows it to generate sympathetic resonances within one's subjectivity.

This, however, is where the paradox beings. The acceptance of the evangelical message is not experienced as the encounter with something entirely new. To some extent, the way has been prepared. In the formulation of the requirements for a truthful existence, the Gospel proposes not an alien, external doctrine, but the clear and concrete expression of what is already known dimly and intuitively. It is the forthright statement of what is already formlessly perceived.

This dynamic is illustrated in Paul's address to the Areopagites: "The God you worship unknowingly is the one whom I now proclaim" (Acts 17:23). The purpose of all Christian preaching and teaching is not the blanket imposition of a complete body of doctrine without reference to subjective factors. It is not brainwashing but *educatio*, the bringing forth of what is latent within, the harmonious interaction of subjective and objective worlds.[3]

This is evident in examining the role played by the Scriptures in the process of conversion. Both Augustine and Antony experience an awakening through the words of Scripture. The external expression gives concrete shape and urgency to the interior inclination and the result is irresistible. Simultaneously occur both the perfect assimilation of the objective text and the adequate expression of the subjective tendency. The text comes alive and the unformulated, inner aspiration becomes urgent and visible in the same moment.

Thus, the search for the heart is not a matter of sustained introspection and self-analysis, but the ability to recognize oneself reflected in realities external to consciousness. *Cardiomimesis* is the activity by which other objects mediate the self to the self. They reflect or echo back to the person the movements of the heart. A person becomes aware of an aspect of the truth of his being by recognizing himself reflected in the world around him. Finding the heart is a matter of perceiving its mirror-image in the objects of experience.

Creation thus reveals not only God but also man. One who is alienated from creation, who does not feel at home in the world, is estranged from himself and without any means of access to God's revelation of himself. Almost anything can serve as a channel of understanding about inner realities provided a person is perceptive.

When Jesus wished to make explicit the realities of divine grace, he drew the people's attention to the realities by which they were surrounded. The parables and similitudes of the Gospels make the connection between everyday experience and the ineffable ways of God. They also provide a key to the understanding of the recipient of grace; for one who reads attentively, they are a means of self-understanding as well.

The Incarnation represents the high point of God's efforts to make material things the carriers of the Unseen. Not only does the person of Jesus convey to us the ultimate mystery of the transcendent God, he also reveals something of the extent of human receptivity. Our contemplation of him brings us closer to God; it also compels us to recognize an important aspect of our own reality—our limitless spiritual capacity.

The whole order of nature and grace is cardiomimetic; it has the capacity to make visible the deepest realities of both communal and individual humanity. It "mimics" the heart of man so that he is able to recognize himself in what is outside consciousness and by living in accordance with what is there reflected, he realizes his own truth.

Without this search for personal truth, man cannot but live an inauthentic life. There are many channels by which he may come to transcend social expectations and roles, but none is more effective than the traditional practice of *lectio divina* well done.

The whole object of applying oneself to the reading of the Scriptures (and other texts which mediate truth) is not to gather information, but to place oneself in a situation where one might hear the divine call and begin to put it into practice.[4] The text which most mediates God's call in the present situation is precisely that which most effectively translates into accessible form, the dark and diffuse promptings of conscience.

Reading is very much like the diagnostic process of palpation. The physician applies pressure on different organs and when he provokes only a routine response, he passes on. Where, however, the patient suddenly erupts with pain, as in the case of an inflamed appendix, the physician realizes that he has found a likely cause of the patient's trouble. In reading, once a basic familiarity with doctrine is established, one reads not in the hope of discovering something new, but in the desire of pinpointing the area of the spirit's prompting. A text read many times and as often passed over may suddenly come alive, throbbing with a message of comfort or challenge. Nothing has changed in the text: what has changed is one's sensitivity. One is gradually becoming aware of God's leading one in a certain direction. Often the same lesson is repeated through different media. A book read, a song heard, a casual remark or a liturgical text may seem to converge, reinforcing the impression of being shepherded in a direction one would not otherwise have taken.

In his letter to Marcellinus on the psalms, St. Athanasius strongly emphasizes the cardiomimetic power of the Scriptures: "It seems to me," he writes, "that these words become like a mirror to the person singing them, so that he might perceive himself and the emotions of his soul."[5] The key to the profitable saying of the psalms is the recognition of their role in the process of self-discovery—including within the "self" thus discovered, the spiritual and godward tendencies God has implanted therein.

It is important, therefore, to view *lectio divina* in this light. It is not a matter of getting the "right" thoughts, nor of building up a store of appropriate attitudes. It is coming into contact with God's call at a particular time. It is directed toward self-knowledge.

The same applies to prayer, the natural outcome of reading. It is not an escape from the reality of life nor a means of covertly compensating for its failures; it brings the person praying into the awareness of reality—pleasant or otherwise. "Your prayer will show you what condition you are in. Theologians say that prayer is the monk's mirror."[6] Our contact with the spiritual world is meant to demonstrate the true character of our life and to force us to decide against complacency and compromise and to submit ourselves to the leading of God's spirit in our hearts.

*   *   *

The heart of man is slippery and hard to grasp. It is not found by introspective analysis, but by progressively learning to recognize the personal content in life. There are precious moments in which the heart manifests something of its distinctive character and these occur when it is confronted by something similar to itself. The heart is called forth only by that which is like itself. God's revelation is powerful enough to penetrate the husk of conscious existence and touch the very center of being; at this the heart springs into life, recognizing in the divine its own proper object. To find the heart is a matter of allowing God's Word to penetrate it and cause it to leap within, like John the Baptist. To find the heart is to follow its leading away from appearances in the direction of unblemished good.

To find the heart is the only means of finding God. We find God only because he has made all things to serve as signposts. This is *cardiomimesis*.

NOTES

[1]Cf. M. Casey, "The Monk in the Modern World," *Tjurunga* 21 (1981), pp. 5-24.

[2]Cf. The Epistle of Stirrings 69.1; quoted W. Johnston, *The Mysticism of the Cloud of Unknowing* (Wheathampstead: Anthony Clarke Books, 1978), p. 12.

[3]Cf. Hermann Hesse, *The Glass Bead Game* (Harmondsworth: Penguin Books, 1972), p. 58: "His was the typical evolution of every noble mind: working and growing harmoniously and at the same tempo; the inner self and the outer world approached each other."

[4]Cf. M. Casey, "Seven Principles of Lectio Divina," *Tjurunga* 12 (1976), pp. 69-74. See above, pp. 3-9.

[5]St. Athanasius, *Letter to Marcellinus*, trans. R. Gregg in the Classics of Western Spirituality Series (New York: Paulist Press, 1980), #12, p. 111.

[6]John Climacus, *The Ladder of Divine Ascent* (London: Faber, 1959), Step 28, 34, p. 255.

Introductory Note

This article is the fruit of research done in the preparation of *Athirst for God: Spiritual Desire in Bernard of Clairvaux's Sermons on the Song of Songs*, CS 77 (Kalamazoo: Cistercian Publications, 1988). Gregory was an important figure in the monastic West, possibly because he was revered as the disciple and biographer of St. Benedict. He was an important factor in the marketing of the spirituality of both John Cassian and Augustine of Hippo and in imbuing the tradition with a strongly affective eschatology. This present article concentrates on his *Gospel Homilies*; the same characteristics are evident also in his *Moral Commentary on Job* and his books *On Ezekiel*. The significance of Gregory for the early Cistercians is signaled by the fact that in the first days of the foundation, the first books to be copied in the scriptorium of the New Monastery after the liturgical texts and the Bible were the *Moralia* of Gregory the Great. This text was published in CS 16 (1981), pp. 297-314.

Spiritual Desire in the Gospel
Homilies of St. Gregory the Great

The *Gospel Homilies* of St. Gregory the Great are ideal material for *lectio divina*. These simple, pastoral reflections on the Sunday Gospels aim at relating the evangelical teaching to the realities of daily life[1] and are a ready source of prayer and understanding. Each homily is a complete unit, which means that the reader does not have to keep in mind a long sequence of ideas and arguments, but can simply relax and allow the text to speak to his heart. Gregory's slow, somewhat repetitious style is most suitable for a calm, leisurely reading and the teaching he extracts from the Gospel pericopes is habitually straightforward and accessible, even to a modern reader.

It is rather unfortunate that, as far as I know, there is no complete translation of the *Gospel Homilies* into English, although 22 of the 40 are available in Martin Toal's *The Sunday Sermons of the Great Fathers*.[2] Those who read some Latin will not find Gregory very difficult. Many passages will be familiar from the readings of the former Breviary, and the general atmosphere of the sermons is something between the Latin version of Origen's writings and the more developed prose of Bernard. Stylistically it is not glamorous Latin, but the meaning of the text and the personality of the preacher are easily apparent.

The *Gospel Homilies* were delivered to various Roman congregations in the first years of Gregory's pontificate (590-591). The principal influence on Gregory's presentation is biblical, and it quickly becomes clear to the reader that Gregory possessed a thorough familiarity with most of the books of both Testaments. There are a number of indications that Gregory was versed in the writings of the monastic tradition and of the earlier Fathers, especially Cassian and Augustine, though there is little evidence to show that he had ever read the Rule of Benedict of Nursia.[3] There is a high degree of cohesiveness with Gregory's other writings, particularly the *Moralia* on the book of Job and the *Ezekiel Homilies*, although the general tone of the *Gospel Homilies* is less intense.

Often, in preaching, Gregory makes allusion to particular facts known to his congregation or of common interest. He speaks about a sore throat,[4] the oppressive heat,[5] and occasionally interpolates remarks about the length of the sermon.[6] Often he reinforces his teaching with stories of cures, conversions and other marvels on the grounds that such concrete examples have more power to move his hearers than abstract reasoning.[7] We find a number of Gregory's personal theological preoccupations intruding on his presentation from time to time, his interest in angels and their functions,[8] the rules for the interpretation of Scripture,[9] and his concern about the imminent end of the world.[10] Generally, however, Gregory stays close to the Gospel text he is commenting on, and his teaching is of wide applicability.

One of the themes which is often touched on in the *Gospel Homilies* is desire for God. Although he was at various times in his career an administrator, a pastor and a diplomat, Gregory remained very much a monk at heart. There is a mystical tenor in his exhortations that seems to spring from experience, which enables us to see a man of deep personal prayer behind the *persona* of an effective man of affairs and leader of men. Desire for God and devotion to heaven were dominant themes in Gregory's personal philosophy, and it is with good reason that Jean Leclercq speaks of him as "Doctor of Desire."[11]

I. Spiritual Desire

Although desire for God is an important strand in Gregory's thought, he approaches the theme with a fair amount of flexibility. At the center of his thought is the experience of a longing for God, for heaven and for spiritual realities. Associated with this is a growing disaffiliation for worldly and fleshly values, an abhorrence of evil and a strengthening of inner, personal unity. On a more visible level, dedication to spiritual realities expresses itself in a characteristically Christian approach to life, in good works and in an unfeigned and unrestricted love. To speak about Gregory's teaching on spiritual desire is to intimate something of the dynamic which binds together these disparate elements.

1. Theological Bracketing

Gregory's understanding of man's desire for God needs to be appreciated within the context of his theological standpoint with regard to human reality. Like so many of the Church Fathers, he took his basic assumption about man from the Genesis account of creation in which man is said to have been formed to God's image, *ad imaginem Dei*.[12] This fundamental, pre-elective affinity with God means that it is natural for man to seek God insofar as he is absent, to desire his presence and to feel incomplete without him. Man was made to contemplate the uncreated

Light; orientation toward God is, therefore, a basic imperative of his nature.[13]

Man's situation, however, changed with the Fall: *aliud sumus per peccatum lapsi, aliud per naturam conditi.*[14] In being expelled from the garden of delights, the human race has become blind.[15] The flesh became dominant, with the result that man's spiritual aspect was perverted[16] and bent.[17] If man was to make any headway in fulfilling his natural potential, he would have to struggle continually against the flesh and even despise the "dung-heap" which is his own body.[18] Growth in spirituality was seen by Gregory to involve learning to live not according to the body and its instincts, but according to the soul or spirit, *(mens)* which transcends corporal realities[19] since everything that is inner is more potent than external realities[20] and because the soul is, in fact, the dwelling of God, his temple.[21]

Gregory does not speak often about the role of Christ in the rebuilding of human nature; he seems to take it for granted. There is a sustained awareness in his writings of the power of grace to energize man in his search for God and to sustain him in the practice of good. Desire for God is, in fact, Christ's gift,[22] it is also his command.[23] For Gregory, it is an integral part of being a Christian. A short passage in the second homily combines some of these themes.

> The human race is blind since in its first father it was expelled from the joys of Paradise. It is without knowledge of the transcendent light and is made to experience the darkness of its condemned state. Nevertheless, through the presence of its Redeemer, it is enlightened so that it may, even now, through desire, catch sight of the joys of inward light and so be able to walk, by good action, on the path of life.[24]

Desire thus appears as an interim reality which does service for man's direct participation in uncreated light and which serves to guide his steps along the way to fulfillment.

2. The Nature of Desire

The essential characteristic of desire for God is that it belongs with a preference for heavenly or spiritual realities. Gregory uses phrases such as *coeleste desiderium,*[25] *studium coelestis desiderii,*[26] and even *disciplina studii coelestis.*[27] It is the object of such a desire that differentiates it. Desire for God indicates a fundamental turnabout in personal orientation; it involves the renunciation of earthly desires,[28] including the flesh, acquisitiveness and ambition,[29] and even control lest the thoughts linger over such subjects and arouse concern for them in the heart.[30] The reason Gregory gives for leaving aside earthly desire is simple and straightforward. Concern with earthly things desensitizes a person to spiritual realities with the result that he becomes incapable of responding to grace and of going beyond the dictates of instinct and expedience.

> We who are intent on worldly cares gradually lose inner sensitivity in the proportion that our interests are aroused by external things. When the soul (*animus*) becomes involved in earthly care it becomes hardened against heavenly desire.[31]

> It is impossible for those to perceive the Kingdom of Heaven who, here below, although established in the heavenly faith, yet seek the earth with their whole desire.[32]

> Love for fleshly things breaks up the concentration of the mind (*intentionem mentis*) and blunts its cutting edge.[33]

For Gregory, yearning for the things of heaven involves insulating oneself against the attractions of transitory pleasures.

Yet the growing distance between the spiritual man and earthly satisfaction is not entirely the result of will-power and effort. Gregory recognizes that spiritual experience, which is like a foretaste of heaven,[34] causes many earthly delights to lose something of their former savor.

> One who knows perfectly the sweetness of the heavenly life, happily leaves behind everything he previously loved on earth. In comparison with this, everything is devalued. He abandons his possessions and scatters what he had amassed since his soul (*animus*) is on fire for heavenly things and he has no pleasure in the things of earth.[35] The mind of the man who does not seek the beauty of his Maker is unnaturally hard and remains frigid within itself. But if that man begins to burn with the desire of following the One whom he loves, then he runs, melted by the fire of love. Desire becomes restless, and everything in the world that previously made him happy, loses its value, Now he takes delight in nothing outside his Maker, and what previously brought pleasure to his soul subsequently becomes an intolerable burden.[36]

> If we keep in mind what are the things which are promised us in heaven and how great they are, then everything which we have on earth is devalued for the soul.[37]

Desire for God indicates that we appreciate the value of the precious pearl entrusted to us,[38] for "whoever desires God with his whole mind already possesses the object of his love."[39] To the extent that a person allows himself to be governed by this desire for heaven he is already in heaven, a fellow citizen of the angels,[40] only his body is on earth.[41]

In a homily on the parable of the great supper (Lk. 14:16-24), Gregory is at pains to distinguish between spiritual and carnal desire.

> There is a great difference, dear brothers, between the pleasures of the body and those of the heart. Bodily pleasures set alight a strong desire when they are not possessed, but when he who has them partakes of them, he becomes satiated and tires of them. On the other hand, spiritual pleasures are tiresome when they are not possessed, when they are possessed they cause greater desire. He who partakes of them hungers for more, and the more he eats the hungrier he becomes. In carnal pleasure the appetite is more pleasurable than the experience, but with regard to spiritual pleasures the experience of them is more rewarding; the appetite for them is nothing. In carnal pleasures the appetite causes satiety and satiety generates tedium, but in spiritual pleasures when the appetite gives birth to satiety, satiety gives birth to even greater appetite. Spiritual delights increase the extent of desire in the mind even while they satisfy the appetite for them. The more a person experiences their taste, the more he recognizes what it is that he loves so strongly. Therefore we cannot love what we do not have because this would involve ignorance of the taste…. You cannot know his sweetness if you have never tasted it. Rather, touch the food of life with the palate of the heart so that having made trial of his sweetness you may be empowered to love.[42]

The idea of man's continuing penetration of the divine reality and the theme of unending progression in desire are common among the Eastern Fathers, especially Gregory of Nyssa.[43] There is, however, no indication in the present text that Gregory the Great was familiar with any of the classical formulations of this theme in the Cappadocian's writings.

There is movement in desire; it is uneasy and restless as long as it is separated from its object. The very fact of delay only causes it to grow stronger.[44] It is the positive force of desire that motivates both the renunciation of sin and self-satisfaction, as we have already noted, and serves as the stimulus to all manner of good works.[45] Desire is, as far as Gregory is concerned, more than a simple nostalgia for God and for heaven; it is the central principle of integral Christian living. It is desire which locks together the various actions and restraints which are expected of a follower of Jesus and relates them firmly to the person's center of understanding and decision.

3. The Vocabulary of Desire

Jean Leclercq has already compiled a first listing of Gregory's vocabulary of desire.[46] There are the expected images of hunger,[47] sighing,[48] and panting (*anhelare*);[49] there are straight synonyms such as *concupiscere*[50] and *inhiare*,[51] there are spatial metaphors such as *festinare*,[52] *transire*,[53] and *sublevare*,[54] and he makes use of the more active image of seeking God.[55] Occasionally he strings several different terms together to form a chain, a fact which leads one to suspect that the various words used are virtually interchangeable.[56]

Perhaps most characteristic of Gregory's vocabulary is his use of the images of fire and heat. The "fire of charity"[57] burning in the heart of the believer causes him to grow hot (*aestuare*,[58] *inardescere*,[59] *ardere*[60]) and to catch fire (*ignescare*[61]) and burn (*accendere*[62]) with the passion of desire[63] for heavenly things.

Two important usages will be examined separately: that of *intentio* and the theme of compunction.

4. The Object of Desire

Man is moving toward eternal life and it is for heaven that he yearns above everything else. The idea of heaven as the goal of the Christian's pursuit is very strong throughout Gregory's writings. In the fourth book of the *Dialogues*, Gregory spells out a detailed eschatology as a means of confirming simple readers in the faith and protecting them from both cynicism and despair. His teaching has been presented and analyzed by J.P. McClain in *The Doctrine of Heaven in the Writings of St. Gregory the Great*.[64]

In the *Gospel Homilies* the prospect of heaven forms the backdrop of nearly all Gregory's considerations. "To this end let us move with all our love, for it is there that we shall be gladdened forever. In that place is the holy community of the heavenly citizens, there is certain festivity and unendangered rest; there true peace is no longer 'left' for us, but 'given' to us...."[65]

It is love for the heavenly homeland (*patria*) which ought to dominate our attitudes.[66] Our thoughts should tend toward it each day,[67] and firmly fix the anchor of our hope there.[68] If we are animated by this prospect then our progress will be faster and more fearless (*robustius ten-datur*)[69] and we will be less dismayed by the hardships experienced in fighting for the heavenly King.[70]

The Christian is chiefly characterized by the way in which he has turned away from earthly realities and allowed his interests to be captivated by the prospect of heaven. The more complete his emancipation from the tyranny of world, flesh and devil, the more aware he will be of his yearning for eternal life and the stronger will this desire grow.

There is an element of "realized eschatology" in Gregory's thought. In his comments on the parables of the Kingdom, he makes it clear that he regards them as applicable to the present reality of the Church.[71] For him, the Church is, even now, the "threshold" of heaven.[72] At the same time, he recognizes the limits of human perception. It is unable to attain now to the *supercoelestia*;[73] God remains "incommunicable" since men cannot see through to his Godhead.[74] This is why the preferred object of spiritual desire is not God but heaven.

If it is true that it is only when he allows himself to be shaped by his desire for heaven that man is true to his nature, then it means that the Christian is a pilgrim;[75] for as long as he remains in the flesh,[76] only his body is here below.[77] Because he is on the way, his manner of living is dictated by his pilgrim status. A beautiful passage in the *Moralia* develops this thought.

> The present life is but a road by which we advance to our home-land. Because of this, by a secret judgment, we are subjected to frequent disturbance so that we do not have more love for the journey than for the destination. Some travelers, whenever they see pleasant fields by the road, contrive to linger there and thus deviate from the course undertaken in the journey. As long as they are charmed by the beauty of the journey, their steps are slowed. It is for this reason that the Lord makes the path through this world rough for his chosen ones who are on their way toward him. This is so that none may take pleasure in this world's rest or find refreshment in the beauty of the journey and thus prefer to continue the journey for a long time rather than to arrive quickly. It is also to prevent one who finds delight in the journey from forgetting what he had desired in his homeland.[78]

5. Intentio

The term *intentio* is a rich and evocative one within the monastic tradition.[79] Although its range of meanings is wide, it habitually has reference to a concentrated outflow of energies from a person's center in a particular direction. It is distinct from action,[80] but it is what gives to any particular action its specifically human or moral dimension. An action is qualified by what the doer of the action intends. *Intentio* is something that comes from within the person; in Gregory it often comes from the *mens*.[81] It is not to be confused with outwardly imposed obligation,[82] or mere chance.[83] It is the essential personal content of behavior, containing elements of deliberateness,[84] motivation,[85] and decision.[86] An *intentio* bridges the gap between spiritual aspiration and concrete behavior; it gives external embodiment to the inner dynamics of personal choice.

The whole movement of the Christian's being is toward God. The momentum behind it stems from the action of grace in his heart; ahead of it, as its goal, is eternal life. Thus, very often in monastic literature, desire for God in its ontological sense is often referred to by *intentio*. "Hasten with all the energy (*tota intentione*) of your being toward the glory of this resurrection and flee from earthly desires which place distance between you and your Author."[87] Gregory tells us to fix the *intentio* of our mind on the true light,[88] and to have the heavenly homeland as its goal.[89] This is to say that it is necessary for the Christian to ensure that the fundamental direction of his life is toward God; to the extent that this is so, everything will be well, otherwise no good can be expected. Gregory is harsh toward those whose energies are consumed by less worthy objects: work,[90] worldly cares,[91] or illicit actions.[92] The only worthy goal for the Christian's thoughts and endeavors is the heavenly kingdom. "The eyes of the mind go on ahead of us; with complete concentration (*tota intentione*) they look upon the goal at which we will arrive."[93] In gauging an action's value, what has to be examined is whether it is directed toward God; only such an *intentio* is capable of pleasing him.[94] Love sharpens the focus of the *intentio*,[95] whereas carnal involvement renders it dull.[96]

In Gregory's *Gospel Homilies* the word *intentio* is often used in a sense closely akin to spiritual desire. It signifies an outward movement from man's spiritual center which is deeper than the superficial fluctuations of thought and emotion. It informs behavior and gives it a specific personal imprint. When the *intentio* is appropriately directed, it has heaven as its goal. Its repeated use in tandem with *coeleste desiderium* indicates that when Gregory speaks of spiritual desire he has in mind an ontological movement from the center of man's being, which progressively suffuses his whole life and all his activities with a sense of being drawn toward God. Desire is not a superficial emotion of longing or nostalgia nor a rational response of the will to appropriate inspirational data. It is, rather, an innate, pre-elective quality of being, which is never quite extinguished by sin or infidelity, but which permanently supplies the fundamental motive power for all man's efforts to respond to grace and return to God.

6. Compunction

Something of the wealth of traditional, monastic teaching on *compunctio* has been lost in recent centuries by limiting its meaning to sorrow for sin. While contrition is certainly an element in compunction, the traditional understanding of the term involves a lot more.

At the heart of compunction is a sense of pain, a stinging, a sensation of being pricked. It is a question of being pierced (*punctio*), aroused from torpor and complacency and stimulated to action. It has nothing to do with an obsessive and depressive sense of guilt, with endless reviewing of past failures and sins. There is regret for previous actions, but it is of a specific kind. It is the dissatisfaction that rises in a person's heart only when he is deeply convinced that he is capable of something better. The dissatisfaction, regret or anger is a secondary manifestation; the primary content of the experience of compunction is the recognition of a deep personal attraction for God and of his love drawing one on. The depth of the divine compassion makes an impression on our hard hearts and we can experience only regret at our present level of performance. The poignancy we experience in our resistance to God's overpowering love causes us to yearn ever more strongly for the grace of conversion and to desire with greater vigor that compromise might cease.

Compunction is, therefore, a dual sensitivity. It places before us both the reality of our sinful condition *and* the urgency of our desire to be possessed totally by God. Compunction is the feeling we have when, having experienced something of our fulfillment in union with God, we allow ourselves to become once more immersed in activities which inhibit or frustrate our spiritual potential. It is active disgust at our low-level living, knowing that we were made for something better and that nothing less than God can bring us what our nature craves.

Sometimes he is admitted to a particular, unaccustomed experience of inner sweetness and for a moment he is, in some way, a new man, set afire by the breath of the spirit. And the more he tastes the object of his love, the stronger grows his desire for it. Within himself he craves what he had experienced through the inner sense of taste and from love of that sweetness he becomes of less value in his own eyes. For after he discovers that sweetness he becomes able to perceive what sort of a person he is without it. He tries to prolong the experience but he is driven back from its strength because he is still weak. And because he is incapable of contemplating such purity, he weeps sweet tears and then falls back and lies down on the tears of his weakness. For the eye of the mind is unable to fix itself firmly on what it had so fleetingly glimpsed. It is subject to the constraint of inveterate habit which holds it down. In this state he is filled with yearning and he ardently tries to transcend himself, but each time he is beaten by fatigue and falls back into his familiar darkness. A soul so moved must endure a serious inner struggle against itself.... When we are thus pierced (*compuncti*) we seek to distance ourselves from what we have made of ourselves so that we may be refashioned according to what we were originally.[97]

It is precisely the comparison between what we are and what we could be which constitutes the triggering cause of the experience of compunction. It can be seen, therefore, that Gregory recognizes two complementary aspects of compunction: a negative apprehension of the presence of sin and fear of punishment which gives birth to its opposite—hope for eternal life and frustration at being kept far from it.

There are two main types of compunction. First the soul thirsting for God is pierced (*compungitur*) by fear and afterwards by love. In the beginning the soul is moved to tears at the remembrance of its evil deeds and fears the prospect of eternal punishment. But when, after a long and anxious experience of pain, this fear works itself out, then is born in the soul a calmness coming from the assurance of forgiveness and the soul is inflamed with love for heavenly joys. He who previously wept at the prospect of being led to punishment now begins to weep most bitterly because he is far from the Kingdom. For the mind contemplates the choirs of angels, the community of the blessed spirits and the splendor of the unending vision of God and then he is more downcast because he is separated from these eternal goods than he was when he wept because he was afraid of unending evils. When the compunction of fear is complete it draws the soul into the compunction of love.[98]

A different approach occurs in the same passage from the *Moralia* already cited.

> There are four situations in which the soul of the good person is strongly moved by compunction. Firstly, when he remembers his sins and thinks about where he was (*ubi fuit*); secondly, when searching his heart and fearing the sentence of divine judgment he takes thought of where he will end up (*ubi erit*); thirdly, when he seriously considers the evils of this present life and grieves at the thought of where he is (*ubi est*); finally, when he contemplates the good things of the heavenly homeland which he has not yet obtained he mourns because of where he is not (*ubi non est*).[99]

Gregory writes often about compunction, and it is clear that it constitutes a single reality with spiritual desire, although viewed from a different angle. It too is a "fire"[100] and a "flame"[101] and once he uses an epexegetical genitive to indicate its compatibility with *intentio*.[102] Compunction, for Gregory, is more than contrition for sin; it is also desire for God. It is the "machine" (to use one of his favorite terms) by which the soul is lifted up to lofty things.[103]

It is important to appreciate Gregory's overriding concern with compunction in order to have a context in which to locate the various texts in the *Gospel Homilies* which speak about this quality.

Compunction is a gift of divine love[104] which is aimed at bringing us to salvation.[105] It causes in us a salutary pain and fear[106] which keeps us from forgetting the possibility of eternal death,[107] and thus serves as a check on carnal desire,[108] a remedy for depravity,[109] and destroys any lack of seriousness or concern with trivialities (*curiositas*).[110]

At the same time, compunction is closely akin to spiritual desire. "Sometimes, those who remember that they have done things which are wrong are pierced (*compuncti*) with pain at the recollection and become afire with love for God.... They are consumed with a passion of desire as they yearn for their heavenly homeland."[111] When we baptize our consciences with its tears,[112] we daily wash away our sins,[113] and progressively make our way back[114] to paradise[115] and to eternal joy.[116]

Compunction comes into our lives through various channels. Primary among them is the attentive reading of the Scriptures,[117] by the comparison of our lives with those of our fathers,[118] and by heeding the rebukes which spiritual men hurl at us.[119]

Gregory is especially insistent that we do not take our salvation for granted once we experience compunction,[120] but strive to allow it to become an ever more potent force in our attitudes and behavior. It is possible to forget our moments of being touched by the grace of God and return to our former lukewarmness,[121] especially during periods of sustained temptation.[122] Hence Gregory reiterates the need for the Christian to ensure an element of vigilance in his approach to life.[123]

II. The External Factors in Desire

Although Gregory conceives of desire as something flowing from the nature of man and coming from his deepest zone of personal being, he recognizes that spiritual desire cannot possibly exist without stimulation, support and expression through outward forms.

In the first place it is the task of pastors to nurture desire in the hearts of those for whom they are responsible, healing the wounds of sin with their tongues (like the dogs in the story of Lazarus)[124] pronouncing absolution on those who have received the grace of compunction,[125] and continually pointing out to them the path back to the heavenly homeland.[126] The power of the preacher's word comes from its reliance on the Scriptures, which are, for the Christian, food which sustains the soul in its progress toward God,[127] the eating of which is a source of correction,[128] compunction,[129] and instruction in fulfilling his will,[130] and resisting the clamorous demands of the flesh.[131]

Once a person becomes aware of the power of spiritual desire it is necessary for him to allow the fullest scope to its expression in his daily life. Although desire naturally seeks embodiment in good works,[132] this is not a necessary process; the person must actively will and contribute to this conclusion.[133] Real love for God is always active; it is never lazy,[134] even the reception of the sacraments is without effect unless they have impact on our lives.[135] Works of kindness nourish the spirit[136] and provide example and encouragement to others.[137] It is important for the Christian to be intent on all good works, especially hospitality,[138] to put down roots of humility[139] and patience,[140] to endure hard times when they come,[141] and to submit his life to the governance of God's Word,[142] and to the processes of purification which he sends.[143] For external works well performed, a generous reward is to be expected in the world to come.[144]

It is often said that Gregory was much concerned with the interaction of the active and contemplative aspects of Christian life.[145] Yet, in one sense this was no problem at all. The binding principle was love: love is the epitome of the Christian program of good works; it is also the essence of spiritual desire and contemplation. In love, action and contemplation merge.

In speaking of desire for God, Gregory often uses one or other of the terms for love.[146] Desire is itself a first step of love,[147] it is the specific form which loves takes while the Christian is yet on pilgrimage. Love is the energy that gives strength to desire,[148] and is already a sort of knowledge[149] and possession of the beloved.[150]

There is no real tension between the life of desire and the active service of the neighbor. The love which is expressed in spiritual desire is itself incomplete unless it serves others,[151] loving our friends in God and our enemies for God's sake.[152] A pithy sentence in the 39th homily summarizes Gregory's position. *Neque enim aliter Redemptoris nostri membri efficimur, nisi inhaerendo Deo et compatiendo proximi:* "There is no other way of becoming the members of our Redeemer except by staying close to God and having compassion for our neighbor."[153]

On the other hand good works lead back to spiritual activity. Desire is kindled by virtuous action. This is because all activity tends toward rest,[154] whatever we do is ordered to bring us to the delight of experiencing something of the stillness of God's eternal rest[155] and to remove us from the tumult of temporal involvement.[156] Through contemplation, inner grace lifts us above the clamor of the flesh[157] to where there is perfect peace.[158] "For we seek the beloved on our beds when, in this present life, we sigh with desire for something of our Redeemer's rest."[159]

*   *   *

For St. Gregory the Great, desire is an ontological force inserted into man's nature to give him a permanent yearning for heaven. To the extent that he refuses to be dominated by lesser desires, a person comes under the sway of this fundamental movement of his being. He is led to regret the power sin holds over him and to desire salvation with great ardor. As such love grows in his heart, it begins to find expression in the way he lives, in the priorities he establishes, in the way he acts and in the manner in which he resists temptation. It becomes a shaping force in his life, ordering everything toward heaven and toward the God who draws him to himself.

NOTES

[1]Ev 40.1-2; PL 76, col. 1302B. Gregory distinguishes the levels of exposition and opts to order his discourse *ad moralitatis latitudinem*. Throughout this article, where no other indication is given, the references are to Gregory's *Gospel Homilies* in PL 76. All translations are my own.

[2]Four volumes: London 1954, 1958, 1959, 1963. The homilies presented in these volumes are numbers 1, 2, 6, 7, 8, 10, 14, 15, 16, 18, 19, 20, 21, 26, 27, 28, 29, 30, 34, 36, 38, 39. Five other Gregorian texts are also given. In St. Gregory the Great, *Parables of the Gospel*, (Dublin, 1960), twelve homilies are translated: 9, 11, 12, 14, 15, 17, 19, 31, 34, 36, 38, 40. Cistercian Publications has published a complete translation of the *Gospel Homilies* in its Cistercian Studies Series, #123.

[3]For general information on Gregory and his sources, the following may profitably be consulted. R. Gillet, art. "Grégoire le Grand (saint)," in *Dict. Spir.* 6 (1967), col. 872-910. This includes three columns of bibliography. *Id.*, Introduction to: Grégoire le Grand, *Morales sur Job* (Livres 1 et 2) (SC 32), Paris, 1950, pp. 7-113. J. Leclercq, in *The Spirituality of the Middle Ages* (HCS 2), London, 1968, pp. 3-30. A.C. Rush, art. "Gregory I (The Great), Pope St," in *Cath. Encycl.* vol. 6, pp. 766-770. The classic work, C. Butler, *Western Mysticism*, [2]1926, retains some value. On the relationship between St. Gregory and St. Benedict, cf. K. Hallinger, "Papst Gregor der Grosse und der Hl. Benedikt," in B. Steidle (ed.), *Commentationes in Regulam S. Benedicti* (SA 42), Rome, 1957, pp. 231-319. A looser and less satisfactory treatment of the same issue is O. Porcel, *La doctrina monastica de San Gregorio M. y la Regula monachorum*, Madrid, 1950.

[4]21.1, 1169CD.

[5]34.1, 1248A.

[6]23.1, 1182B; 39.1, 1294A.

[7]39.10, 1300B: *quia ad amorem Dei et proximi plerumque corda audientium plus exempla quam verba excitant.*

[8]Cf. 8.2, 1104D; 11.1, 1115A; 21.7, 1174A; etc. See also L. Kurtz, *Gregors des Grossen Lehre von den Engeln*, Rottenburg, 1938.

[9]Cf. 38.2, 1282D; 39.3, 1295C; 40.1, 1302B; etc. See also H. de Lubac, *Exégèse médiévale*, Paris, 1959-61, *passim*.

[10]Cf. 1.3, 1079C; 4.2, 1090B; 5.1, 1093B; 36.2, 1267A; etc. Cf. R. Manselli, "L'escatologismo di S. Gregorio Magno," in *Atti del primo congresso internationale di studi Longobardi*, Spoleto, 1952, pp. 383-387.

[11]J. Leclercq, *The Love of Learning and Desire for God*, New York, 1962, pp. 33-43. J. de Guibert gives Gregory the title "Doctor of Compunction"; cf. *infra*, note 97, p. 229 of the article cited there.

[12]28.2-3, 1211C-1212C; 34.6, 1249A. Cf. *In Cant.* 1.28, PL 79.490B.

[13]31.7, 1231B. *Contemplatus namque quod ad supernam lucem intuendam homo conditus fuerat, sed peccatis exigentibus, foras missus, mentis suae tenebras portat, superna non appetit, infimis intendit, coelestia numquam desiderat, terrena semper in animo versat.* Cf. *Moralia* 8.18; PL 75.821C. *Ad contemplandum quippe Creatorem homo conditus fuerat, ut eius semper speciem quaeret.*

[14] 32.2, 1233B.

[15] 2.1, 1082C.

[16] 39.3, 1296A.

[17] 31.6, 1230C: *a mentis suae rectitudine curvatur.*

[18] 40.11, 1312A: *sterquilinium…hanc ipsam corruptibilitatem corporis appello.* A good treatment of this theme with ample reference to Gregory is P. Daubercies, "La théologie de la condition charnelle chez les Maîtres du haut moyen âge," RTAM 30 (1963), pp. 5-54.

[19] 34.11, 1253C: *Et sunt nonnulli qui, supernae contemplationis facibus accensi, in solo conditoris sui desiderio anhelant, nihil jam in hoc mundo cupiunt, solo aeternitatis amore pascuntur, terrena quaequae abjiciunt, cuncta temporalia mente transcendunt, amant et ardent.*

[20] 36.13, 1274C.

[21] 39.7, 1298A: *Templum quoque et domus Dei est ipsa mens atque conscientia fidelium.*

[22] 29.11, 1219D: *non autem deserit desiderium nostrum ipse qui dedit, Jesus Christus.*

[23] 18.1, 1150B: *Coelestem patriam desiderare Veritas jubet…*

[24] 2.1, 1082C.

[25] 10.6, 1113B; 17.14, 1146B; etc.

[26] 11.1, 1115A. Cf. 37.5, 1277C, *pro studio aeternae intentionis…*

[27] 11.1, 1115C.

[28] 5.2, 1093C; 11.1, 1115C; 26.12, 1204C: *Ad huius resurrectionis gloriam…tota intentione festinate. Terrena desideria quae ab auctore separant fugite;* 31.7, 1231B; 33.7, 1244A: *In illis ergo cordibus Deus requiescit, quae amor praesentis saeculi non incendit, quae carnis desideria non exurent, quae incensa suis anxietatibus in huius mundi concupiscentiis non arescunt;* 37.4, 1277A: *Si ergo ad aeterni solis habitationem tendimus, dignum profecto est ut de Deo itinere pro carnalibus affectibus non declinemus;* 38.4, 1284B; 40.11, 1312B: *Discite…temporalia cuncta despicere, discite honorem transeuntem contemnere, aeternam gloriam amare.*

[29] 18.1, 1150B: *carnis desideria conteri, mundi gloriam declinare, aliena non appetere propria largiri.*

[30] 9.1, 1107A: *Talentum in terra abscondere est…cor a terrenis cogitationibus nunquam levare;* 10.6, 1113B: *Omnis peccator terrena cogitans, coelestia non requirens, sursum respicere non valet;* 36.6, 1269A: *Dum hunc terrena cura occupat, illum alieni actus sagax cogitatio devastat, alterius etiam mentem voluptas carnalis inquinat, fastidiosus quisque ad aeternae vitae epulas non festinat.*

[31] 17.14, 1146B.

[32] 19.5, 1157C.

[33] 37.3, 1276C.

[34] 38.4, 1284B.

[35] 11.2, 1118A.

[36] 25.2, 1191A.

[37] 37.1, 1275A.

[38] 11.2, 1118A.

[39] 30.1, 1220C: *Qui ergo mente integra Deus desiderat, profecto iam habet quem amat.*

Neque enim quisquam posset Deum diligere, si eum quem diligit non haberet.

[40]21.7, 1174A: *Ecce in resurrectione auctoris nostri ministros ejus angelos concives nostros agnovimus.... His cum necdum visione possumus desiderio et mente jungamur.*

[41]38.15, 1292A: *Cum solo hic essent corpore, quotidie animo ad aeterna transire.*

[42]36.1, 1266. The whole 36th homily is translated in Toal, *op. cit.*, vol. 3, pp. 180-189.

[43]Cf. Daniel O'Donovan, "Gregory of Nyssa's *Epektasis*," in *Colloquium* 4 (1970), pp. 54-61.

[44]22.5, 1177A: *Tanto validius teneat cum invenerit quanto tardius invenerit quod quaerebat*; 25.2, 1190D: *Prius ergo non inveniendus quaeritur, ut post inventus strictius teneatur. Sancta enim desideria, ut praediximus, dilatatione crescunt.* The idea is frequent in Augustine.

[45]2.1, 1082C.

[46]This is at the end of his article, "Un Centon de Fleury sur les devoirs des moines," *Analecta Monastica* I (SA 20), Rome, 1948, pp. 75-90. I have expanded this list somewhat, although restricting myself to terms occurring in the *Gospel Homilies.*

[47]36.7, 1269D.

[48]25.2, 1190B; 27.4, 1207A: *per aspirationem.*

[49]12.1, 1119B; 34.4, 1248B; 34.11, 1253C; 38.10, 1288D.

[50]37.3, 1276B: *aeterna concupiscit.*

[51]36.10, 1272B; 40.2, 1304A: *...uni tamen singulariter bono inhianter aestuabat dicent, "Mihi autem adhaerere Deo bonus est."*

[52]36.12, 1273C.

[53]37.10, 1281C; 38.15, 1290A.

[54]38.4, 1284B.

[55]25.2, 1190D; 25.4, 1192B.

[56]34.4, 1248B: *Nonnunquam hi qui se aliqua illicita egisse meminerunt, ex ipso dolore compuncti, inardescunt in amorem Dei...flagrant desiderio, ad coelestem patriam anhelant.*

[57]5.4, 1095A: *Mens nostra accenditur igne charitatis*; 25.2, 1191A: *liquefacta per ignem amoris...*

[58]12.6, 1122A: *cum magno aestu desiderii* (an epexegetical genitive); 24.6, 1188B; 25.2, 1191A; 25.4, 1192B; 40.2, 1304A.

[59]11.2, 1115C: *inardescit in coelestibus animus*; 34.4, 1248B; 34.11, 1253C; 37.1, 1275B.

[60]25.2, 1190D; 25.4, 1192B; 36.13, 1274C: *sed ardenter interius ad aeterna destinate.* A similar usage is *incalescere*, 26.2, 1191A.

[61]20.13, 1167C: *ad bonorum coelestium desiderium ignescat.*

[62]30.5, 1223A: *in desiderium suae aeternitatis accendit*; 31.5, 1230A.

[63]34.4, 1248B: *flagrant desiderio.*

[64]Washington, 1956.

[65]30.10, 1227C. Cf. 24.4, 1186C: *Omnis nostra operatio in fide Trinitatis exhibita ad requiem tendit.*

[66]3.3, 1088A; 35.8, 1264A: This text concerns the sanctity of Abbot Stephen.

...Erat autem huius lingua rustica, sed docta vita. Hic pro amore coelestis patriae cuncta despexerat, possidere aliquid in hoc mundo fugiebat, tumultus devitabat hominum, crebris et prolixioribus orationibus intentus erat.

[67]37.10, 1281C; 38.15, 1291A: *quotidie animo ad aeterna transire.*

[68]29.11, 1219C: *Iam tamen spei vestrae anchoram in aeternam patriam figite; intentionem mentis in vera luce solidate.*

[69]17.7, 1142A.

[70]6.3, 1097A.

[71]38.2, 1282D: *In sancto Evangelio regnum coelorum praesens Ecclesia nominatur.*

[72]38.10, 1288B: *vestibulum dicitur.*

[73]27.4, 1207A. This term is often associated with Ps-Denis, though see the reservations of E. Boissard, "Saint Bernard et le Pseudo-Aréopagite," in RTAM 26 (1959), pp. 214-263, especially pp. 217-218. Note, however, that Gregory had read Ps-Denis and quotes him once in connection with the angels. He calls him *antiquus et venerabilis Pater*; 34.12, 1254B.

[74]22.4, 1176B: *(Deus) qui in se quidem semper quietus atque incommunicabilis permanet...*; 26.8, 1202A: *A mortali quippe homine divinitas videri non potuit.*

[75]2.8, 1085B; 11.1, 1115A: *In praesenti etenim vita quasi in via sumus, qua ad patriam pergimus*; 17.7, 1141D.

[76]9.1, 1106B: *Carnis enim locus proprius terra est quae quasi ad peregrina ducitur, dum per Redemptorem nostrum in coelo collocatur.*

[77]38.15, 1291A.

[78]*Moralia* 23.47, PL 76.279D-280A.

[79]I have discussed the evolution of the meaning of *intentio* and its use in the monastic tradition in "Intentio Cordis (RB 52.4)," RBS 67 (1981), pp. 105-120.

[80]11.1, 1115B: *Sic autem sit opus in publico quatenus intentio maneat in occulto...*; 22.7, 1178B.

[81]22.7, 1178B; 26.11, 1203C.

[82]36.13, 1274A: *magis ex debito quam ex intentione.*

[83]17.5, 1141B: *quia ex occasione, et non ex intentione.*

[84]31.5, 1230A: *intentionem contra se dirigit.*

[85]22.1, 1174C.

[86]3.4, 1088B.

[87]26.12, 1204C.

[88]29.11, 1219C.

[89]9.1, 1107A: *pro intentione...supernae patriae.*

[90]38.5, 1284D: *intentus labori terreno.*

[91]17.14, 1146C: *curis enim saecularibus intenti.*

[92]33.2, 1240A: *illicitis actibus...intenta.*

[93]36.11, 1272D.

[94]11.1, 1115B.

[95]25.2, 1189D: *Sed amanti semel aspexisse non sufficit, quia via amoris intentionem multiplicat inquisitionis.*

[96]37.3, 1276C.

[97]*Moralia* 23.43, PL 76.277-278. The whole section of the *Moralia* on the theme

of compunction is one of the classic *loci* for a study of the concept. It is translated in Toal, *op. cit.*, vol. 4, pp. 193-199. An old, but still useful presentation is, J. de Guibert, "La componction du coeur," in RAM 5 (1934), pp. 225-240. Valuable material is also contained in the four-column entry of *Thesaurus Linguae Latinae (editus iussu et auctoritate consilii ab academicis societatibus diversarum nationum electi,* Leipzig, 1918) *sub voce.*

[98]*Dialogues* 3.34, PL 75.300A. The same thought can be found in *Moralia* 24.6, PL 76.291; *In Ezech.* 2.10.20-21, PL 76.1070; *Ep.* 7.23, PL 77.879.

[99]*Moralia* 23.41, PL 76.276A.

[100]*Moralia* 1.48, PL 75.349A: *Holocaustum igitur dare, est totam mentem igne compunctionis incendere, ut in ara amoris cor ardeat.*

[101]*Moralia* 3.59, PL 75.628D: *Quia afflata a Redemptore spiritus, tanta cor nostrum flamma compunctionis concremat, ut omne quod in eo est illicitum et operis et cogitationis exurat.*

[102]*In Ezech.* 1.8.13, PL 76.859D.

[103]*Moralia* 1.47, PL 75.548C.

[104]17.10, 1143C.

[105]26.6, 1200C; 36.9, 1272A.

[106]27.4, 1206D.

[107]15.2, 1132A: *Aeternae igitur mortis periculum formidate*; 20.13, 1167C.

[108]39.1, 1294C; 39.3, 1295D.

[109]34.6, 1249B: *prava mens si no prius per timorem evertitur, ab assuetis vitiis non emundatur.*

[110]36.4-6, 1268-1269: *Grave namque curiositatis est vitium.*

[111]34.4, 1248B.

[112]10.7, 1114B.

[113]39.9, 1300A: *Mala quae fecimus per quotidiana lamenta diluamus*; 17.10, 1143C.

[114]39.5, 1297A: *aut dolore compuncta, redeat.*

[115]10.7, 1113D: *Quoniam qui a paradisi gaudiis per delectamenta discessimus, ad haec per lamenta revocamur.*

[116]2.8, 1085D: *Per fletus quippe ad aeterna gaudia ducimur.*

[117]18.1, 1150B.

[118]17.10, 1143C: *Tunc autem de nobis vere compungimur, si studiose patrum praecedentium facta pensamus...*

[119]20.13, 1167C.

[120]13.3, 1124C-D.

[121]15.2, 1132D; 18.1, 1150B.

[122]30.2, 1221A: *Per compunctionem quidem Dei respectum percipiunt, sed tentationis tempore hoc ipsum quod compuncti fuerant obliviscuntur.*

[123]13.3, 1124C-D.

[124]40.2, 1303A.

[125]26.6, 1200C: *...ut quos omnipotens Deus per compunctionis gratiam visitat, illos pastoris sententia absolvat.*

[126]24.4, 1186A.

[127]15.2, 1132A: *Cibus enim mentis est sermo Dei*; 38.11, 1289B: *qui Scripturae sacrae*

epulis pascimur…; 38.14, 1290B.

[128]22.8, 1180A: *In quo devorationis Verbo quid aliud quam pigritiae nostrae torpor reprehenditur?*

[129]18.1, 1150B: *Et sunt nonnulli qui libenter verba Dei suscipiunt ita ut etiam in fletibus compungatur…*

[130]40.10, 1309D: *Verba sacrae lectionis debent nos instruere ad implenda mandata pietatis.*

[131]39.5, 1297B: *Adversarius noster in via est sermo Dei, contrarius nostris carnalibus desideriis in praesenti vita. A quo ipse liberatur qui praecepta eius humiliter subditur.*

[132]2.1, 1082C.

[133]36.9, 1271A: *Viderit quae agere debeant, sed haec ex desideriis non sequuntur.*

[134]30.2, 1221B: *Numquam est Dei amor otiosus…*

[135]22.8, 1178D.

[136]4.5, 1092B: *pro opere spiritus nutriatur.*

[137]11.1, 1115B: *ut de bono opere proximis praedeamus exemplum.*

[138]36.13, 1273D: *…bonis operibus intentus…hospitalitati praecipue studens.*

[139]7.4, 1103A: *In cunctis ergo quae agitis…radicem boni operis humilitatem tenete.*

[140]35.4, 1262D: *Radix omnium custosque virtutum patientia est.*

[141]6.3, 1097A.

[142]39.5, 1297B.

[143]15.2, 1132A.

[144]9.5, 1108C: *Intellectum…illi dari debuit qui bene exteriore…ministravit*; 17.7, 1141D-1142A.

[145]Cf. J. Leclercq, *The Spirituality of the Middle Ages*, pp. 10-12.

[146]"We see how, again for St. Gregory, *desiderare, amare* and *diligere* are synonymous." J. Morson, "Seeking God By Desire," CS 2 (1967), pp. 175-185; p. 180.

[147]29.11, 1219D.

[148]30.10, 1227C.

[149]27.4, 1207A: *Amor ipse notitia est.*

[150]30.1, 1220C.

[151]6.5, 1298B-C: *In via Dei socios habere desiderate…si ad Deum tenditis, curate ne ad eum soli veniatis*; 38.10, 1288D: *Omnis itaque homo inter homines vivens, sic ad eum anhelet quem desiderat, ut tamen hunc non deserat cum quo currebat.*

[152]The same principle is enunciated in three places in the *Gospel Homilies*: *Charitas est amicum diligere in Deo, et inimicum diligere propter Deum*; 9.6, 1108D; 27.1, 1205B; 38.11, 1289A.

[153]39.9, 1300A.

[154]24.4, 1186C.

[155]22.4, 1176B.

[156]24.2, 1184D-1185A.

[157]38.4, 1284B.

[158]30.10, 1227C.

[159]25.2, 1190B.

Introductory Note

This article attempts to describe the traditional stages of awareness through which a person passes in the process of arriving at an undivided heart. Joyful communion with God is a long journey which has its beginnings at the level of seriousness about avoiding sin and practicing active virtue, keeping a guard over one's life. It progresses by sustained efforts in the field of meditation, opening the mind and heart to God's word and allowing oneself to be educated in seeing things differently. It reaches its perfection in an abiding sense of communion with God that rapidly transforms the whole person.

The term "mindfulness" (or *memoria Dei*) attracted me because of its use in different spiritual traditions, the theme of remembering in Deuteronomy and the liturgical connotations of *memoria* in the New Testament.

The article was published in CS 17 (1982), pp. 111-126.

Mindfulness of God
in the Monastic Tradition

A point at which western monasticism makes contact with many other currents of spiritual teaching is its emphasis on the role of mindfulness in spiritual growth. What is common to all these diverse traditions is the realization that, of themselves, external actions achieve nothing. If divinization is to take place, it can only be by means of a profound change which makes the human mind or heart progressively attuned to the divine self-manifestation and so capable of guiding behavior in accord with its perception of truth. Spiritual growth demands a change of heart by which a person is simultaneously the passive receiver of revelation and an active follower, who strives to render life responsive to its dictates.

Mindfulness or *memoria* is a significant theme in the various strands of thought and practice which constitute the Benedictine tradition. Monastic *conversatio* is not viewed as a pre-determined complex of attitudes and activities which relieves the monk from any responsibility from the distinctive fashioning of his life. Monasticism is, rather, a constant flight from mindless and comfortable routines and evasions and the cultivation of contrary habits of mind: openness to grace, sensitivity, vigilance for the coming of the Lord. Monastic regimen is seen primarily as a structure of mindfulness through which the monk grows in his ability to perceive truth—about himself, about God, about the world in which he lives.

The greatest obstacle to this work is *oblivio*, heedlessness, a consciousness so saturated with tangible employments that its capacity to absorb the unexpected is inhibited. Other sins and vices will eventually yield to growth and to the grace of God: to be immured in untruth not only retards growth, it is a positive factor in decline. The monk who forgets God forgets himself. He ceases to be concerned about the things which serve his ultimate welfare and habitually fails to take those steps which are required by the reality of his own situation. He falls not through malice or overt weakness, but through thoughtlessness and unconcern (*acedia*). Unless he is roused by the sharp sting of compunction, his spiritual senses atrophy and salvation itself is placed in jeopardy. Heedlessness inevitably issues in death: *Mors animae oblivio*.[1] In monastic tradition the memory of God is more than a pious practice; it is the very dynamic of a life which is subordinated to the divine process of transformation.

This ascetic doctrine has its foundation and principal point of reference in the Bible. This remains true even though the influence of other trains of thought (such as Stoicism and Platonism or Neo-Platonism) has colored some formulations of the theme. In the monastic tradition, the admonitions of Deuteronomy and of the Psalms to mindfulness were seriously pondered in the light of the New Testament, with the result that *memoria* became a principle not only of liturgical celebration but also of effective Christian living. In their worship and in their prayer the monks strove to realize the memory of Christ.

In this paper, three stages of mindfulness will be discussed. In the first, *memoria* is very close to the notion of fear of the Lord; it connotes a seriousness in the ordering of life and a care to live within the limits fixed by the commandments. In the second stage, *memoria* becomes an active effort of mind and heart to retain and enter into the riches of revealed truth through *meditatio*. Finally, mindfulness of God appears less as an action than as a transformed state of consciousness, in which every thought and word and deed take place within the context of the divine. Such is the purity of heart attained by one who has reached this level that his whole being is habitually possessed and transfigured by the presence of God; he has been "divinized."[2]

1. Mindfulness as Praxis

The fundamental dynamic in the process of humility, according to St. Benedict, is fear of the Lord.[3]

> The first step of humility is that, having the fear of God always before his eyes, he entirely flees from forgetfulness and is always mindful of everything that God has commanded. He constantly turns over in his mind that those who despise God burn in hell for their sins and how eternal life has been prepared for those who fear God.[4]

Before any positive progress can be expected, the monk has soberly to assess the extent of the labor to which he is committing himself. No effort is made to shield him from the difficulty of the journey to God (58.8) nor to pretend that an undemanding enthusiasm will much profit him. Instead, he is confronted immediately with the stark reality of his own sinfulness and he is expected, at the very beginning, to take practical measures to diminish its control over him. In the monastic tradition, *compunctio, contritio* and *timor Dei* are unequivocally declared to be the foundations of spiritual growth.[5]

The scope of Benedict's demand becomes clear from his insistence that the monk's religious endeavor be considered a full-time occupation. Eight times in describing the first step of humility he uses the adverb *semper*, four times the phrase *omni hora* occurs, and he also uses *cotidie* once.[6] The point he seems to be making is that a genuine religious response to life cannot be a part-time or eclectic project, sometimes to be indulged, at other times to be judiciously deferred. The first thing that a monk must do is to win control over his own life; to succeed in this he must exercise surveillance over all its details.

A life characterized by forgetfulness is often not overtly sinful. Its danger lies in its capacity to engender sins of omission coupled with an unseeing sense of complacency. Peer pressure is normally sufficient to ensure that the monk complies with the visible obligations of his state, with the result that there are usually only rare infractions of major precepts. At the same time, however, the very struggle which the monk makes in order to upgrade his observance often leads him into hidden sins. Either he becomes complacent and judges harshly those that cannot attain his standard or, alternatively, he begins to relax, preferring to rest on the plateau instead of continuing his climb. In both cases, growth is stopped without the monk's becoming aware that such is the case.

Fear of the Lord is the goad which keeps the monk moving and prevents his being lulled into *oblivio*. If he must regress, then it is fear of the Lord that keeps him aware that he is doing so and eventually prepares the way for his recovery. It is his mindfulness of the ultimate values in his life and of his own personal precariousness which makes a monk tireless in doing good and in avoiding evil. The first requirement for upright living is an upright understanding; if his mind has lost the capacity for distinguishing truth, then behavior inevitably deteriorates. Fear of the Lord is the beginning of wisdom because it sets the monk in the way of sober self-esteem, alerting him to what needs to be done and giving him the energy to translate theory into practice. When a monk is unaware of his actual state, he tends to become smug, locked into his private routines and somewhat removed from an appreciation that Christian life is a sustained struggle.[7]

Fear of the Lord compels a monk to protect himself, first of all, from sins and vices. This is the negative aspect of spiritual endeavor, already touched upon in the enumeration of the tools of the spiritual craft:

To fear the day of judgment. To dread Gehenna. To desire eternal life with the whole longing of one's spirit. Each day to place death before one's eyes. To know for certain that in every place God is watching one.[8]

Thus motivated, the monk begins to take steps to eliminate actions and behavior patterns that militate against evangelical living. His appreciation of his own impairment leads to a willingness to accept guidance from outside himself, to conform to an external code of conduct by keeping the commandments and by desiring to walk according to the judgment of another (5.12). Conversely, a frequent reason why monks experience problems in their obedience either to a rule or to an abbot is a failure to appreciate personal sinfulness and the havoc wrought interiorly by years of heedless living. The monk who sees himself as a sinner is likely to be conscientious in fulfilling all justice before he sets his sights on loftier goals.

The avoidance of sin goes further than achieving a level of blamelessness in external conduct. Benedict and the Master here draw on the tradition of psychological sophistication built up in the desert and insist that the monk also mount guard over his instinctual desires and that he make some effort to exercise control over his thoughts and imaginings. It is here that memory beings to mean a little more than merely remembering to make an effort. Evagrius notes that it is often from the undisciplined memory that sin begins, making the monk restless and dissatisfied and inclining him to instinctual behavior.

> Sadness tends to come up at times because of the deprivation of one's desires. On other occasions it accompanies anger. When it arises from the deprivation of desires it takes place in the following manner. Certain thoughts drive the soul to the memory of home and parents, or else to that of one's former life. Now when these thoughts find that the soul offers no resistance but rather follows after them and pours itself out in pleasures that are still only mental in nature, they then seize her and drench her in sadness, with the result that these ideas she was just indulging no longer remain. In fact they cannot be had in reality, either, because of her present way of life. So the miserable soul is now shriveled up in her humiliation to the degree that she poured herself out upon these thoughts of hers.[9]

The effective negation of sin must, therefore, begin with the countering of instinctual thoughts and memories. The best means of doing this is to fill the mind with loftier contents. " 'Psalms and hymns and spiritual canticles' invite the spirit to the constant memory of virtue by cooling our boiling anger and by extinguishing our lusts."[10]

The motivation alleged by Benedict and the Master for vigilance regarding one's innermost thoughts (*ut sollicitus sit circa cogitationes suas perversas*, 7.18) is the fact that these are constantly subject to divine scrutiny and liable to judgment. This is a theme which occurs frequently in the *Small Asceticon*, the "Rule of our Holy Father Basil" to which Benedict refers in RB 73.5.[11]

> How can one who is slack about (observing) the commandments be made industrious and vigilant?
>
> If he is certain that the Lord God is present everywhere and that he sees everything. And let him keep before his eyes the threat which has been uttered against those who are slack as well as the hope of God's great reward which the Apostle Paul promised saying, "Everyone will receive an appropriate reward according to his labor." Other texts like this may be found in Holy Scripture which relate patient labor and careful work to God's glory.[12]

In a similar vein he responds to a query about avoiding anger by suggesting that the monk "believe that God watches all things and perceive that the Lord is always present."[13] To rid himself of distractions at prayer he has to strengthen his conviction that he stands before the eyes of God.[14] The cause of his problem is that "he does not believe that God is present, probing hearts and reins."[15]

> How can one escape the vice of seeking to please human beings and to win approval from them?
>
> If he is certain of the presence of God and has the fixed intention of being careful to please God. Let him be bound by a great desire for the happiness which the Lord has promised. If he is aware of God's presence he will not try to please his fellow servants at the Lord's expense and to his own detriment. He will, instead, depend on the Lord's behest, not that of his fellow servants.[16]

A long answer at the very beginning of the *Small Asceticon* demonstrates Basil's conviction that *memoria* is a fundamental means of living according to the commandments of God and of thus arriving at perfect charity.

> ...Therefore we ought to keep our heart with all watchfulness lest the desire for God be dislodged and driven from our souls by evil desires and filthy thoughts. On the contrary let each one of us set on

our souls the seal of the divine form and figure by the assiduous recollection and memory of God, so that it cannot be removed by any disturbances whatever. If the fire of desire for divine charity burns in us, then the mind and the soul will be illumined by the frequent memory of him and we will be lifted up and raised for the task of keeping his commands...

In this life crafts are exercised according to a certain mental viewpoint (*prospectus animi*); the work of the hands is guided by the way the mind conceives things. In the work which we have undertaken there is the same need for a single viewpoint, and that fixed point of reference is our obligation to please God. It is in accordance with this that we give ourselves to the work of keeping the commandments. For it is impossible to make any meaning of it unless one retains in the memory the will of God who has given us the task. It is a fact that while we are ever mindful of God we will observe his will, give ourselves to the labor of the task with industry and skill and we will always be joined to God.... If anyone does not keep the rule and fails to observe what is commanded it may be inferred that he is one who is forgetful of God.[17]

Basil then goes on to suggest practical means for maintaining oneself in mindfulness: living apart, not mingling with unbelievers, prayer, work, self-denial in imitation of Christ and, generally, a realistic acceptance of the need for the amendment of life. Without these, mindfulness is impossible.

Then, once the obstacles, disturbances and occupations which are usual in human life are accepted, he is not able to maintain that which is greater than all and more precious: the memory of God. Once this is driven out and excluded from the soul, all divine joy and gladness is lost. His capacity to find delight in the Lord is diminished and he no longer experiences the sweetness of the divine promises.... So he comes into the neglect and forgetfulness of the divine judgments and falls into a habit of counting them as unimportant. There is no state worse or more destructive than this.[18]

The theme is repeated frequently throughout subsequent monastic tradition. Forgetfulness of God causes the monk to degenerate and opens the door to all sorts of aberrations. What is even more dangerous is that it cuts him off from the sources of spiritual nourishment, so that even if he continues to follow monastic observances, he ceases to gain much profit from them.

Bernard of Clairvaux describes the condition produced by such forgetfulness.

> Brothers, you will find very many, even among those who wear the religious habit and are professedly seeking perfection, in whom the fearful sentence of the Prophet seems to be realized: "If I forget you Jerusalem, let my right hand be given to oblivion." They devote their whole attention to looking after the left side. They become experienced, somewhat, but it is in the wisdom of this age which they ought to have given up, in those things which flesh and blood reveal and which, according to the Apostle, they should be unwilling to accept. See how eagerly they grasp at any present gain, how, like seculars, they enjoy fleeting conveniences, how their souls are so easily upset by earthly loss or deprivement of goods. See how carnally they dispute over such things, how shamelessly they pursue them, how they deny their religion to become involved in worldly business as if this was all they had, their entire substance.[19]

Once the *memoria abundantiae suavitatis eius* vanishes, the residual observances begin to pall. Guerric of Igny describes the result thus:

> Now they come to the divine office and doze, they give themselves to idle and pernicious thoughts, they sit down to read but yawn at the book, they listen to the sermon but find it difficult to pay attention.[20]

Monastic life is not only ineffectual without mindfulness; it rapidly becomes intolerable.

The first stage of mindfulness gives to the monk's life the character of seriousness. He honestly confronts the liabilities inherent in his personal history and the necessary hardship of Christian discipleship and decides that he is not going to attain the goal he has set before him without sustained and painstaking application. There is no possibility of reaching God either through a short burst of initial enthusiasm or by occasional forays into spirituality when the mood takes him. Fear of the Lord makes the monk realize that in his particular case, responding to God's call involves a long, uphill struggle. From the monastery he expects not a foolproof system which will minimize the effort and anguish of the pursuit, but support from like-minded brothers and discretion from those wiser than himself.

This is not to say that the monk embarks on a program of maximal asceticism. *Memoria* is not a mechanism of the superego for arousing guilt feelings and for impelling the monk to keep exceeding the natural limits of his ascetical performance. Fear of the Lord has no interest in quantitative asceticism; its concern is with the quality of what is done: whether an action is done mindful of God and for the sake of the Kingdom or whether it simply flows from instinctual prompting, from ambition or from the chaos of interior inconsistency.

Fear of the Lord simplifies the monk's life by motivating him consciously to channel the bulk of his energies in a single direction. A life which responds to inner and personal imperatives is less likely to be rendered uncreative by the vagaries of external circumstance. Without some progress toward such undividedness, spiritual growth is impossible, or in traditional terms, nobody can realistically expect to attain the Kingdom of God without striving after purity of heart.[21]

2. Mindfulness and "Meditatio"

The stages of mindfulness are not perfectly sequential. The care for the ordering of life and the practice of asceticism do not consume the whole of the *memoria*'s energies, even in the initial phases. The drudgery of amendment is constantly lubricated by moments of awareness which prevent the desire for God being quenched by weariness. Even while the monk is mindful of his own shortcomings and lack of resources, he is constantly strengthened by his perception of the bounty of God and the boundless possibilities opened up by grace.

Experience soon reveals that the labor of living under discipline is lightened by keeping in mind the loving kindness of God and the power of his grace.

> Therefore my advice to you, friends, is to turn aside from troubled and anxious reflection on your own progress, and escape to the easier paths of remembering the good things which God has done; in this way, instead of becoming upset by thinking about yourself, you will find relief by turning your attention to God…. Sorrow for sin is, indeed, a necessary thing, but it should not prevail all the time. It is necessary, rather, that happier recollections of the divine bounty should counterbalance it, lest the heart should become hardened through too much sadness and so perish through despair.[22]

The work of amendment is complemented and motivated by the effort to set life in perspective through reflection on the realities of Christian faith. There has to be an active turning of the mind to the things of God, otherwise consciousness will be overwhelmed by the insistent impressions of sensate experience or by the subtle demands of unresolved inner processes. It is only by positively placing before his eyes the memory of God and the ultimate truths of human existence that the monk is able to avoid succumbing to the dispiritedness and inertia which are engendered by concentration on the immediate situation.[23]

Monastic life, from its inception, has been geared to promoting mindfulness. The purpose of *fuga mundi* is not escape into a different set of distractions, but to make provision for that solitude, disengagement and creative monotony which are necessary for heightened awareness. When the emphasis is on doing things instead of on the personal content of every action, there is danger that monasticism will degenerate into a mindless program of endurance and good works, loosely legitimated by reference to hierarchical authorities. When monasticism merely substitutes for the real concerns of secular life the imagined urgencies of its own microcosm, it is not only encouraging immaturity in its members, it is depriving them of the very reason for their coming—leisure to seek God and to grow in his love.

In general, then, the kinds of activities undertaken by monks should be such that they bring their doers closer to truth. In the first place, the manifold truth of human existence: its social and individual aspects, its labor and its delight, its moments of creativity and its hours of routine, its bodily aspect as well as its intellectual and spiritual values, its different rhythms of development and the mellow familiarity that stems from stability. Such a balanced life predisposes the monk to grow in his appreciation of the truth about God. Thoughtfully undertaken, it provides the possibility that, at the end of his life, he will have come close to wisdom.

Yet even within such a privileged atmosphere of leisure, the monk needs consciously to advert to the presence of God, to lift up his heart in the midst of living and to open his mind to God's revelation. Opportunity for this comes, structurally, through the Hours of the *Opus Dei* in which the monk is able to give himself more explicitly to converse with God than is possible in the diffuse moments of prayer which season his daily activities. At this time the monk is able to live more intensely and consciously the values he embodies in his other occupations. The Hours of the *Opus Dei* are aids to a more general mindfulness, reminders of the presence of God and vehicles for his Word.[24]

Perhaps even more important, because it flows more completely from free choice, is the monk's regular practice of holy reading. Mindfulness of the economy of divine grace in the midst of activities is largely dependent upon some time having been devoted to concentrating on nothing else. It is from his long hours spent in *lectio divina* that the monk derives that special character which he imprints on all he does. By exposing his life to the thrust of the Word, he sets his situation in a broader perspective according to which ultimate values can assume a rightful priority over short-term issues.

It is not sufficient simply to read; the Word must be received into a reflective heart. The essential component of monastic *conversatio* is that it gives the monk an opportunity to ponder over the Word, to relate it to the circumstances of his own life and to experience that extra discovery which comes only through the effort to put it into practice.

It is the practice of *meditatio* which is the characteristic feature of the second stage of mindfulness. Monastic tradition sees meditation in the same way as the writers of the Old Testament.[25] It is not so much an exercise in discursive thought or construcive imagination, as the low-voiced recitation of what has been read, a process of rumination which forms a background to other activities and which opens the whole of life to the *memoria Dei*. William of St Thierry describes the process in a well-known passage.

> Some part of your daily reading should, each day, be stored in the stomach (i.e., the memory) and be allowed to be digested. At times it should be brought up again for frequent rumination. You should select something that is in keeping with your calling and in line with your personal orientation, something that will seize hold of your mind and not allow it to think over alien matters.[26]

The effort involved in thus allowing life to be seasoned by the Scriptures is not to be underestimated. The monk has to make a deliberate choice to put aside other thoughts and fantasies and to overcome a curious reluctance which makes it difficult for him to turn his mind to God. The power of sin is experienced concretely in the obstacles thrown up to prevent prayerful reflection. There is no way of avoiding the conclusion that strengthening the memory of God within one's heart is a long and arduous process.

It is the slowness of the conversion which guarantees that it is not artificial. If there were some gimmick available which rendered recollection of God easy, then the likelihood is that the result would be contrived—a distortion of personal existence. The years invested in the struggle to turn the mind around so that it regularly includes God within its natural horizons effect a change within the personality itself so that, in time, it is possible to accomplish naturally and easily what would have been very difficult in the beginning. There is no advantage in praying beyond one's level. Genuine prayer is always tailored to the reality of the person's situation. Furthermore, the process of becoming aware of God is dependent on a more general growth in recognizing truth and penetrating to the meaning of existence. There is no question of the *memoria Dei* being a substitute, alternative or rival to common sense and practicality, at least not often at this stage. Instead, awareness of God curiously co-exists with mundane mental processes, sometimes permeating them with its own distinctive fragrance.

What characterizes this stage of mindfulness is a fair degree of discipline, though the monk lives from inner values rather than merely because of external constraints. Having once internalized monastic *conversatio*, it is necessary for him to proceed apace with the evangelizing of his own consciousness. He needs to keep making the effort to lift up his heart to God, to exercise some control over his thoughts and to be ready to recall his mind to its goal through the practice of *meditatio*. With practice and through the grace of God, this becomes easier with the years, and even sporadic periods of backsliding seem to add something to the quality of the final blend. Prayer becomes habitual: the memory of God lives in the heart and the name of Jesus becomes as the air that is breathed.

3. Mindfulness as Transformation

In the early monastic Fathers and among the Cappadocians, the *memoria Dei* was viewed in terms of a recurring effort of the heart to make contact with God, especially through the active recall of the words of Scripture, the teachings of holy persons and the manifold benefits which come from the hand of God. The practice was, they affirmed, accessible to all. In Hausherr's view, there was nothing "mystical" about it.[27]

In the Cistercians of the twelfth century, the term seems to have a more intense connotation. Instead of being a sporadic exercise which punctuated the daily round, it is understood as a state of being in which the one who has faithfully struggled throughout the years becomes progressively immersed. "*Memoria*," writes Aelred, "is like the soul's embrace by which it clings to God without any trace of forgetfulness."[28] "It is by memory that the soul embraces God without any sense of weariness."[29] For William of St Thierry, understanding *memoria* in the Augustinian sense of faculty rather than act, the memory is the site of the soul's communion with God. When the memory is filled with God, then joy, grace and love flood the soul,[30] understanding and love are activated,[31] and temptation and infidelity are kept at bay.[32] The very act of memory is already an act of love, the desire to make present the absent Object of one's affection.[33] "Love is kindled anew when it remembers the One whom it loves so exclusively, and the great desire of the one who so remembers is itself a loving prayer."[34]

At this point it is clear that the emphasis is no longer on the specific contents of the act of remembering, but on the fact of memory itself. The action of recall is seen as a means of stimulating a faculty which had been dormant until then. It is an awakening of the person's spiritual outreach. Here the thought manifests clear dependence on Augustine's development of Neo-Platonic ideas. Memory is seen not simply as a faculty or skill for retrieving stored information; it is understood as a means for making contact with ultimate reality which although always present is habitually "forgotten" or ignored. The activation of memory is a necessary concomitant of a person's growth in spiritual sensitivity.

Thus, through mindfulness, a person becomes in fact what he is already in nature. Formed in God's image and stamped with a likeness to his Creator, he fell through sin into the "Region of Unlikeness," where his own state and the environment in which he lived conspired to induce forgetfulness. But through the work of Christ and the labor of discipleship he is progressively re-formed to his pristine likeness and by the grace of his active presence he is gradually transformed and trans-figured from glory to glory.[35]

Consciousness follows being. The monk's labor to reform his life by cooperating with grace and by raising his mind to God gradually effects a change in what he is. His life becomes simpler and more innocent, he is less under the control of passion and less impelled by furious inner storms. He retains his capacity for sin, but even his falling seems to serve his growth through the depth of his repentance and the humbled sense of his own unworthiness. He is not quite the "New Man," but he is moving in that direction.

At such a stage of growth, mindfulness of God is almost an habitual thing. It is like the sap that keeps a tree supple. Most of the time it does not seem to be a distinct thing in itself; it appears more as a hidden fac-tor which changed the quality of what is done. Actions performed in mindfulness somehow have the power to produce a disproportionate effect on the recipient. A cup of cold water given in mindfulness becomes a torrent of salvation which cleanses and carries with it both giver and receiver. There is a unity of inner actuality and outer behavior which renders actions translucent. An inner radiance transforms the humblest service.

In the monk who has been admitted to this level of mindfulness, Christ is powerfully active. His life is characterized by wisdom, the "outshining of eternal light,"[36] and he develops an affinity for things spiritual and divine. He has no sense of achievement because all is gift, he is merely aware of a profound sense of joy which is not related to carnal or worldly events. From all of these he finds himself detached. Once initiated into spiritual delights, he finds himself losing interest in tangible pleasures. At this point he can truly say: *Conversatio nostra in coelis est* (Phil. 3:20).

*   *   *

In the monastic tradition mindfulness is a strong emphasis. The monk is one who is called upon to abandon the heedless ways of unchristian society and to walk the humble paths that lead to truth. He begins his liberation from falsehood by the practice of humility in fear of God; he reinforces it by repeated acts of turning his mind and heart to God in response to his Word; he brings his part in the process to completion by opening himself to be fully possessed by *memoria Dei*. There is a progression from morality to psychology to spirituality, from action to consciousness to being. But in all this the monk's own contributions are minimal; it is God who acts, bringing to completion the image of himself presaged at creation.

NOTES

[1]"Forgetfulness brings death to the soul. From this death we rise thus: by memory we become sensate, by obedience we hear, by understanding we see, by caution we smell and we experience taste through love." Bernard of Clairvaux, Sent. 2.19; SBO 6b.29.16-18.

[2]For a basic treatment of the several aspects of this rich theme see the following: H. Eising, art. "Zakar" in TDOT 4.64-82. O. Michel, art. "Mimneskomai" in TDNT 4.675-683. H. Sieben, art. "Mnèmè Theou" in DSp 10.1407-1414. A. Solignac e.a., art. "Mémoire" in DSp 10.991-1008. O. Casel, *Faites ceci en mémoire de moi* (Lex Orandi n. 34), Paris: Cerf, 1962. M. Thurian, *Eucharistic Memorial* (Ecumenical Studies in Worship n. 7-8), London: Lutterworth Press, r.p. 1968. J. Gribomont, "La preghiera secondo S. Basilio," in C. Vagaggini and G. Penco, *La preghiera nella bibbia e nella tradizione patristica e monastica* (Biblioteca di cultura religiosa n. 78), Rome: Edizioni Paolini, 1964, pp. 373-397, esp. pp. 387-393. I. Hausherr, *The Name of Jesus* (Kalamazoo: Cistercian Publications, 1978, pp.

158-165. *Id.*, *Hésychasme et Prière* (Orientalia Christiana Analecta n. 176), Rome: Pontifical Institute of Oriental Studies, 1966, pp. 275-277. R. Javalet, *Image et ressemblance au douzième siècle: De saint Anselme à Alain de Lille*, 2 vols., Paris: Letouzey & Ané, 1967. G. Webb, "The Cistercian Memoria: William of Saint Thierry VI," *New Blackfriars* 48 (1966), pp. 209-213. W. Hiss, *Die Anthropologie Bernhards von Clairvaux* (Quellen und Studien zur Geschichte der Philosophia n. 7), Berlin: W. De Gruyter, 1964, pp. 112-115 and *passim*.

[3]This is clear from the fact that RB follows RM in adding the first and twelfth "degrees" to the series of ten *indicia* adduced by John Cassian in Inst. 4.39.2 (SChr 109, p. 180). Fear of God is the basis and inspiration of humility just as transformation and perfect charity are its goal. The ground had already been prepared by Cassian's statement: *Principium nostrae salutis eiusdem custodia, timor Domini est.* (Inst. 4.29.1; SChr 109, p. 178, adapting Prov. 9:10 or Ps. 110:10). Cf. Conl. 11.7, SChr 54, pp. 105-107. On the relationship of *memoria* and *timor Dei*, cf. Inst. 6.13.31; SChr 109, p. 278.

[4]RB 7.10-11: *oblivionem omnino fugiat et semper sit memor omnia quae praecepit Deus....* Some influence of Cyprian of Carthage is postulated by André Borias, "L'influence de saint Cyprien sur la Règle de saint Benoît," Rev Bén 74 (1964), pp. 54-97, esp. pp. 70-71. The onward dynamic of mindfulness as obedience to precept is indicated by Bernard: "The memory of God is the pathway to the presence of God. Whoever keeps the commandments in mind so that he may observe them will be rewarded, from time to time, by the perceiving of his presence." Sent 1.12; SBO 6b.9.17-21.

[5]"The first task of a faith working through love is compunction of heart" thus Bernard of Clairvaux, Asc. 1.3; SBO 5.125.9-10. Bernard often refers to the sequence: compunction, devotion, piety; e.g., Sent 1.9; SBO 6b.9.15-17, Sent 2.169; SBO 6b.56.1-4, Div 87.6; SBO 6a.333.9-12, Div 90.1-4; SBO 6a.337-340. All these texts are related to SC 10-12, being expositions on the theme of the three unguents. Other listings which state the negativity of the first phase of spiritual development include SC 12.1; SBO 1.60.9-11, SC 16.4; SBO 1.91-92, SC 18.6; SBO 1.108.4-6, p Epi 1.4; SBO 4.317.1-10, Div 48; SBO 6a.268.10-11, Div 118; SBO 6a.396.8-11, Div 88.1; SBO 6a.334.4-7. Texts which highlight the role of fear of the Lord include Sent 1.34; SBO 6b.18.20-19.6, Asspt 4.3; SBO 5.245-246. Div 40, covering much the same area designates as the first phase *cognitio sui*, SBO 6a.236-243.

[6]*Semper* occurs in vss. 7, 10, 11 (*bis*), 13, 14, 18, 23, 27, corresponding to RM 10.10, 11 (*bis*), 13, 14, 19, 20, 24, 34, 38. *Omni hora* is in RB 7.12, 13 (*bis*), 29, corresponding to RM 10.10, 12, 13, 40. *Cotidie* is at RB 7.28 = RM 10.39. A. de Vogüé notes that both *semper* and *omni hora* recur in the twelfth degree, also added to Cassian's basic outline; cf. La Règle de saint Benoît IV, SChr 184, p. 288, note 21.

[7]The Vulgate text of Job 7:1 is often quoted in this respect: *Militia est vita hominis super terram.* On this theme see E. Manning, "La signification de 'militare-militia-miles' dans la Règle de saint Benoît", Rev Bén 72 (1962), pp. 135-138. Thomas Merton approaches the subject from a different angle in his

treatment of the role of dread in the practice of prayer. Cf. *The Climate of Monastic Prayer* (Cistercian Studies Series n. 1), Spencer: Cistercian Publications, 1969.

[8]RB 4.44-49.

[9]*Praktikos* 10, SChr 171, p. 514; translated by J.-E. Bamberger, *Praktikos, Chapters on Prayer* (Cistercian Studies Series n. 4), Spencer: Cistercian Publications, 1970, pp. 17-18. Benedict follows the tradition in seeing such mental delights as the gateway to more external sins: *Quia mors secus introitum delectationis posita est* (RB 7.24). Through the agency of the demon of *acedie*, other memories can also trigger temptations, such as those which bring to mind the difficulties of perseverance (*Praktikos* 12, SChr 171, pp. 520-526), those which recall the sufferings of other monks (*Praktikos* 7, p. 510) or the pleasures of one's own pre-reformed past (*Praktikos* 34, p. 518). Cf. Cassian, Inst. 6.13.2; SChr 109, p. 276.

[10]*Praktikos* 71.3; SChr 171, p. 658. Cf. Cassian Inst. 1.4.13-14, SChr 109, p. 48 and Inst. 6.13.31, p. 278.

[11]The *Small Asceticon*, comprising 203 questions and answers of varying lengths, is probably an earlier (*circa* 365) form of the *Great Asceticon* which is made up of both the "Long Rules" and the "Short Rules." The *Small Asceticon* is found only in Latin and Syriac renderings; the original Greek is not extant. In the Latin version of Rufinus, probably known to Benedict, it is given in Benedict of Aniane's *Codex Regularum*, located in PL 103, 484-555.

[12]Reg 66, PL 103, col. 518a.

[13]Reg 46, 514b; cf. Reg 79, 521c.

[14]Reg 108, 527c.

[15]Reg 34, 511c.

[16]Reg 60, 516d.

[17]Reg 2, 492b, 492d, 493a.

[18]Reg 2, 494a.

[19]QH 7.14; SBO 4.422.21-423.2.

[20]Serm 38.4; SChr 202, p. 292. Translated by monks of Mount Saint Bernard Abbey, *Liturgical Sermons Volume Two* (Cistercian Fathers Series n. 32), Spencer: Cistercian Publications, 1971, p. 114.

[21]The classical *locus* for a statement of this theme is the first conference of Abba Moses, SChr 42, pp. 78-108.

[22]Bernard of Clairvaux, SC 11.12; SBO 1.55.12-19.

[23] Cf. *Id.*, SC 32.4; SBO 1.228.16-20: "There are people who grow tired in their zeal for spiritual things and, as a result, they gradually become lukewarm. Defective in spirituality, they walk sadly along the ways of the Lord. With a heart that is dry and without enthusiasm, they do what they are instructed, but they grumble often.... It may happen that he who is from heaven may begin to speak to us about heaven, singing the dear songs of Zion and telling us all about the city of God and the peace of that city and about the permanence of that peace and about eternity itself. Then, I tell you, such a happy account will carry the sluggish and sleepy soul along with it. The result will be that it will remove all disgust from the soul of the hearer and all tiredness from his body, as well." Cf. SC 14.6; SBO 1.79-80.

[24]Cf. M. Casey, "St. Benedict's Approach to Prayer," CS 15 (1980), pp. 327-343; esp. pp. 331f. See above, pp. 17-34.

[25]Cf. A. Negoitâ, art. "Hagah," TDOT 3.321-324.

[26]Ep Aur 122, SChr 223, p. 240. In the tradition which stemmed from Cassian's conferences on prayer, a short prayer or formula was often used to encapsulate the message extracted from the reading. "This formula of prayer and discipline is proposed to you so that every monk who is moving toward the permanent memory of God may accustom himself to its use. By continually turning it over in his heart he can preserve himself from that mobility of thoughts which comes from thinking about all manner of things" (Coll. 10.10; SChr 54, p. 84. Cf. Inst. 2.6.5-9, SChr 109, p. 68 and Inst. 5.10.1-3, p. 204).

[27]*The Name of Jesus*, p. 158.

[28]Sermo in Nativitate Domini, ed. C.H. Talbot, *Sermones Inediti* (Series Scriptorum S. Ordinis Cisterciensis n. 1), Rome: Editiones Cistercienses, 1952, p. 38.

[29]Sermo in die Pentecosten, *ibid.*, p. 108; cf. *De Anima* 2.3 *CChr Med* 1, p. 707.

[30]William of St Thierry, In Cant 30, SChr 82, p. 114.

[31]*Ibid.*, 64 (p. 162), 79 (p. 192), 81 (p. 198), 153 (p. 324).

[32]*Ibid.*, 80, p.196. Cf. Guerric of Igny, Serm 30.1.11-13, SChr 202, p. 172: "What is more promotive of the experience of love among the faithful or more effective as a remedy for behavior than the *memoria* of the crucified One? Such mindfulness destroys sins, crucifies habits of sin and fosters and strengthens the virtues."

[33]Guerric, Serm 10.5, SChr 166, p. 234.

[34]William of St Thierry, In Cant 127, SChr 82, p. 272.

[35]On divergences of thought between Bernard of Clairvaux and William of St Thierry, cf. E. Gilson, *The Mystical Theology of Saint Bernard*, London: Sheed and Ward, 1955, p. 239, note 178. The basis for this twelfth-century development is already given in Benedict's treatment of the final step in the climb to humility, where the monk is understood to manifest some signs of a burgeoning heavenly existence—Benedict here deviating from his major source. At the end of his progression from renunciation to perfect love, the monk appears as one totally permeated by a sense of God, wholly possessed by mindfulness. He becomes a living prayer. By the work of the Holy Spirit and the labor of decades, such a monk has been so seized by the love of Christ that *oblivio* is banished; all that he does is done in awareness of the presence of God. The early Cistercians followed Augustine's example in linking the themes of *memoria* and *imago*. At the pinnacle of humility, the monk abandons his attempts at self-deification and willingly accepts and asserts his creatureliness and his utter dependence on God. As a result, his latent likeness to God is laid bare and his innate imagehood is manifest in all its splendor.

[36]Cf. Bernard of Clairvaux, SC 70.5 SBO 2.210.11, SC 85.7; SBO 2.311.20-21, SC 69.2; SBO 2.203.2, SC 50.8; SBO 2.83.11-16.

Introductory Note

"The Prayer of Psalmody" (CS 18 [1983], pp. 106-120) was an exploration of the role of psalmody in the development of a prayerful life as a complement to a more silent, solitary prayer. Without distinguishing between liturgical usage and personal saying of the Psalms, it aimed to outline practical tactics in making use of the Psalter as a means of finding God and living from the heart. I had intended supplementing this essay with another on the Liturgy of the Hours, but have not yet done so.

The Prayer of Psalmody

Psalmody is a traditional form of prayer located somewhere on the continuum between the active exercise of prayerful reading and the more intense state of being which is associated with moments of contemplative prayer. It is the prayer which grows to fill the interstices between daily dedication to *lectio divina* and those brief instants of spiritual concentration which bring into temporary harmony the disparate elements of a complex individual life. As such it is an important element not only in the sanctification of the day but also in the preparation of the heart for the gift of contemplation.

It is a shame that psalmody is not much propagated nowadays as a means to prayerful living. It is not dramatic enough to attract much interest: a treasuring in the heart of familiar texts rather than the searing insight into hitherto unperceived truth, a mere murmuring of the mouth while the "wild wanton wits" remain dormant. "Vocal" prayer has, after all, fallen into disrepute these past four centuries. As a result, the practice of psalmody has been banished to the liturgy, where it suffered a long estrangement from the deep inner movements of love, aspiration and prayer. So it has come about that the Psalms are sometimes regarded with suspicion as part of a formalist package of religious observance, which bears little relationship to the genuine Godward movements of the heart.[1]

Such a dismissal of the Psalms is unfortunate. When the components of the liturgy are divorced from personal devotion, the result is, on the one hand, a less prayerful liturgy and, on the other, an impoverishment of the range of practices available to the individual for the expression of different facets of a religious response to life. Conversely, progressive familiarization with the Psalms on a personal basis is not only an easy way of extending mindfulness of God; it is, perhaps, the only way to render fruitful their use during the liturgy.

Any Scripture can, of course, be stored in the memory and brought forth for rumination, but the Psalms have traditionally been regarded as ideal for this purpose. This is true not only in monasticism but in the Church at large and, before that, in Judaism. Psalmody has been a tested component of Judeo-Christian piety for almost three millennia and should not, therefore, lightly be left aside. The parallel use of *sutras* in East Asian traditions is a reminder that there is something peculiarly conducive to prayer in the passive recitation of familiar texts, which conclusion is tentatively confirmed by the findings of audio-psycho-phonology.[2] In this matter also, the medium is perhaps as significant as the message.

In this article I would like to examine some of the problems associated with psalmody and to suggest some tentative remedies for some of the difficulties experienced by our contemporaries in its practice. Love for the Psalms is too characteristic a feature of monastic spirituality and devotion to be allowed to weaken and wane without regret.[3]

1. A Sense of Alienation

There are considerable difficulties to be overcome in acquiring the habit of psalmody, especially during the first phases of growth. Many, after a period of initial attraction to a limited number of "easy" Psalms, find their enthusiasm inhibited by the overwhelming strangeness of the bulk of the Psalter. The result is that the Psalms are often experienced as an obstacle rather than as an aid to prayer. When this leads to the abandonment of the personal use of the Psalms so that the only time the Psalms are used is in the liturgy, the sense of estrangement is intensified.

The primary reason for this discomfiture is the massive givenness of the Psalter. It stands there, aloof in its centuries-old sameness, with no reference or relevance to the present or to the one attempting to make use of it. Many of our contemporaries come to feel excluded by the low self-expression factor of the Psalms and cannot find prayer in them. It is not only that they are confused by such images as "the bulls of Bashan"; there is often a fundamental dissonance with certain fundamental themes such as law, exile, kingship, warfare, enemies, historical recital and primitive cosmology. The so-called "cursing Psalms" are not isolated examples of incomprehension; they are the climax of a number of different strands of thought with which many of our contemporaries find themselves profoundly out of sympathy. It is true that each of these difficulties can be explained and located within its proper context, but too often such instruction is presupposed rather than actually given. The recognition that the intelligent use of the Psalms demands a biblical formation proportionate to the individual's aptitudes is not realistically acted upon. As a result, the practice of psalmody is often bedeviled by the effort of sustained transposition, which occupies the mind, exhausts the energies and effectively inhibits the flowering of interior prayer.

A particular aspect of this difficulty is the low Christological content of psalmody. Those accustomed to a form of prayer which revolves around the person of Christ often find it difficult to relate this to the less focused piety of the Psalter. This seems to have been no great problem to the ancient monks, if the patristic commentaries are any indication of their approach.[4] They prayed the Psalms *to* Christ or *about* Christ; if this was not directly possible, then they changed their approach to the text until it was. The Psalms were, for them, profoundly Christian prayer.

Such an approach is often difficult to reconcile with the demands of critical exegesis, especially if one is only vaguely and imperfectly aware of the content of recent scholarship. Uncontextualized fragments of interpretation can easily destroy a devotional approach to psalmody without themselves being able to serve as the stuff from which prayer devolves. Hence it is important to develop a comprehensive view of psalmody which recognizes the distinction between literary analysis and prayerful utilization, and fosters the balanced development of both rather than the unilateral concentration on one or the other. Undisciplined allegorization and hyper-scientific theorization are equally to be restrained.

It remains sadly true that there are few substantial books on the Psalms which achieve such balance. It is not enough for experts to write watered-down commentaries interspersed with pious asides. What is needed is work which grows out of and, in some way, encapsulates years of scholarly attention and decades of prayer. Considering the fact that, within the Church, the Book of Psalms must be the most frequently read of all the books of the Bible, it is a singular tragedy that there is such a dearth of worthwhile introductory material. This certainly makes the task of initiation into the Psalter much more difficult.

The individual who wishes to make psalmody a structural element in his response to grace has really to work very hard. The core of the problem is, perhaps, to be found in the fact that the Psalms lack the fresh impact of a hitherto undiscovered passage and yet have not reached the point where they exude the mellowness that comes with years of use. This difficulty can be overcome only through perseverance, staying with the Psalms during the transition from one stage to the other, allowing them to weave themselves into the fabric of spiritual experience, building up a friendship which renders their spiritual force accessible. This last point is one which William of St Thierry noted.

> You will never grasp the meaning of the Psalms of David until, through experience, you make his sentiments your own.... There is the same gulf between attentive study and mere perusal as there is

between friendship and acquaintance with a transient, or between close affection and a passing word of greeting.[5]

Patience and perseverance are necessary if potential for enhancing prayerfulness is to be realized.[6]

It should be pointed out, however, that whatever problems are caused by the technical difficulties inherent in psalmody, those caused by subjective dispositions are both more serious and more fundamental.

Sometimes blame is laid on the obscurity of the Psalms or the difficulty of their melodies for a person's inability to find prayer therein. Often the basic cause is the person's own attitudes. Whatever blocks prayer will certainly render psalmody fruitless: non-reconciliation, distractedness, *acedia*, physical or emotional tension, self-display, domineering. These will inevitably impede a profound concordance of heart and lips. Furthermore, a person cannot *pray* the Psalms without a desire to pray and to the extent that such a desire is effective during psalmody, prayer will ordinarily result—notwithstanding the continuing operation of the various external impedances noted above. The operation of subjective factors is especially to be noted in psalmody which is part of prescribed or communal prayer. This is probably why St. Benedict concludes that a novice who is habitually able to find prayer in the *Opus Dei* is probably substantially faithful in other areas of his life (cf. RB 58.7).

2. Fusion of Horizons

Nothing is gained by denying the difficulties inherent in making use of the Psalms as vehicles of personal prayer. It would be a mistake, however, to think that these problems cannot be overcome or lessened through intelligent effort and perseverance. Strange they may appear to our contemporaries, but this alienation can be reduced and some merging of sensibilities achieved.[7] There is no real reason why our generation also should not be trained in making use of this traditional aid to prayerful living.

There is no doubt that the Psalms are complex; the texts are often obscure, with further complications added by their being successively overlaid by variant and even divergent meanings. This means that it is scarcely possible to appropriate their meaning without serious study, according to the individual's needs and resources.

On a first level there is question of achieving a familiarity with the texts of the Psalms, with the nuances and rhythms of psalmic language and with the range of images there employed. It was probably with a view to such familiarization that the ancient monks studied the Psalter, learning it by heart and gradually achieving some form of overlap between their own inner processes and the thought of the Psalms. The result was that they spoke and wrote the language of the Psalter spontaneously and naturally. A glance at the scriptural index of much monastic writing reveals the extent to which the Psalms influenced the thought and expression of those who had been reared in this way.

The studious zeal of many Fathers of the Church with regard to the Psalms is manifested by the sermons and commentaries which they composed about them. Of these, Athanasius of Alexandria's *Letter to Marcellinus* is most likely to impress a modern reader both with its depth and its surprising "modernity."[8] In a short compass St. Athanasius offers a complete conspectus of the Psalms and of the role which they can play in the life of the Christian. He relates individual Psalms to their mother-lode in other parts of Scripture. He notes the variety of dispositions necessary for reciting the different Psalms. He traverses the whole Psalter, explaining and introducing everything. It is impossible to read such a *tour de force* without being powerfully impressed by the profundity of such patristic exegesis, notwithstanding its not having access to the resources of modern scholarship.

The example of such inspired industry should encourage the contemporary practitioner of psalmody to keep studying the Psalms, making use of the expanded resources which recent scholarship has yielded. Anything that we do in this matter to heighten our interest in the Psalms and deepen our love for them will eventually bear fruit in the context of our whole life. There are, however, three particular areas of study where any effort expended is likely to be abundantly repaid.

A first field of fruitful operation is the *language* of the Psalms. That more monks and nuns do not avail themselves of opportunities to acquire some elementary Hebrew seems to me to be an undermining of the tradition of Psalm-study which we have inherited. It is not so much a matter of producing large numbers of professional exegetes as of giving the ordinary, thoughtful person some insight into a world of image and expression which can never be fully transposed into a modern Indo-European idiom. There are sufficient aids in instruction available to render basic Hebrew a realistic proposition for anyone who really wants it. Even Stephen Harding approached the rabbis for help when he was revising the Vulgate.

If it is not possible to learn even a little of the language, one can still develop an appreciation of the distinctiveness of Hebrew. To discover the rugged and concrete emotiveness of the Psalms can be a refreshing change for one immersed in the slick informational functionality of today's *lingua franca*.

The daily recitation of the Psalms in the vernacular can be considerably enhanced by an awareness of the wealth of meaning which underlies a simple, perhaps banal, equivalent. Appreciating more fully the rich significance of certain words and their linkage with other themes and contexts is a valuable counterbalance to the desacralizing effect which necessarily accompanied the transition from a Latin to a vernacular Psalter. In addition, it is possible to elucidate verbal forms through sharper visual images, and this process also is an aid to rendering the Psalms more real.[9]

A second worthy area of study is the classification of Psalms into *categories* (*Gattungen*). Since the pioneering work of Hermann Gunkel, many different systems of division and grouping of Psalms have been advanced. This is not the place to discuss their respective merits. Familiarity with one particular system, however, does make the work of approaching the Psalter very much easier. It means that, in advance, one has some general knowledge of the structure and purpose of the Psalm and, more importantly, some basic idea of what spirit pervades it and in what disposition it ought to be sung. This is extremely important. By breaking the Psalter down into Songs of Praise, Laments, Thanksgivings, Sapiential and Didactic Psalms, and so forth, one is easier able to latch onto the wave-length of any particular Psalm. In this way the Psalter is less an impenetrable mass of confused and confusing elements than an anthology comprised mainly of about half a dozen loose categories of Psalms. One approaches the individual Psalm through its whole group, so that whatever is learned about one Psalm is somewhat transferable to others in the category. This facilitates understanding both in the self-learning situation and in the more formal educational context.[10]

Once the general idea of dividing up the Psalter according to the types of Psalms is grasped, it becomes possible to ensure that the way the Psalms are used corresponds to their nature. In this way the mode of recitation and even the music employed can be fashioned so that they take their cue from the fundamental movement of the text. Such an orientation is recognized in the *General Instruction on the Liturgy of the Hours*.

> Whoever sings a psalm opens his heart to those emotions which inspired the psalm, *each according to its literary type*, whether it be a

psalm of lament, confidence, thanksgiving or any other type designated by exegetes.[11]

The psalms can be recited in various ways taking into account: whether they are said in Latin or in the vernacular, and especially whether they are said by an individual or by a group, or recited in a celebration with the people. A way should be chosen to enable those who pray the psalms *to appreciate more easily their spiritual and literary flavor*. Psalms are not used just to make up a certain quantity of prayer; a consideration of variety and the character of each enters into their choice.[12]

...Variety is introduced not because of external circumstances but on account of *the various types* of psalms which occur in any one celebration. Thus it may be better to say sapiential and historical psalms, while the hymns and psalms of thanksgiving are best sung. It is very important for us to be concerned with the meaning and spirit of what we are doing....[13]

It probably does not matter which system of division is espoused, since all are imperfect. One should perhaps look for something that is critically based, which does not assume such a rigidity that the Psalms themselves have to be mangled to conform to it, and which does not depend on hypothetical reconstructions of supposed situations for its basic rationale. I have always found a gentler and modified version of Gunkel's basic division reasonably satisfactory, but there are other acceptable alternatives.

A third area in which effort may be profitably invested is *application*. Once having developed some sensitivity to the language of the Psalms and some awareness of the literary forces which shaped them, it becomes possible to attempt that fusion of horizons which is the harbinger of genuine understanding. Bridges have to be built between the concrete facticity of the Psalm text and the basic elements of our own situation. At times this will be easy; lamentation or thanksgiving will fortuitously accord with our own emotions and so we will be able to render the Psalm with appropriate conviction. At other times, perhaps, the text of the Psalm will appear to be antipathetic to how we feel, and this is when we have to be prepared to transcend ourselves and to see things from a higher viewpoint. A certain detachment or self-effacement is required so that we can pray the Psalms not merely from the viewpoint of our own transient emotions but in the Church and on its behalf. There is, accordingly, always scope both for praise and for threnody in the life of

the Church, and any Psalm can be used wholeheartedly from this perspective. Indeed viewing the Psalms from an ecclesial standpoint has the
effect of raising us above a limited preoccupation with the self which
often reveals itself as the major obstacle to praying the Psalter.

Furthermore, there is a dynamic inherent in psalmody which leads
us to fuller self-understanding, if we give ourselves to it. The Psalms
can reveal to us hitherto hidden aspects of our own reality; in the image used by St. Athanasius, they are like a mirror in which we suddenly
catch a glimpse of something of our own inner processes.

> And it seems to me that these words become like a mirror to the
> person singing them, so that he might perceive himself and the emo-
> tions of his soul and, thus affected, he might recite them. For in fact
> he who hears the one reading receives the song as being about
> him…. And so, on the whole, each Psalm is both spoken and com-
> posed by the Spirit so that in these same words, as was said earlier,
> the stirrings of our souls might be grasped, and all of them be said as
> concerning us, and the same issue from us as our own words, for a
> remembrance of the emotions in us, and a chastening of our life.[14]

If we limit the Psalms to the role of expressing the way we feel *before*
giving ourselves to them, it is likely that their cardiomimetic aspect will
remain dormant and that we will be unchanged by our prayer.[15]

An exercise that can facilitate the application of the Psalms to our own
life can easily follow work on the categories. This is to go through the
Psalter and note the *a priori* applicability of certain Psalms to particular
recurrent situations of human life. Then for each vicissitude, we have at
hand Psalms that are peculiarly appropriate. This seems to have been the
approach of Evagrius Ponticus.[16]

3. The Psalms as Poetry

Many difficulties in psalmody derive from a failure to appreciate the
poetic nature of the Psalms. They are not, despite the practice of early
monasticism, readings. They are songs: rhythmed compositions intended
to be accompanied by musical instruments. They cannot be assayed sole-
ly on the basis of their rational content. They are poems, with all the
non-rational components typical of the poetry of every culture: strong
imagery, exaggeration, exuberance, the occasional triumph of form over
content, repetition, antithesis and a frequent divergence from the canons
of rational thought. Something is lost if one approaches the Psalter

merely as a literary text to be expounded; to be understood the Psalms must be sung. Cardinal Garrone makes this point well.

> The psalms are prayers in *poetry*. This could be a somewhat discouraging fact since so much that is essential in poetic expression is found in the genius of the language and the magic of its sounds. It is doubtful that even the best translation can retain the perfection of the original. Besides, the text of a prayer which has been conceived and written as a poem, as a song, loses its intrinsic value and hence its efficacy for prayer if it is stripped of its precisely poetic structure.
>
> The Church is certainly aware of this problem. But she gives them to us to sing because she is convinced that their religious strength, their power as prayer, is independent, to a certain extent, of the intellectual content of the texts. On the other hand, when one takes up the psalms, it is important to realize that they are poetry; otherwise they will be devoid of all meaning. Remember that the particular attitude one needs to apprehend the charm of a poem is not the same as that needed for the study of a philosophical treatise. We must be able to abandon ourselves to a certain enchantment of combined sounds and images, an almost musical experience which is perplexing to our ordinary thinking processes. We must be ready to situate ourselves in a certain region of the unknown, out of which the prayer of the psalms rises with irrepressible fervor. Otherwise the psalms as prayers are unattainable.[17]

This means that in psalmody one has to be less active and analytic than one would be in dealing with a merely rational text. The way to read the Psalms is to relax and allow oneself to be immersed in them so that their meaning as a whole gradually penetrates. It is not a question of grasping the parts and scrutinizing them, but of embracing the whole and consenting to be formed by it.

> You stayed on one of the syllables of a great song; consequently you are disturbed when the all-wise singer goes on with his song. For the syllable which alone you loved is taken from you, and others follow in their proper order. For he is not singing for you alone, nor according to your will, but his own. And the syllables which follow are an obstacle to you for this reason, that they clash with the one you loved wrongfully.[18]

In psalmody, as in life, one has to yield oneself to be molded by the action of God, letting the words create an atmosphere as they wash over one, now lifting one to the heights, now casting one down to the depths, giving expression to the hidden facets of prayer within the heart even when these are not fully owned in thought.

Bernard of Clairvaux makes the point that everything must be subjected to the rhythm of the Psalm's meaning. Psalmody is not a time for disconnected spiritual reflection; it is, rather, a disciplined attention to the Psalm as it unfolds.

> I say that psalmody should be performed with a pure heart to indicate that, during psalmody, you should not be thinking of anything except the Psalm itself. Nor do I mean that only vain and useless thoughts are to be avoided. At that time and in that place are to be avoided those necessary thoughts about necessary community matters which frequently importune the minds of those brothers who have official positions. Furthermore, my advice is that even those thoughts are to be left aside which come from attending on the Holy Spirit before psalmody begins, for example, as you sit in the cloister or read books or as you listen to my conference, as you do now. These are wholesome thoughts, but it is not at all wholesome to reflect upon them during psalmody. At such a time the Holy Spirit is not pleased to receive what you offer apart from what you owe, since you are neglecting to render your due.[19]

The important thing during psalmody, therefore, is to remain vulnerable before the Psalm, ready to receive what its text and the operation of the Holy Spirit inspire, leaving the mind empty and the heart detached. When a Psalm issues into such a void, it is able to produce a disproportionate response.

The beauty of authentic psalmody is not a decorative accretion, nor does it necessarily represent an unmanly and unmonastic deviation from appropriate austerity, as Pambo seems to have believed.[20] Cassian notes that the beautiful singing of a Psalm is often the occasion for the experience of compunction.[21] This was certainly true in Augustine's case.

> What cries did I utter, O my God, as I read the Psalms of David, for these are songs of faithfulness which upbraid the swollen spirit with their melodies of devotion.... What cries I did utter in these Psalms! How they did set me on fire for you! How ardently I desired that, if it were within my power, I would cause the whole world to recite them as a remedy for the pride of humankind.[22]

The Psalms, far from being the expression of a disembodied piety, really require an abundance of physical involvement for their full impact. This is why it is important to attend not only to the philological accuracy of a translation intended for personal or communal use (as distinct from study); one must also pay attention to aural character.[23] Thus many would judge the Vulgate Psalms to be more appropriate for liturgical use than the undeniably more accurate Latin version issued under Pius XII.[24]

A final note on matters having to do with the poetic nature of the Psalms concerns the spirit of *reverence* with which they are approached. These inspired songs deserve more respect than more ephemeral expressions of religious sentiment. Apart from the fact of inspiration and their long acceptance in the Church, they deserve our respect simply because they have served as the mainstay of prayer throughout the history of monasticism. Even if it happens that they do not seem to express my inner feelings, the fact remains that they still deserve my reverence. Indeed, unless we approach them in such a spirit, it is unlikely that they will ever assume their traditional place in sustaining a life of prayer.

4. Tactics

Once we are convinced of the importance of psalmody in the development of a realistic approach to prayerful living, it becomes necessary to discuss what can be done on a practical level to overcome some of the difficulties encountered in psalmody by our contemporaries. Not everything which may be recommended is necessarily helpful to everyone, but some of the following suggestions may prove effective in individual cases.

The most fundamental aid is a continuing confidence in the value of psalmody and a willingness to invest some private energies in coming to know and love them more. When Cardinal Hume was Abbot of Ampleforth, he addressed these words to a group of novices.

> I would finally urge you to spend quite a lot of time looking at, mulling over, praying privately the Psalms. The more you look at them, the more you study them, the more you will see how they express in prayer the things I talk to you about.... Work hard to acquire a love for the Psalms.[25]

In particular, the memorization of Psalms can be most helpful. The Gradual Psalms, for example, are short enough to learn easily through repetition, and can be said going from one place to another, before beginning a task or as expressions of personal dedication in any compatible situation. Other Psalms can be used to initiate or to accompany our reading. Ps. 118 (119), for example, is ideal for seasoning the banquet of the Word; its short aphorisms forming us in a disposition suitable to profiting from our reading. This is very much a matter of individual flair. One does not have to develop a monomania for Psalms; it is simply a matter of recognizing that there are many recurrent situations in our lives in which they can be used naturally and without contrivance, if we wish to.

The practical problems associated with the use of the Psalms in communal prayer must be faced. A certain level of comfort is necessary for good psalmody; if the liturgy is badly designed, if the accidentals are gauche, the standard of performance expected is too high or the general setting is not in continuity with the style of those involved, problems will result. In such circumstances love for the Office and for the Psalms will almost certainly wither. On the other hand, good liturgy is the best possible initiation into the Psalter and can render the Psalms so attractive that when the song has ended, the melody lingers on. Imperceptibly, the Psalms mold awareness and stimulate prayer. In this way, liturgy gives form to life.

In studying the Psalms, it can be useful to supplement the more technical instruction in language, form and background, with exercises not requiring a great deal of arcane expertise yet having the capacity to involve the learner with the Psalms at an intelligent and personal level. Two particular tasks can be assigned; one is the writing of a collect for each Psalm as it is studied, the other involves finding New Testament texts which illuminate or contextualize the Psalm as a whole.

The composition and use of Psalter Collects is a very monastic enterprise. Apart from the role played by such creative writing in the liturgy, the task itself is instructive. It forces the individual to encapsulate the whole thrust of the Psalm, relating it to his own situation or to that of the community or of the Church, and directing it to God. The example of such prayers that have come down to us illustrate how by this means it was possible to lend a Christian and Christological sense to the Psalms by locating them within a more explicitly New Testament perspective, building a bridge between the givenness of the ancient texts and the actual situation of Christian worship.[26] Adherence to the ancient tricursal model for a Collect keeps the prayer tight and compact, and enables a hearer more easily to catch and echo the movement of thought.

A similar function is served by the search for texts from the New Testament which throw light on the meaning of the Psalm for today's Christian. Again, it compels one to accept the Psalm as a whole with a view to finding parallels to one's own circumstances. The resulting texts can often serve to highlight particular facets of a Psalm, in much the same way as an anthem does; introducing the user to a specific approach to the Psalm. The current *Roman Breviary* uses texts in this way.

Whatever tactics are adopted, it is important that means be devised and utilized which promote interest, use and perseverance with respect to the Psalms. There are, undoubtedly, great difficulties associated with feeling at home in the Psalter, but greater difficulties will surely confront those who try to cultivate continuing prayerfulness without having recourse to the method of psalmody. The strain endured will be too great. On the other hand, it may often be inferred that persons and communities who find it almost impossible to practice silence and recollection are simply reflecting the fact that they have been given no practical means of filling the emptiness which discipline has created.

Meditatio, ruminatio and psalmody are characteristic monastic concerns which are at risk in a world of technological efficiency. However, with some basis of common sense, a degree of generosity and much patience, this style of living prayerfully can yet be realized. Would that it were said of us, as it was of St. Wulstan: *Semper in ore psalmus; semper in corde Christus*—His mouth was always filled with Psalms, his heart was filled with Christ.

NOTES

[1]At times, the Psalms have become merely formalities. This is possibly true in many cases where Latin Psalms were prescribed without much attention either to the demands of the situation or to the comprehension of the users. One could question, for example, the appropriateness to grace after meals of the *Miserere*. Cluny seems to have been an example of the excessive multiplication of the Psalms. This, of course, is not to say that authentic prayer cannot take place within such observances.

[2]Instructive in this regard is an interview with Dr. Alfred Tomatis entitled "Chant," published in 1978 by Soundscape Productions Ltd., 33 Gibson Ave., Toronto, Ont., M5R 1T4 Canada.

[3]In this article I am not treating professedly of the use of the Psalms in the Liturgy of the Hours, I am approaching psalmody from a more generic angle.

[4]See, for instance, a number of the articles in Msgr. Cassien and Bernard Botte, *La Prière des Heures* (Lex Orandi, no. 35, Paris: Cerf, 1963). Cf. Joseph Gelineau,

"The Psalms in the Age of the Fathers," in *Liturgy* OCSO 13.1 (Feb. 1979), pp. 53-70. There is also a beautiful article by Soeur Etienne, "Psallite Sapienter," *ibid.*, 11.1 (Jan. 1977), pp. 67-82. A modern statement of a monastic approach is found in Ch. 5 of André Louf's *Teach Us to Pray* (London: Darton, Longman and Todd, 1974), pp. 50-58.

[5]*Ep Aur*, no. 121 (SChr 223, p. 238).

[6]In contrast to many facile assertions to the contrary, the "self" which finds expression in prayer is not primarily that self which is the plaything of the whole gamut of physical, emotional and social conditioning. It is, rather, the self which is manifested at the center of one's being in moments of intensity, the self which is more served by discipline than by abandon, the self which is oppressed by sin and selfishness and comes to life only in disinterested love. To find this self one must lose the other. Sometimes, enthusiasm for "self-expression" overlooks the fact that what has not been realized cannot be expressed and that genuine self-discovery spans a lifetime. Instant prayer may be a very saleable commodity in this generation, but attempts to circumvent the natural rhythms of growth generally produce results which are either short-term or illusory—both possibilities working against the life-long evolution of genuine prayerfulness.

[7]On the title of this section and the context in which I am approaching it, see Hans-Georg Gadamer, *Truth and Method* (London: Sheed and Ward, 2nd edition 1979), especially pp. 272-274.

[8]Translated by R. Gregg in the Classics of Western Spirituality series (New York: Paulist Press, 1980), pp. 101-129.

[9]For the meaning of words, the ongoing publication of the *Theological Dictionary of the Old Testament* (Grand Rapids: Eerdmans) is valuable. For a more pictorial approach, see Othmar Keel, *The Symbolism of the Biblical World: Ancient Near Eastern Iconography and the Book of Psalms* (New York: The Seabury Press, 1978).

[10]A single-volume treatment of the Psalms from this angle which does not tax the reader's indulgence more than moderately is Leopold Sabourin, *The Psalms: Their Origin and Meaning* (New York: Alba House, 1974).

[11]GILH, no. 106; trans. Peter Coughlan and Peter Purdue in *The Liturgy of the Hours* (London: Geoffrey Chapman, 1971), p. 41. Emphasis added.

[12]GILH, no. 121; *op. cit.*, pp. 44-45. Emphasis added.

[13]GILH, no 270; *op. cit.*, p. 69. Emphasis added.

[14]*Letter to Marcellinus* 12, *op. cit.*, p. 111.

[15]Cf. M. Casey, "Cardiomimesis" in *Tjurunga* 20 (1980), pp. 118-122. Above pp. 35-40.

[16]Thus I. Hausherr, *The Name of Jesus* (CSS, no. 44, Kalamazoo: Cistercian Publications, 1978), p. 209.

[17]Gabriel Garrone, *How to Pray the Psalms* (Notre Dame: Fides, 1965), pp. 14-15. For the understanding of the different types of consciousness activated in poetic appreciation and in intellectual analysis, an awareness of the different functions of the left and right hemispheres of the brain is most helpful. Artistic involvement, intuition, facial recognition and synthetic or integrative thought are associated with the right or non-dominant hemisphere. The left brain specializes in

analytic, sequential and logical thought and in language and mathematics. I have discussed elsewhere the possibility that the difference between "monastic theology" and the theology issuing from the Scholasticism of the thirteenth century is explainable in terms of a switch from right-brain to left-brain thinking. Cf. " 'Emotionally Hollow, Esthetically Meaningless and Spiritually Empty': An Inquiry into Theological Discourse," *Colloquium* 14.1 (1981), pp. 54-61. Cf. Robert E. Ornstein, *The Psychology of Consciousness* (Harmondsworth: Penguin Books, 1979). Id. *Physiological Studies of Consciousness* (Tunbridge Wells: Institute for Cultural Research, 1979). Id. (ed.), *The Nature of Human Consciousness: A Book of Readings* (New York: The Viking Press, 1973). Id., "Two Sides of the Brain," in Richard Woods (ed.) *Understanding Mysticism* (Garden City: Image Books, 1980), pp. 270-285; this last item is an extract from the first book mentioned above. Approaching the Psalms from an exclusively left-brain angle may result in a gratifyingly scientific commentary, but it misses the heart of the matter. "To understand many of the psalms it helps a great deal to sing them or at least to regard them from a poetic and musical point of view." GILH, no. 278, *op. cit.*, p. 68.

[18]Guigo, *Meditations* (trans. J. Jolin, Marquette University Press, 1951), no. 149, p. 24. I am, of course, changing the context of this famous aphorism.

[19]SC 47.8; SBO 2.66.17-26.

[20]"Woe to us, my poor boy, for the days are coming when monks will turn away from solid food such as the Holy Spirit provides and give all their attention to chanting and singing. What compunction of heart can such things produce? How can a monk shed tears of compunction when he is singing these hymns? Yes, the day is coming when monks, whether they be in their cells or in the church, will sing, lowing like cattle.... Monks have not come into this solitude to fill themselves with such things, singing songs, putting rhythm into ditties, clapping their hands and jumping from one foot to the other. They should, rather, offer their prayers to God in sighs and tears, with a voice full of reverence and ready for compunction and in an attitude which is both restrained and humble." Translated from I. Hausherr, *Penthos: La doctrine de la componction dans l'Orient Chrétien* (Rome: Pontifical Institute for Oriental Studies, 1944), pp. 120-122. Pambo is speaking particularly of the troparia which had captivated his disciple during a visit to Alexandria.

[21]Three texts from the conferences of Abba Isaac may illustrate Cassian's position. Speaking of the divers factors with give rise to the experience of compunction, he continues thus: "Sometimes some small verse of a Psalm which we are singing provides the occasion for the prayer of fire. Sometimes the beauty of a brother's singing rouses the capacity to increase the fervor of those present." *Conl.* 9.26 (SChr no. 54, p. 62). Speaking of one who has learned to fill the day with prayer through the use of a short formula, and has thus come to be initiated into lofty mysteries, Cassian notes that his use of the Psalms is transfigured; they are no longer alien texts, but seem to come forth from the very depths of one's being. "Thus nourished in a continuous feeding, he receives all the feelings of the Psalms within himself, and so he begins to sing them, not as something

composed by the prophet, but as something issuing forth from himself, as his own prayer inspired by deep compunction of heart. On the other hand, he may think of them as having been written with special regard to himself, so that what is said in them is not merely something that is fulfilled in the prophet's own life, but something that corresponds to what he experiences in daily living." *Conl.* 10.11 (*op. cit.*, p. 92). He goes on to declare that if we share the attitudes of the Psalmist then we will enjoy what Bultmann has called a "pre-cognition," an intuitive perception of what the Psalm is saying even before the rational processes are complete. A third text is a negative one, describing inappropriate use of the Psalms, so that no profound affinity is developed with the text and only superficial impressions result. "The mind is constantly moving from one Psalm to another.... During psalmody he meditates on something else, not contained in the text of the Psalm itself." *Conl.* 10.13 (*op. cit.*, p. 94). The whole question of the importance of beauty in the liturgy cannot be treated here, but cf. Stephen List, "Beauty in the Liturgy," *Tjurunga* 6 (1974), pp. 75-92; a number of other articles in the same issue deal with the topic.

[22]*Confessions*, 9.8.

[23]Cf. John B. Foley, "An Aural Basis for Oral Liturgical Prayer," in *Worship* 566.2 (1982), pp. 132-152.

[24]Thus Christine Mohrmann, "The New Latin Psalter: Its Diction and Style," in *Etudes sur le Latin des Chrétiens*, vol. II (Rome: Edizioni de Storia e Letteratura, 1961), pp. 109-132. There is also the problem that the revised Psalter would have severed the link with the Christian writers of a millennium who had been formed by the older version and allowed it to inform their writings.

[25]Basil Hume, *Searching for God*, (London: Hodder & Stoughton, 1977), p. 51.

[26]Cf. Louis Brou (ed.), *The Psalter Collects, from V-VIth Century Sources* (London: Henry Bradshaw Society, 1949). This volume (written in French despite the title) is based on the researches of André Wilmart and is now out of print. It is, however, available on microfiches from the Microlibrary at Slangenburg Abbey, Doetinchem. For a review, see Christine Mohrmann, "A Propos des Collectes du Psautier," *op. cit.*, vol. III, pp. 245-263. An illustration of how these ancient Collects can be employed is given in A. Rose, *Psaumes et Prière Chrétienne*, (Bruges: Publications de Saint-André, 1965).

Introductory Note

An article on patience may seem out of place in a collection of essays about prayer. However, patience is absolutely necessary not only for arriving at the "immobility" of a mind ready for contemplation (as Evagrius viewed things) but also for achieving that level of soft-heartedness which the Gospels enjoin. St. Bernard sees compassion as the doorway to contemplation; we become compassionate only when we learn to accept, with a quiet mind, that measure of suffering which is our lot. On the other hand, contemplation is quite incompatible with impatience and in many cases the first steps toward deeper prayer involve dealing with anger, resentment and sadness. Only confidence in God and trust in Providence allow patience to grow and patience itself is the seedbed of prayer. This essay was first published in CS 21 (1986), pp. 3-23.

The Virtue of Patience
in Western Monastic Tradition

The overriding ambition of every Christian is to find entry into God's kingdom, to enjoy eternal life, to be established in blissful and unqualified communion with God, the source and fulfillment of all that is good. About the ultimate goal of Christian and monastic life there is no dispute. There is even little enough difference of opinion when it comes to setting forth the ideal complex of values, actions and habits of behavior which, under grace, prepare the heart to receive the final outpouring of God's giving, the means which, as it were, conduct the Christian along the road to God. Where we do perceive a difference in emphasis is among those authors who address themselves to the more common situation, where the whole gamut of moral virtues is practically unrealizable. The question which divides the experts is this: if a choice must be made, in which area of spiritual endeavor is one advised to invest the limited amount of energy available for spiritual pursuits?

John Cassian answers the question for monks and nuns in a typically strong and forthright manner. The major means of growing in godliness and of finding access to the kingdom of heaven is purity of heart.[1] Our task in this life is to work at reducing the level of our inner dividedness.

As we become less inconsistent within ourselves, we begin to find harmony and simplicity where previously there was only conflict and enslavement. So, we need to fight against our vices and to bring our unruly passions under control that we may be possessed by a unity and freedom from which deep prayer may be born and where God's action is uninhibited by human perversity. Our task is to work hard, in the strength of the grace that is available to us, to put ourselves into a state of receptivity. The greatest danger is that we do nothing.

St. Benedict would have had little to cavil at in such a position yet, when he came to make a statement about his own priorities in this matter, he expressed himself in a different vein. In the last verse of the Prologue of his Rule, following closely the conclusion of the *Rule of the Master*, he writes:

> So that, never ceasing to be his disciples, we may, by his instruction, persevere in the monastery until death, becoming participant in the

sufferings of Christ through patience in such a way that we may deserve to become sharers in his kingdom.[2]

There are two nuances here which Benedict has chosen to add to Cassian's understanding of what means are suitable to gain the kingdom. The first is that the achievement of the goal is the result not of individual proficiency, but of sharing in the fruits of Christ's passion and death. Secondly, we share in the victory of Christ by becoming sharers in his sufferings and this occurs principally through patience.

It is probably true that Cassian would not have been adverse to such a statement, yet the whole picture presented in the *Rule of Benedict* is, at once, more Christocentric and less activist than that presented in the *Conferences*. There is a reserve in Benedict about the spiritual athleticism of Cassian. It often seems that he wishes to protect himself from the slightest suspicion of Semi-Pelagianism.

That this reference to patience is a significant element in Benedict's monastic philosophy is clear from other parts of the Rule, specifically his description of the fourth step in the ladder of humility and his exhortation in 72.5. What is surprising is that many learned commentators do not seem to have attributed great weight to his words.

There is a strand in western monastic thought which refuses to view patience as a trivial virtue and faults against it as inconsiderable. On the contrary, it is seen as the principal battleground where the issue of ultimate salvation is decided, the practical expression of faith and hope and an important indication of the genuineness of the interior life. As Gregory the Great affirms, it is "the root and guardian of all the virtues."[3] Impatience, on the other hand, is also taken seriously; it is, in the words of Bernard of Clairvaux, nothing less than the soul's perdition.[4]

1. Christian Background

There is substantial teaching in the New Testament on this subject. It revolves around three foci: the imitation of Jesus, who suffered greatly without resistance, his explicit teaching, especially in the Sermon on the Mount, and the vivid expectation of a proximate return of Christ who would set all things right. The theme is expressed by a cluster of terms of which *makrothumia* (long-suffering) and *hupomone* (endurance) were the most frequent, although other words such as *apedechesthai* and its cognates also figure significantly.[5]

These words were not created; they were already in use. *Makrothumia* is found in the Septuagint, habitually applied to the forbearance of God.[6]

Hupomone had long been associated with manliness and courage (*andreia*) in the heroic and philosophic literature of Greece and had been developed considerably in Stoicism.[7] Whereas it is possible and even likely that the Christian vocabulary of patience had profited from the accumulated connotations of earlier usage, it is important to recognize its distinctive nuances, which owe less to either Judaism or to Hellenism than to the specific content of New Testament faith.

The significance of patience is grounded in the cross of Christ which has become the way of life which Christians follow. This was particularly evident in those times when the following of the Gospel involved the giving up of everything else, including one's life; when the assent of faith involved the prospect of imminent persecution and death. Such Christians had to be ready literally to leave everything behind, even life itself, in order to gain Christ. For them, "the cross" and "dying daily" were not pious clichés but proximate possibilities. In such a climate, it was imperative that the Church proclaim a philosophy which kept before the mind's eye of believers the example of Christ, which dwelt upon his teaching concerning gentleness under persecution and which nurtured a lively and personal faith in the coming of the kingdom. To survive the onslaughts of massive pain and death, a warm devotion was needed, not a cool, abstract logic; it was only passionate devotion to Jesus Christ which could motivate the martyrs to endure and remain loyal to their faith.[8]

So it happened that much of the spiritual devotional teaching of the Church in the early centuries was conveyed through the accounts of martyrdom, written by Christians with a view to strengthening the faith of their co-religionists. The same line of instruction was continued in the celebration of the cult of the martyrs and in the writing and reading of the martyrologies.[9] It was not that the Church hoped that all would become martyrs in fact. Rather, it sought to propagate those attitudes and dispositions which the martyrs demonstrated in an eminent degree. In sharing physically in the sufferings of Christ they truly walked in the way that was his, demonstrating that they were indeed genuine "disciples and imitators of the Lord."[10]

The practical consequences of the Gospel way are evident in the lives of the martyrs. It progressively became clear that of those not facing actual martyrdom, the teaching of Christ yet requires steadfast adherence to the same principles of faith and a comparable willingness to undergo self-sacrifice. Already in Origen's preaching we see the beginnings of a doctrine of spiritual martyrdom.

I have no doubt that in this assembly there are those who, known only to him, are already martyrs in his sight by the testimony of their consciences. These are ready, if they be asked, to pour out their blood for the sake of the name of the Lord Jesus Christ. I have no doubt that these are they who have taken up their cross and have followed him.[11]

If it is true "that monasticism grew out of the most devout circles of the second and third-century Church, the virgins and ascetics, and was strongly marked with the imprint of the spirituality of martyrdom,"[12] then it is likely that the underlying—and perhaps often unstated—presuppositions of monastic spirituality concur with those expressed in the literature of martyrdom. The classic statements of the primitive philosophy revolved around cheerful, Christocentric patience.

> Let us, therefore, become imitators of [Christ's] patience and if it should happen that we have to suffer on account of his name, then let us glorify him for it. This is the model which he has established for us by his own example and we must put our faith in it.
>
> I implore you, therefore, to put into practice, the word of right-eousness and to be patient in all patience (*hupomenein pasan hupomenen*), having before your eyes the example not only of the blessed Ignatius and Zosimos and Rufus, but also of others from among you and of Paul and the rest of the apostles, being convinced that these did not run in vain but in faith and righteousness and so they are now in the place assigned to them by the Lord who suffered with them. They did not love this age but they died for our sakes and it was for us that God has raised them.
>
> Stand fast in these things, therefore, and follow the Lord's exam-ple: firm and immovable in faith, lovers of the brotherhood, loving one another, bound together in truth, manifesting the Lord's meek-ness to the other, despising no one. When it is possible for you to do a good deed, do not postpone it, since almsgiving frees from death. All be subject to one another, having an irreproachable way of life (*conversatio*) among the gentiles so that you might be praised on account of your good works and so that it may not happen that the Lord is blasphemed.[13]

This is the spirituality of the martyrs which was progressively trans-posed beyond the sphere of persecution. Martyr or not, the Christian was seen to be called to reproduce in his life the forbearance and endur-ance of Christ, expressed both in a willingness to die for the Lord and in the honest determination to live a life of self-sacrificing love in accordance with his teaching. This is the universal teaching of the Church in those centuries.

It is patience that makes martyrdom a good thing and without this virtue there is no witness given to Christ, irrespective of the sufferings undergone.[14] The consequence of this is that it becomes possible to understand a life characterized by genuine patience as a martyrdom, a manner of bearing witness to Christ, that was accessible to all.

> The fact is that every single one of the faithful takes part in a contest: his adversary is the devil and God is the umpire. The amphitheatre is filled not only with the Church and with the angels, but also with unbelievers.[15]

Thus, every Christian has a cross to bear.[16] If he does so with equanimity, then his patience entitles him to take rank among the martyrs.

> If, with God's help, we struggle to maintain the virtue of patience and to live peaceably within the Church, we will, at the end, lay hold of the palm of martyrdom. For there are two types of martyrdom, one mental, the other both mental and in fact. Hence it is possible for us to be martyrs even though we are not slain by the persecutors' sword.[17]

It is at this point that it becomes necessary to recall the explicitly Christian content of patience. It is more than mere *andreia*: manliness, endurance and courage. It is a gift of God,[18] closely associated with the theological virtues of faith, hope and charity.[19] More importantly, Christian patience is part of a program of *imitatio Christi*.[20] It is only the heat of a love for Christ which is able effectively to counteract the natural heat of vindictive or recriminatory anger.[21] Patience is not timidity or insensibility; it is the strength of a love which is not overcome by evil, which "endures all" (1 Cor. 13:7). Patience is not mindless endurance but the fruit of the Spirit (Gal. 5:22).

2. Patience in a Monastic Context

Impatience and irascibility are so patently foreign to the monastic pursuit that it is no source of surprise that the ancient monastic authors repeatedly advocate the practice of patience.

There are many kindly stories emanating from Egypt which illustrate the esteem in which patience was held by the Desert Fathers. Furthermore forty-seven anecdotes are gathered together in the *Verba Seniorum* under the general title of *De patientia seu fortitudine*, which give an idea of the ample scope of the virtue. Patience is seen as the opposite of giving up the fight;[22] it means persevering with the struggle to acquire virtue, maintaining one's stability of place, and being prepared for a long, long engagement.[23] "Believe me," Abba Theodore is quoted as saying, "I have been seventy years in this monastic habit and I have never been able to find even a single day of rest."[24] Monastic life is viewed as a continuing struggle with temptations: it is only through grappling with temptations that a monk's virtue becomes evident.[25] If he remains patient under the steady erosion of self-exaltation that such a process achieves, then the enemy is destroyed.[26] It is staying constant throughout the whole weary succession of struggles that makes a man a real monk. Instead of trying to grasp what will be the outcome of it all, the monk is invited to sit quietly, to carry on as normal and to preserve himself in patience and charity.[27] The underlying motivation for this endurance is not often stated, but it can be found: it is the desire to follow the crucified Christ.[28] Patience is certainly highly regarded, but its theory is not expounded in any depth.

Evagrius Ponticus mentions patience occasionally but gives it no particular emphasis. One who is sick is to give thanks for his pain and to be patient with those who attend him.[29] *Apatheia* is said to proceed from endurance (*hupomone*),[30] and *makrothumia* is listed along with psalmody and mercy as the cure for anger.[31] Even stranger still, Evagrius evidently considers *hupomone* as something eventually to be transcended. The perfect man does not need to practice self-control or to put up with suffering, because he is beyond all that pertains to the realm of the passions.[32] The point he is making is probably that as a monk develops good habits and his heart is more firmly set on God, minor upsets bother him less, so that it can be inferred that one who is perfect would not be subject to contrary suggestion. If spiritual growth were a linear progression this would be fine; in practice, the opposite is the case. More often than not it seems that the one who is far advanced has to be detached precisely from such "perfection" in order that God alone is the basis of confidence, not progress secured.

John Cassian was much more fully aware of the importance of patience, even to the point of making some measure of it the condition for entry into monastic life.[33] In general he associates it with humility:[34] its components are seriousness,[35] obedience and meekness,[36] longanimity,[37] gentleness,[38] discretion[39] and the whole gamut of Christian virtues.[40] Its opposite is pride,[41] expressed particularly in anger and sadness.[42] "Anger lays waste to patience."[43] Patience is the monk's way of imitating the example of the martyrs,[44] and so it is through the *fratrum frequentatio* that vices are healed;[45] and such communal living is impossible without patience. In fact he understands the monastery as a school of patience. Cassian laments the fact that many go off into the wilderness to avoid the pangs associated with acquiring this virtue. As if patience depended on the absence of provocation![46] In fact, withdrawal from social interaction may reduce the level of conflict, but it does not heal the inner disorder which is its source.[47] Concealed, it may escape notice, but its hold over the person is unchallenged. If an opportunity presents itself impatience manifests itself as vigorous as ever, and perhaps its potential for harm is increased, since such an outburst is perceived as coming from one previously perceived as a model of holiness.

> The fact that we do not become angry ought not to be due to the perfection of someone else; it should derive from our own virtue which is acquired not through another's patience but by our own forbearing.
>
> Accordingly, the desert should be for those who are perfect, purified of every vice and, as it were, with their vices burnt away by fire in a community of brothers. It should not be an escape for the faint-hearted but for those who desire to attain to the contemplation of God and the perception of higher realities, which can be grasped only by those who are perfect and only in solitude. We carry with us into the desert whatever vices we have that have not been cured. We know that although they do not show themselves in the open, yet they are not extinguished. For those whose vices have been corrected, solitude offers the occasion for the purest contemplation and to communicate knowledge by the unblemished perception of spiritual mysteries. But for those who have not amended their lives, what usually happens is not only do their vices remain, they even get worse.
>
> Somebody who has no dealings with other human beings may seem to himself patient and humble, but as soon as there is an occasion of some disturbance, he immediately reverts to his former nature. In fact the vices that were in hiding suddenly show themselves. They come forth like unbridled horses, well fed and too long left uncontrolled; eagerly and fiercely they break from their stalls and cause the downfall of the one driving the chariot. When the opportunity for giving expression to our vices in human company ceases, our vices grow stronger, unless we have previously been

purged of them. The semblance of patience which we thought we had when we lived among brothers, which came from respect for them and public expectations, is lost through the carelessness which follows complacency.[48]

As, perhaps, is indicated by the far greater emphasis given to patience in the *Institutes*, compared to the *Conferences*, it was understood by Cassian as a virtue which was of particular relevance to the monk living in community.

The teaching of RB on patience follows closely that of RM, though it could be argued that Benedict's doctrine is both more pervasive and deeper. There are three principal texts in RB. The first on patience as a mode of participating in Christ's passion has already been quoted.[49] The second is the exposition of the practicalities of patience in the fourth step of humility;[50] this will be discussed in the next section. The third major reference is the statement in the chapter on good zeal. "Let them tolerate most patiently their infirmities, be they bodily or behavioral."[51] If Benedict were a strict Latinist it would seem that he was admonishing his disciples patiently to bear *their own* (*suas*) weaknesses. In the context of this chapter, so reminiscent in content to the text of Polycarp quoted above, the theme is clearly fraternal charity. The text calls on monks to recognize that weaknesses exist in members of the community (Benedict himself makes provision for all manner of faults ranging from oversleeping to murder). Instead of being scandalized,[52] real monks (those with the good zeal) continue to tolerate the evil which remains in their brothers. They do not complain or campaign for their amendment, but remain steadfast and unshaken in their affection for them. There is more than endurance here; there is a wisdom and serenity which enables the genuine monk to accept painful consequences of another's sin rather than abandon love.

The other occurrences of patience and its cognates are varied. It is combined with meekness and obedience to conjure up the picture of a monk with whom the abbot is able to use reason rather than rebuke.[53] Rather than injure others, the good monk bears his own injuries patiently.[54] Those who attend the sick are to be patient with their demands.[55] The newcomer to the monastery is expected to demonstrate by his patience that he has the grit to deal with the hardships that will inevitably come his way.[56] Another text speaks about the novice being tested in all patience. It is not immediately clear whether there is question of trying the novice's patience through hardships to see if it is adequate, or of the senior (and the community) being patient in their testing of the novice in line with the directives given to the abbot in 64.12.[57] The fact that the phrase "in all patience" occurs in 2 Tim. 4:2 in the context, *increpa in omni patientia*, lends a certain weight to the second option. The final example is found in the chapter on difficult and impossible commands: the monk is counselled to make his representations "patiently and at the right time"; he is to bide his time until an approach has some possibility of succeeding.[58]

There are a number of texts in RM which Benedict has not, for some reason, made his own. Patience is mentioned three times among the qualities desirable in a potential abbot.[59] The monastic candidate is cautioned about the difficulties he will encounter and advised to make joyful patience his offering to God.[60] Finally, there is a text in the chapter on obedience relating patience and martyrdom. Perhaps the reason for Benedict's omission of it is simply that the whole passage is somewhat repetitious; for instance RM 7.61-64 is almost the same as RM 10.57-58. "Each day their will is frustrated in the monastery and they patiently bear with whatever is enjoined on them for their testing as if it were martyrdom."[61] We will, however, return to RM-RB in the following section.

Gregory the Great was himself a monk, the biographer of St. Benedict, the heir of Cassian and one of the principal patristic influences on medieval monasticism. The fact that he lived in a period of history in which scourges (*flagella*) predominated, meant that patience assumed a great importance for him.[62] Small wonder, too, that his greatest work was a commentary on the Book of Job, whom he saw as a type of the Church of his age.[63]

For Gregory, patience is the root of all virture.[64] Notwithstanding his own considerable interest in miracles, he declares bluntly: "I believe that the virtue of patience is greater than signs and wonders."[65] For him, patience was a matter of keeping faith with God in times of difficulty and temptation. "There is no virtue of patience in prosperity. Only he is really patient who is crushed by adversity and yet does not deviate from the straight course of his hope."[66] Patience is the ultimate test of holiness. "He only is truly perfect who is not impatient with the imperfection of his neighbor. The one who ceases to bear another's imperfection is his own witness that he has not advanced to perfection."[67] "None of the Saints attained to heavenly glory except through maintaining patience."[68]

The trials that are the potential source of disturbance either come from God or are permitted by him.[69] Patience also is his gift.[70] At the same time Gregory is, as always, interested in the practicalities of the virtue. He recommends that we have patience abiding in the mind, ready to be called into operation when the situation warrants it.[71] We should prepare ourselves for hardships in advance, by accepting them theoretically before they happen; in this way we will be protected "by the breastplate of patience."[72] When troubles strike and we suffer loss, he bids us remember how we used to get along well enough without the things of which we have recently been deprived.[73] Patience involves endurance, not for its own sake, but because it follows on the recognition that present troubles are only part of the total picture. The wise man does not allow himself to break out in spontaneous irritation against his suffering. He cools the situation and reserves judgment until later.[74] There is an element of discipline and self-control here.[75] He also needs to remain alert to the challenge of patience, not allowing himself to be hurried by circumstances into its opposite.[76] What he aims at is to put up with inevitable adversities *aequanimiter*—with a quiet mind.[77] Gregory is insistent that patience is not a matter of cold self-containment.[78] If it is real, it continues to love those who are the source of suffering: "True patience also loves the one whom it bears."[79] Gregory, with his usual perceptiveness, adds one further note: It is not enough to be patient during the time of suffering; one must also ensure that no residue of bitterness remains. Subsequent vindictiveness cancels out all previous merit in accepting manfully.[80]

Throughout medieval monastic literature patience continues to be regarded as an outstanding virtue,[81] and the equivalent of martyrdom.[82] On the understanding that patience if left unexercised soon disappeared,[83] the monastery was viewed as a "school of patience."[84] Bearing with the various difficulties experienced in corporate life and in remaining faithful to discipline developed one's capacity to endure and cultivated interiorly a deeper patience that was close to peace, a "patience of heart,"[85] a "patience of mind."[86] This virtue, along with contrition, mortification and the practice of good works, was understood as one of the principal means of purification for the monk.[87] Likewise, the solid good habits it generates make it a source of final perseverance.[88]

Patience is associated with other virutes: with humility,[89] with longanimity,[90] but especially with eschatological hope.[91] It derives its positive power and confidence from a recognition of the victory of Christ.[92] He remains the prime example and model of patience for the monk to imitate.[93] It is through him that the monk can hope to pass from patience to glory.[94] It is to him that the monk must look to draw that inner strength and quiet that will enable him to be undefeated by his troubles. As Aelred of Rievaulx beautifully concludes, "Lest this divine fire be cooled by the winds of injury, one should gaze constantly with the eyes of the mind on the tranquil patience of the dear Lord and Savior."[95]

The teaching of Bernard of Clairvaux is, perhaps, worth reviewing separately. For a man not naturally much gifted in this field, his insights into the dynamics of patience are profound. No righteousness is possible, as far as he is concerned, without this virtue.[96] At its most basic level it consists in the ability to absorb hardships as a dumb beast is passive under a rain of blows.[97] Irrespective of the source of trouble, and Bernard recognizes that there are different sorts of suffering, with different provenances,[98] the Christian strives to preserve his heart from rancour,[99] and to avoid all semblance of grumbling.[100] In this, his model is Christ who was for him a model of patient endurance, *speculum patiendi*.[101] It is patience which enables one to bear what is burdensome in others,[102] mindful of the reward Job received for his patience,[103] and confident that this is a sure road which leads to glory.[104] Yet there is more to patience than suffering and endurance and anticipation of future relief. For Bernard, patience must be suffused with a buoyancy which makes it a positive force for good.[105] In particular, instead of merely allowing the conflict to continue and enduring its effects, patience needs to become active in making peace. The *pacificus* is more advanced than one who is merely *patiens*, even if the latter remains without bitterness toward the source of his troubles.[106] Patience is not an end in itself; there are limits to endurance so that avoidable burdens are not to be sought. "Patience is a great virtue, but I would not have wished such things on you; on occasion it is more praiseworthy to be impatient.... *That patience is not good which allows you to become a slave when you could have been free.*"[107]

From the beginnings until the twelfth century there is steady evidence that the writers of western monasticism gave great importance to the practice of patience in the life of a cenobite. It is now time to look more closely at the experience and practice of patience and to try to understand something of its theology.

3. The Practice of Patience

There is little doubt that for many western monks patience appeared as the battleground *par excellence* of the spiritual life. The real test of the genuineness of a person's endeavor is to be found in the way he deals with difficulties. St. Benedict, in line with antecedent tradition, recognized the importance of making trial of novices in this respect,[108] and of telling them quite clearly that the way to God was characterized by *dura et aspea*.[109]

It is in his description of the fourth degree of humility that Benedict gives the clearest indications of what one can expect to encounter in monastic life: harshness, things which go against the grain, injuries, suffering, "being tormented by death all day long," "being reckoned as sheep for the slaughter," "being tested like silver in the furnace," "being led into a trap," "having afflictions laid upon one's back," "having men walk over one's head" which means being under a superior, adversities, being "struck on the cheek," having one's clothes stolen, being forced to walk long distances and having to endure false brothers, persecution and being cursed.[110] Nobody can say that no warning was given. These are the elements of which monastic life is made—as they are also the stuff of most human experience. Instead of asking himself why he has to endure them, who is responsible for them and how such trials are to be eliminated, the monk would do better to take for granted that they, or something very similar, will always be with him and so devote his energies to the task of living creatively despite them.

It is worth noting that Benedict locates the main thrust of patience in the realm of obedience to a superior. A monk demonstrates his humility, his openness to being exalted by God, by the manner in which he copes with the problems posed by obedience. Probably there is not so much question of fulfilling particular commands given as the whole business of having to live under the authority of another, of being an inferior vis-à-vis a superior. It is an emphasis which constantly recurs in monastic literature right up to our own times, as witness an incisive, if indelicate, aphorism of Thomas Merton: "Poverty, that's a cinch. Chastity, well, that takes a little getting used to, but that's manageable. Obedience, that's the [expletive deleted]."[111] This is the "labor of obedience" which the Rule, in its opening phrases, sharply distinguishes from the easy-going ways in which obedience is absent.[112]

At the same time, it is important to recognize that patience embraces an area far broader than that of the subordination of a monk to his abbot. There are five principal areas where patience is tried and where the monk has to deal with the temptation either to hurry the process to an uncreative termination or precipitately to abandon it and try his hand at something else.

A) Harsh Treatment

There is no doubt that people's sensibilities are often violated in monastic life. In our own case we feel that this is because nobody has bothered to come to an understanding of us and so we are asked to render inappropriate service, we are overlooked and neglected, we are the victims of the neuroses of others and are sometimes the object of violence and injustice. With regard to others we are a little more sanguine. We can see that the harsh treatment they receive somehow counteracts and corrects their vices and neuroses, helps them to re-focus their attention on the one thing necessary and keeps them from becoming complacent and unbearably conceited. Both viewpoints contain elements of the whole truth. There is no doubt that objective unfairness occurs in monastic life and occasionally monstrous injustices are committed, but the more usual grinding down of sensibilities can be understood as serving a creative role in monastic life insofar as it contributes to the downfall of the ego, which is a necessary cataclysm before the advent of total prayerfulness. Generally such difficulties result not from malice or coldness but from the thoughtlessness and selfishness of others. This is simply part of human life which the normal sane adult learns to cope with. There is no point in making a great lamentation and drowning in self-pity; it is a fact of life.

B) Liabilities of Personal History

One of the most tyrannical fantasies which can paralyze the human being is the idea that somehow or other it might be possible to wipe the slate clean and make a brand new start. Alas, there is no way that this can be done. We are left with a cumulative burden of personal liabilities: decisions made, opportunities missed, guilts born and nurtured, mistakes committed, reputations made and broken, sickness, weaknesses, skills left undeveloped, fears and anxieties collected. Often our greatest irritations come from ourselves and from the residue of our own past. We may rail against circumstances and administrators but the problem is not theirs but ours alone. Monks are not immune to this inrush of regret; it can help if they realize that wherever they go they will carry it with them. Creative living, however, begins with understanding and accepting such limits, compensating for them where possible, and making the most out of the good things which are often their counterface.

C) Slowness of Real Growth

Only babies grow quickly. Genuine growth for human adults is slow.

Monks often bewail the fact that after many years of solid effort they appear to be less advanced than they were before they entered. It is especially hard for those who live in a culture which maximalizes speed and has created scores of "instant" products, to appreciate that the best things in life take time. Perhaps what is lacking in current monastic theory is an accurate phenomenology of growth—a means of communicating to the newcomer a general outline of what is likely to transpire in the years ahead. Conversion may be a relatively instant event, but it does not bring with it all the values, attitudes and habits which render the ideal practically possible. Years intervene while the convert struggles to become what he is. The same is true of prayer; after the initial fireworks, decades of plodding fidelity follow before prayer becomes instinctual. A contemplative, as Bernard of Clairvaux reminds us, is not merely one for whom to live is Christ, but one for whom this has been the case for a long time.[113] The practical effect of this is that a monk has to endure living with his own patent imperfections, even though he desires nothing more than to be quit of them.

D) Alteration

An associated source of difficulty can be found in the intrinsic changeableness of spiritual life. This theme, addressed under the headings of *alternatio* and *vicissitudo*, is one of Bernard's most characteristic emphases.[114] Life can be difficult simply because, as soon as we develop the skills to handle one set of circumstances, everything changes, our aptitudes become irrelevant and we are confronted with new and fearsome challenges. The temptation is either to stop trying altogether or to go back to doing the things which used to work, blocking out from our mind the thought that such wooden "fidelity" seems to be accomplishing little. It seems to be part of God's pedagogy for the monk that he is always left wrong-footed; he is not allowed to save himself, no matter how desperately he desires it.

E) The Incomprehensibility of God's Ways

The lesson learned through years of living with God is that his interventions are beyond prediction and outside the range of human comprehension. Retrospectively, perhaps, glimmers of understanding may relieve the enigma, but almost always the meaning of God's present actions eludes us. This is a call to faith and in some cases it demands heroism to continue trusting and loving and not losing hope.

Patience extends its influence through all these zones in such a way that it becomes an indicator of the quality of one's whole spiritual response. It is no trivial domestic virtue, but the practical working out of faith and love in the arena of the real.

There is one further aspect which may bear mentioning here. Often the lack of sound spiritual theory can increase the burdens of life —sometimes to an intolerable limit. The fact is that concomitant with the difficulties listed above is an intensifying element. Ordinary difficulties can become exaggerated simply due to defective understanding of the rhythms of Christian life. There is a mental confusion at the time of trouble or temptation with the underlying assumption that these difficulties should not be taking place. The chill realization that despite one's efforts, something is radically wrong, begins a process of fear and anxiety which exacerbates any minor problem that happens to be present.

In fact it is a failure to put an end to such dread that causes the most death-dealing of all monastic faults. A monk can allow himself to become depressed to the point of desperation, or he can punish himself and others by becoming angry at everything which he sees as a factor in his sorry condition, or he can dedicate himself to a life of unceasing escapism, throwing himself into work and hobbies and mindless entertainments to such a degree that the pain is temporarily assuaged. In any case he has ceased to operate as a monk; he is the plaything of his own anxieties.

The solution, if he retains any interest in finding one, is to be found in a realistic confidence in the providence of God, who leaves even serious faults in persons otherwise holy,[115] and allows those whose confidence is in themselves to perceive the hollowness of their boast.[116] All that comes from the hand of God is good, even when it bares to the light the ignominy of human weakness.

Patience, as its derivation from *pati* (to suffer) indicates, is a passive virtue in the sense that it does not generate its own content but works with what life brings. It is *not* a passive virtue in the sense that it involves doing nothing, but simply practicing resignation. Christian patience is far more than this, as Benedict clearly demonstrates in discussing the fourth degree of humility. He distinguishes four stages of patience.

A) Endurance

Being able to bear with suffering is part of patience; it is its beginning. It means more, however, than collapsing into a cocoon of pain. It means being tireless in doing good even when the practice of virtue is more a matter of good habit than of present pleasure: *non dulcedo sed habitudo*. It means setting aside feelings and adhering to the objective teaching of faith: *Iudicium fidei sequere, et non experimentum tuum*.[117] There is a lot of activity here. It is not a depressive state of paralysis, but hard work, labor, carrying on after the initial novelty has worn off, persevering in a task which, though worthy, brings no pleasure.

B) Equanimity

It is in asking for more than endurance that Benedict distinguishes himself from the Master. He qualifies the idea of patience by the addition of the phrase *with a quiet mind*.[118] Real patience does not seethe interiorly. There is an inner stillness which accepts the imposition, even though it may judge it to be unfair. The truly patient monk is less concerned about the external details of the situation than about his own handling of it. He needs to come to the realization that this is God's will for him at this moment, even though he is aware of the sordid politics that have contributed to its fashioning. Patience is really a matter of faith in the providence of God. If the monk can accept in his heart that this unpleasant moment is a vehicle of God's concern, then he will be less angry or depressed because of human idiocy and more able to avoid inward rebellion. Perhaps it needs to be said that we are often defective in the formation we give to younger monks. We do not spend enough time teaching them the skills of finding peace and of making peace. Maybe we give them a double dose of theology, but we don't seem too concerned about training them how to rest in peace in difficult circumstances and how to be a force for peace and reconciliation with others. Without such skills patience becomes an illusory goal.

C) Joy

It is not enough to accept harsh treatment with equanimity; Benedict wants his disciples to be glad about it. Like the apostles who went forth from their punishment "rejoicing that they were found worthy to suffer dishonor for the Name" (Acts 5:41). Even the descriptions of being tried by fire and counted as sheep for the slaughter come from a psalm which begins: *Iubilate Deo omnis terra* and ends with a blessing on God who hears the prayer of the afficted and brings salvation (Ps. 65 [66]). The joy of the patient monk comes from his hope in the final outcome of his struggles and the realization of divine love. "Secure in their hope of God's retribution, they continue joyfully: 'But in all these things we have overcome because of him who has loved us.' "[119]

D) Asking for More

Benedict requires of the monk no less than Christ does of his followers. Quoting the Sermon on the Mount, he tells us to accept more pain
than was originally offered, to give up more of our goods than were
originally taken and spontaneously to offer more when pressed into service. True patience is not only persevering, tranquil and even cheerful, it
gives the impression of an unsatisfied appetite for more of the same.

The practice of patience is, in reality, no more than a realistic living of
the Gospel. It is not, however, to be found in the mere implementation of
individual evangelical injunctions. The factor in patience which gives it
power is the monk's personal relationship with Christ. He is borne up
during his troubles by a sense of solidarity with his Lord. But there is
even more than this. The ability to love one's enemies and to pray for
one's persecutors goes beyond human skills; it is only possible when one
evacuates the ego so that Christ is able to love within one and from the
midst of pain to reach out and negate the malice of sin.

4. The Meaning of Patience

There is a mystery involved in patience. It may be explained thus.
Often when we know the full story behind some set of circumstances we
are happy to endure inconvenience and even pain. Once we have perceived that the hostile actions of others really derive from their own
suffering and not from malice in our regard, it becomes easier to anticipate and endure rough treatment at their hands. In fact, in dealing with
another individual, we are encountering somebody who is severely
scarred by the malice and indifference of others. If we really understood
how much a victim this other person is, we would be compassionate and
not condemnatory. What he is doing is handing on the evil that was
done to him and we are the recipients. Our pain has its ultimate origins,
perhaps, in the first human beings. Each generation is wounded and
perpetuates its pain by inflicting it on others. Genuine Christian patience
calls a halt to this seemingly inevitable transmission. It receives evil and,
instead of passing it on, absorbs it. This line of malice is not continued; it
goes no further. Injuries are not repeated; the process is halted. Patience
puts an end to the endless cycle of mutual hurt.

In his lifetime this is what Christ did and it is to this that he calls us.
Not to render evil for evil, but rather patiently to bear hurt that is done
to us.[120] We have before us the example of the Lamb of God who bears,
who takes upon himself the sins of the world, who, in Paul's adventur-

ous image, became sin for us,[121] who did not think that the shame of the cross was even worth taking into consideration.[122]

Thus Paul was to write to the Colossians: "Now I rejoice in suffering for your sake and in my flesh I bring to completion whatever is lacking to the afflictions of Christ, for the sake of the Church, his body" (Col. 1:24). Paul views his sufferings as contributing to that fixed quantum of tribulations which are the harbingers of the Parousia. "The apostle, through the sufferings which he painfully bears in his own flesh, contributes to foreshortening the eschatological afflictions. This, in turn, brings the dawning of the future glory all the closer."[123] Tribulations borne in the name of Christ reduce the level of suffering to be endured by others for the purification of sin. To accept pain cheerfully is not mere stoicism; it is ultimately altruistic.

Yet, all is not negative. There is a strange economy which transforms pain into an encounter with God. As Dom Helder Camara notes somewhere: God "is far less lilkely to abandon us in hardship than in times of ease." Ambrose of Milan has the same thought: "There are many who seek Christ in times of quiet and do not find him, but they find him in persecutions and find him quickly. The same is true after temptations since God is present to his faithful in their dangers."[124] It goes against all our theoretical conceptions of lineal progress in the spiritual life, but the strange fact is that God seems most present when things are at their worst. Negative situations have the potential to be transformed by the impress of the cross of Christ.

For the patient monk the conflicts and pains of the human situation can become the exercise-ground for his faith and open up to him the possibility of finding eternal life by allowing his grasp on present life to be loosened. It is the clear mandate of Christ that to gain life, we must lose life. The grain of wheat must die before it becomes fruitful. And for us, so many of our problems in the spiritual life come simply from our unwillingness to die. "Who could have believed," cries one of Camus' characters, "that crime consists less in making others die, than in not dying oneself."[125] The start of Christian life is baptism in which we die to sin and to selfishness and the progressive realization that God is found in many situations which, at first, seem to be vehicles of death, not life. Therefore, "bear one another's burdens, and so you will fulfill the law of Christ: *Alter alterius onera portate, et sic adimplebitis legem Christi*" (Gal. 6:2).

NOTES

[1]John Cassian, *Conferences*, 1.7; SChr 42, pp. 84-85.

[2]RB Prol. 50; cf. RM Ths 46; SChr 105, p. 326. This follows an earlier statement not used by Benedict. "Therefore it is right that we should become sharers in his passion so that we may deserve to become co-heirs to his glory." RM Thp 11; SChr 105, p. 302. Benedict has changed RM's "*this* instruction" to "*his* instruction" —a significant alteration.

[3]Gregory the Great, Ev. 35.4, PL 76.1261d. There is a similar statement in the *Regula Pastoralis: Ipsa namque mater est omnium custosque virtutum* (c. 9, PL 77.59d).

[4]Bernard of Clairvaux, Div. 2.5; SBO 6a.83.11-12: *Impatientia animae perditio est.*

[5]Cf. TKNT 2.56, 3.374-387, 581-588. For a different approach see William Barclay, *New Testament Words*, London: S.C.M. Press, 1964, pp. 143-145 and 196-198.

[6]In the Septuagint *hupomenein* usually relates to Hebrew verbs associated with hope and "messianic" expectation. There is a good statement of the difference between the two terms in R.G. Trench's 1889 book, *Synonyms of the New Testament*. *Makrothumia* has to do with persons and *hupomone* with circumstances. The man who has *makrothumia* "having to do with injurious persons, does not suffer himself to be provoked by them or to blaze up in anger," but the man who exercises *hupomone* is the one "who, under a great siege of trials, bears up and does not lose heart or courage.... Thus while both graces are ascribed to the saints only *makrothumia* is an attribute of God." (As quoted by E.J. Cooke, in *The Interpreter's Dictionary of the Bible*, vol. 3, p. 676.)

[7]For the Hellenistic background of the concept of patience and much else besides, see Michel Spanneut, art. "Patience," DSp 12 (1983), col. 438-476.

[8]One might add an *obiter dictum* from Karl Rahner, "On Martyrdom," in *On the Theology of Death*, New York: Herder and Herder, 1960, p. 126: "One might think that Christian life can be understood only in the light of Christian death in its absolute sense, i.e., in martyrdom, and that the poverty and aridity of our modern Christian existence is revealed in the discouraging fact that there is so little courage in us for such a vocation as martyrdom." An alternate source of western interest in patience may be exemplified in *The Shepherd of Hermas* which gives such priority to this virtue. Cf. Mand 5.2 (34); SChr 53, p. 166.

[9]Cf. Willy Rordorf, art. "Martyre," in DSp 10 (1978), col. 718-732.

[10]*The Martyrdom of Polycarp*, 17.3; SChr 10, p. 266. Like many of the primitive witnesses, there is evident dependence on 1 Pet. 2:19-22.

[11]Origen, *In Numeros homilia*, 10.2, PG 12.639a.

[12]Claude Peifer, in *RB 1980*, Collegeville: Liturgical Press, 1981, p. 361.

[13]Polycarp, *Letter to the Philippians*, 9-10; SChr 10, pp. 214-216. The first paragraph is preserved in Greek, the second only in Latin.

[14]Cf. Clement of Alexandria, *Stromata*, 4.4.14.1; GCS 15, p. 254. Tertullian, *Apologia*, 27.3; CChr 1, pp. 138-139. Cyprian, *De Bono Patientiae*, 16, PL 4.657a.

[15]Pseudo-Cyprian, *Ad Fortunatum: De Duplici Martyrio*, 33, PL 4.981a.

[16]Pseudo-Cyprian, *op. cit.*, 32, PL 4.981a. Cf. Bernard of Clairvaux, Sent. 3.74; SBO 6b.112-115. Some important qualifications to this assertion are given in Dietrich Bonhoeffer, *The Cost of Discipleship*, London: S.C.M. Press, 1959, pp. 78-79.

[17]Gregory the Great, Ev. 35.7, PL 76.1263b. The phrase *in pace Ecclesiae vivimus* is difficult to interpret. I am taking it to mean that we do not disturb the *pax Ecclesiae*. Augustine regards the struggle with invisible enemies as the greater test of patience. Cf. *De Patientia* 10 (9), PL 40.615d. On the theme of spiritual martyrdom cf. E.E. Malone, *The Monk and the Martyr: The Monk as the Successor of the Martyr*, Washington, D.C.: Catholic University of America Press, 1950. A.C. Rush, "Spiritual Martyrdom in St. Gregory the Great," *Theological Studies* 23 (1962), pp. 569-589. Anselme Stolz, *L'ascèse chrétienne*, Chevtogne: Editions des Bénédictins d'Amay, 1948, pp. 120-143.

[18]Augustine, *De Patientia*, 1, PL 40.611b, 15 (12); 617d, 26-27; 623-624. *Sermo.* 323, PL 38.1463-1464. Cyprian, *De Bono Patientiae*, 3, PL 4.648a.

[19]Cf. Clement of Alexandria, *Stromata*, 2.6.31.1; GCS 15, p. 129. Cyprian, *De Bono Patientiae*, 20, PL 4.660a. Augustine, *De Patientia*, 18 (15), PL 40.619d. Ambrose, *De Officiis*, 1.48.237, PL 16.93c.

[20]Cyprian, *De Bono Patientiae*, 16, PL 4.657a. Pseudo-Cyprian, *Ad Fortunatum*, 34, PL 4.981d.

[21]William of St Thierry, *De Natura Corporis et Animae*, 8, PL 180.718c. Cf. Bernard of Clairvaux, Par. 5.1; SBO 6b.282.8-9.

[22]*Verba Seniorum*, 7.8, PL 73.894a.

[23]*Ibid.*, 7.11 (894d), 7.15 (895c), 7.24 (900a), 7.26 (900a), 7.30 (900d), 7.34 (901c), 7.36 (902a).

[24]*Ibid.*, 7.5 (893c).

[25]*Dixit abbas Pastor: Quia virtus monachi in tentationibus apparet. Verba Seniorum* 7.13 (895b). Cf. 7.32 (901a).

[26]*Quoniam et ipse inimicus patientia tua destruetur. Verba Seniorum* 7.18 (896d).

[27]*Verba Seniorum*, 7.45 (904c).

[28]*Ibid.*, 7.35 (901d-902a).

[29]Evagrius Ponticus, *Praktikos*, 40; SChr 171, p. 592.

[30]*Ibid.*, Prol. 8, SChr 171, p. 492.

[31]*Ibid.*, 15; SChr 171, p. 536.

[32]*Ibid.*, 68; SChr 171, p. 652.

[33]John Cassian, *De Institutis Coenobiorum*, 4.3.1; SChr 109, p. 124. Cf. *Inst.*, 4.7, p. 130. *Inst.*, 4.36.2, p. 176.

[34]Humility and patience are linked in the following texts. *Inst.*, 4.3.1 (p. 124), 4.7 (p. 130), 4.36.2 (p. 176), 4.39.2 (p. 180), 4.42 (p. 184), 5.36.1 (p. 246), 6.15.1 (p. 280), 7.31 (p. 332), 8.18.2 (p. 358), 10.22 (p. 420). *Conlatio* 18.8; SChr 64, p. 22, 18.13 (pp. 23-25).

[35]*Inst.*, 5.4.1 (p. 194).

[36]*Inst.*, 4.39.2 (p. 180).

[37]*Inst.*, 4.42 (p. 184).

[38]*Conl.*, 12.6; SChr 54, p. 127: *in lenitate ac patientia cordis*.

[39] *Inst.*, 5.36.1 (p. 246).

[40] Cf. *Inst.*, 6.15.1 (p. 280), 8.20.2 (p. 362): ...*ita mens poterit iugiter in omni patientia et sanctitate durare*, 8.16 (p. 358): *ad patientiae ac perfectionis calcem*....

[41] *Inst.*, 8.16 (p. 356).

[42] *Inst.*, 6.3 (p. 264).

[43] *Ira patientiam vastat. Inst.*, 12.3.2 (p. 452).

[44] "The patience and discipline (*districtio*) of the coenobites, by which they continue with their profession once they have taken it so that they never fulfill their own wills, render them each day crucified to this world and living martyrs." *Conl.*, 18.7; SChr 64, p. 21.

[45] *Inst.*, 6.3 (p. 264). Cassian argues that community life provides the occasion for the manifestation of hidden vices. Once out in the open they are negatively reinforced both by the rebukes of others as also, it may be inferred, by a certain self-disgust. In this way one is moved to work positively for the suppression of the vices. This wholesome outcome would not have taken place without the provocation provided by community living. Thus hermits may be deluded about the level of virtue they have achieved; whereas community living monks are never left long to congratulate themselves on their progress. Cassian's conclusion is that God teaches us not to leave aside fraternal interaction: *non deserenda praecepit fratrum consortio. Inst.*, 9.7 (p. 374). Cf. *Conl.*, 19.10; SChr 64, p. 47.

[46] "Therefore your patience ought not to depend on the virtue of others. This is to say that you would only have it on condition that you are annoyed by nobody." *Inst.*, 4.42 (p. 184). On the other hand, "we make the excuse for our negligence by saying that the cause of our upset is not our impatience but that it is generated by the viciousness of the brothers." *Inst.*, 8.16 (p. 358).

[47] "Perfection of heart is acquired not so much by separation from human beings as by the virtue of patience." *Inst.*, 9.7 (p. 374).

[48] *Inst.*, 8.17-18 (pp. 358-360). Cf. *Conl.*, 18.8-15; SChr 64, pp. 21-31.

[49] RB Prol. 50.

[50] RB 7.35-43.

[51] RB 72.5.

[52] RM 92.18; SChr 106, pp. 412-414.

[53] RB 2.25 from RM 2.25; SChr 105, p. 356.

[54] RB 4.30 from RM 3.35; SChr 105, p. 366.

[55] RB 36.5. Benedict seems to be approaching the matter from the opposite direction to Evagrius, see note 29. On RB's approach to the sick, cf. Einar Molland, "*Ut Sapiens Medicus*: Medical Vocabulary in St. Benedict's *Regula Monachorum*," *Studia Monastica* 6 (1964), pp. 273-298.

[56] RB 58.3

[57] RB 58.11. Anselmo Lentini translates this: *e di nuovo sia provato in ogni esercizio di pazienza; La Regola*, Montecassino, 1980, pp. 517-519. Most translators seem to leave it ambiguous.

[58] RB 68.2

[59] RM 92.18; SChr 106, p. 414, RM 92.24 (p. 414), RM 92.80 (p. 422).

[60] RM 90.31; SChr 106, p. 384.

[61]RM 7.59; SChr 105, p. 394. On the theme of obedience and martyrdom in RB, cf. Georg Holzherr, *Die Benediktsregel: Eine Anleitung zu christlichem Leben*, Zurich: Benziger, 1980, p. 128.

[62]*Flagella* occur in *Moralia* praefatium 11; SChr 32, p. 134, praefatium 13 (p. 136), 14.37.45; SChr 212, p. 388, Ev. 35.9, PL 76.1264d-1265a. Gregory would have known, among other scourges, Goths, Lombards, recurrent plagues, floods, famines and drought. No wonder he thought the end of the world was coming! Cf. Jeffrey Richards, *Consul of God: The Life and Time of Gregory the Great*, London: Routledge and Kegan Paul, 1980, esp. pp. 4-16.

[63]*Moralia*, 13.1.1; SChr 212, p. 246.

[64]Ev. 35.4, PL 76.1261d; cf. *Regula Pastoralis*, 3.9, PL 77.59d.

[65]*Dial.* 1.2.8; SChr 260, p. 30.

[66]*Moralia*, 2.34.47; SChr 212, p. 108.

[67]*Ibid.*, 5.16.33; CChr 143, p. 241.

[68]Ezek. 1.7.12; CChr 142, p. 91.

[69]Ev. 35.9, PL 76.1264d-1265a.

[70]*Dial.*, 4.11.2; SChr 265, p. 46.

[71]Ev. 35.9, PL 76.1265b.

[72]*Moralia*, 5.45.81; CChr 143, p. 279.

[73]*Moralia* 2.17.30; SChr 32, p. 203.

[74]*Sapiens autem differt et reservat in posterum. Regula Pastoralis* 3.9, PL 77.60d-61a.

[75]Ev. 35.4, PL 76.1261d.

[76]Ev. 35.9, PL 76.1264d-1265a.

[77]Ev. 35.4, PL 76.1261-1262a.

[78]Although he does see in the meekness and lack of ferocity of the donkey, a sign of patience. Cf. *Moralia*, 2.46.72; SChr 32, p. 231.

[79]*Patientia enim vera est quae et ipsum amat quem portat.* Ezek. 1.7.12; CChr 142, p. 91. The same phrase is found in Ezek. 2.5.14 (p. 287) and 2.8.15 (p. 347). *Patiens namquae est ut aliena mala toleret, benigna vero est ut ipsos etiam quos portat amet*: Ev. 35.4, PL 77.1262a.

[80]*Regula Pastoralis*, 3.9, PL 77.62a.

[81]Bruno, Ep. 3.2; SChr 88, p. 84.

[82]Thomas of Froidmont, *Liber de modo bene vivendi*, 101, PL 184.1261a.

[83]Peter of Celle, *De Conscientia*; Jean Leclercq (ed.), *La spiritualité de Pierre de Celle*, Paris: Vrin, 1946, p. 218, lines 28-30.

[84]Adam of Perseigne, Ep. 64; Jean Bouvet (ed.), *Archives historiques du Maine*, t. 13, p. 629.

[85]Guerric of Igny, *First Sermon for Lent*, 5; SChr 202, p. 20. Guerric is quoting Rom. 5:4. Immediately before the citation of this text he recognizes that trials which are excessively severe can break the *patienta cordis*.

[86]*Habeto semper patientiam mentis. Esto benigna, esto prompta affectu, esto affabilis in sermone, grato animo appare ad omnes.* Thomas of Froidmont, *op. cit.*, PL 184.1261b.

[87]Guerric of Igny, *Fourth Sermon for the Purification*, 4; SChr 166, p. 362.

[88]Guerric of Igny, *First Sermon for the Feast of St. Benedict*, 3; SChr 202, p. 42.

[89]Guerric of Igny, *First Sermon for Palm Sunday*, 3; SChr 202, p. 170.

[90]Guerric of Igny, *Fourth Sermon for the Epiphany*, 3; SChr 166, p. 292. *First Sermon for Palm Sunday*, 2; SChr 202, p. 166. The latter letter is a citation of Col. 1:11.

[91]"Patience is bitter without hope," *sine spe amara patientia*. Peter of Celle, *De disciplina Claustrali* epilogue; SChr 240, p. 318. See also 17.42 (p. 216). Cf. Guerric of Igny, *First Sermon for Advent*, 3: *Si enim quod non videmus speramus, per patientiam expectamus*; SChr 166, p. 98. In a similar vein the *Fourth Sermon for the Feast of St. Benedict*, 3; SChr 202, p. 100.

[92]Peter of Celle, *De Disciplina Claustrali*, 19; SChr 240, p. 234: *vincens per patientiam ut vinceret per potentiam.*

[93]"Whoever living in righteousness and finding himself crushed by trials has only to follow the footsteps of Christ so that at the end he is not cheated of his inheritance." Peter Damian, *De Patientia in insectatione improborum*, PL 145.796b.

[94]Adam of Perseigne, Ep. 20, PL 211.652d.

[95]*Sed ne divinius his ignis iniuriarum flatu tepescat, dilecti Domini ac Salvatoris sui tranquillam patientiam oculis mentis semper aspiciat.* Aelred of Rievaulx, *De Speculo Caritatis*, 3.16; CChrM 1, pp. 112-113.

[96]"One who does not maintain patience loses justice, that is, he loses life, that is, he loses his soul." Bernard of Clairvaux, Ann. 3.6; SBO 5.39.1-2.

[97]QH 7.3; SBO 4.414.18.

[98]Bernard considers that there are three sources of suffering: from oneself, from one's neighbor and from God. PP 1.4; SBO 5.190.18-19. Gregory also distinguishes a triple origin for suffering: from God, from the ancient ememy and from the neighbor; Ev. 35.9, PL 76.1264d. Bernard enunciates a different triad in Sent. 2.75; SBO 6b.40.7-8.

[99]SC 34.3; SBO 1.247.2-3.

[100]"If you murmur in your heart, even if externally you do what is commanded, this is not the virtue of patience but veiled malice. It is needful that the day of patience must dawn whereby you embrace with a quiet mind everything hard and rough" (*omnia dura et aspera tacita amplectaris conscientia*). Circ. 3.8; SBO 4.288.17-20, with reminiscences from RB 48.8 and 7.35.

[101]IV HM 3; SBO 5.58.12.

[102]*Utrumque es mihi, Domine Jesu, et speculum patiendi, et pretium patientiae.* SC 47.6; SBO 2.65.8-9.

[103]"How great is the praise which is his due! With what feeling do you think that brother is to be embraced who lives among brothers without a quarrel, whose whole concern is that there is nothing in himself that has to be borne by others and yet he carries most patiently whatever is burdensome in others." OS 1.14; SBO 5.340.20-24.

[104]Dom I Nov 1.2; SBO 5.305.16-21.

[105]"To bear patiently with bodily troubles is sufficient for salvation; the summit is when they are also embraced gladly, in fervor of spirit." Div. 35.5 = *Sermo ad Abbates*, 5; SBO 5.291.21-22. The same idea occurs in PP 1.4; SBO 5.190.13-15, with the same term *libenter*. He is speaking about the requirements for living a community life; a monk must be self-controlled, sociable and humble. "To live socia-

bly (*sociabiliter*) you must have a care to be loved and to love (*ut studeas amari et amare*), show yourself mild (*blandum*) and affable, supporting the infirmities of your brothers, both bodily and behavioral, not only patiently, but gladly." There is a reference here to RB 72.5.

[106]SC 34.4; SBO 1.247.2-3. Cf. Conv. [c. 18] 31; SBO 4.107-108.

[107]Csi 1.4; SBO 397.15-398.1: *Non bona patientia, cum possis esse liber, servum te permittere fieri.*

[108]RB 58.3, 11.

[109]RB 58.8.

[110]RB 7.35-43. I am taking some liberties with the text.

[111]Quoted by W.H. Ferry in Paul Wilkes (ed.), *Merton: By Those who Knew him Best*, San Francisco: Harper and Row, 1984, p. 89.

[112]RB Prol. 2.

[113]Bernard of Clairvaux, SC 69.1; SBO 2.202.11-12.

[114]I have developed Bernard's teaching on *alternatio* in *Athirst for God: Spiritual Desire in Bernard of Clairvaux's Sermons on the Song of Songs* (CS 77), Kalamazoo: Cistercian Publications, 1988, pp. 244-314.

[115]"The dispensation of almighty God is large. It often happens that those to whom he grants the greater goods are denied the lesser so that their minds might always have something with which to reproach themselves. Hence although they long to be perfect, it is not possible for them. They work hard in the areas where they have not been given the gift and their labor achieves no result. So they are less likely to have a high opinion of themselves in the areas in which they have been gifted. Because they are not able to be victorious over small vices and excesses they learn that the greater goods do not derive from themselves." Gregory the Great, *Dial.* 3.14.12; SChr 260, p.312.

[116]"Is it not true that such a fall contributes to our good, if it makes us humbler and more wary?" Bernard of Clairvaux, QH 2.2; SBO 4.390.21-22. Cf. SC 17.2 SBO 1.99.14-21: "For it is a fact that the Spirit does come and go and that the one who stands with his support *necessarily* falls when this support is withdrawn. But he does not collapse completely since the Lord, once again, stretches out to him a helping hand. For people who are spiritual, or rather, *for those whom the Lord intends to make spiritual*, this process of alternation goes on all the time. God visits by morning and subjects to trial. The just man falls seven times, and seven times gets up again. What is important is that he falls during the day so that he sees himself falling and knows when he has fallen and wants to get up again and calls out for a helping hand, saying: 'O Lord, at your will you made me splendid in virtue, but then you turned away and I was overcome.' " A similar point was made by Pope John Paul I in a general audience on 6 September 1978: "I run the risk of making a blunder, but I will say it: the Lord loves humility so much that, sometimes, he permits serious sins. Why? In order that those committing these sins may, after repenting, remain humble." *L'Osservatore Romano* (Weekly Edition in English), 37 (546), 14 September 1978, p. 8.

[117]Bernard of Clairvaux, Quad. 5.5; SBO 4.374.20-21.

[118]RB 7.35 replaces the *constantiam* of RM 10.52 with *conscientia* to make a sen-

tence which translates thus: in difficulties "his conscience/consciousness quietly embraces patience." The critical texts keep the adverb *tacite*, also found in RM. Traditionally, the *textus receptus* was *tacita conscientia*, which made a lot of sense.

[119]RB 7.39.

[120]RB 4.29-30 following RM 3.34-35; SChr 105, p. 366. The first part seems to be based on 1 Pet. 3:9.

[121]2 Cor. 5:21.

[122]Heb. 12:2.

[123]Eduard Lohse, *Colossians and Philemon: A Commentary on the Epistles to the Colossians and to Philemon*, Philadelphia: Fortress Press, 1975, p. 71. I am basing my interpretation of this text on Lohse's arguments, cf. pp. 68-72.

[124]Ambrose, *Liber de Isaac et anima*, C. 5, 41, PL 14.541d-542a.

[125]Albert Camus, *The Fall*, Harmondsworth: Penguin Books, 1963, p. 83.

Introductory Note

This article (first published in *Tjurunga* 31 [1986], pp. 3-14) flowed almost spontaneously from reflection on the phrase of Gertrude the Great quoted at its beginning. About half of it is concerned with the interactive relationship between chastity and an undivided heart. As such it is not irrelevant to the theme of this collection. On the level of experience it seems that chastity is an essential component of that unifying of inner energies from which contemplation springs. It suffers from being considered too negatively. It can be helpful to view chastity as contributing something positive to the enrichment of spiritual life and not merely enduring it as an impoverishment or imposition.

Consecrated Chastity:
Reflections on a Text of
Gertrude of Helfta

In a devotional exercise designed to deepen her experience of religious consecration, Saint Gertrude the Great has a paragraph which merits close attention. It reads as follows:

> After that there is the act of consecration by which the soul who is faithful to Christ consecrates and offers herself entirely. She is married to one husband, a chaste virgin offered to Christ. By the observance of virginity or chastity she commits herself to remain united to her spouse and to keep faith, *with a pure heart, a chaste body and a love that draws ever closer*, so that it will not be spoiled by the love of any earthly thing.[1]

Although it would be profitable to reflect on the meaning of the strong spousal imagery found in this text and throughout the whole exercise, in this article I would like to concentrate on a single clause describing the complementary aspects of religious chastity: *puro corde, casto corpore et amore unitivo*: with a pure heart, a chaste body and a love that draws ever closer.

I. A Pure Heart

The whole concept of purity is currently not in much favor, probably because it was used, in the immediate past, in a way that seemed to make the noble virtue of chastity both unattractive and unattainable. The major effect of a discussion of chastity was a sense of guilt; it inspired dread rather than generosity. Implicit in many such discussions was often a nostalgia for pre-pubescence and the corresponding implication that becoming sexually aware was a development somehow unworthy of those who felt drawn to a celibate ideal. Much emphasis was placed on virginity, an absolute that once lost could never be regained. Now it is certainly not true that the image of purity was totally to blame for the extent of guilt and unnecessary repression among religious in sexual matters, yet purity has somehow come to seem typical of an approach to chastity which is untheological, unhealthy and pastorally unrealistic. For many, the concept of purity was a cult of whiteness. Theoretically it was splendid and radiant but, in practice, it was nearly impossible to maintain. As with anything white, one is more conscious of the spots and stains than of the considerable areas which remain unblemished.

Even without the difficulties caused by a less-than-perfect use of the image of purity in the past, there are other difficulties with it. Firstly, like all words ending in -*ity*, it is an abstraction. In an area which is eminently practical its import is general and unrestricted. Its goals are vague and, as a result, they become tyrannical; we can never be quite sure that all possible demands have been fulfilled. Secondly, the symbol of purity operates at the level of taboo and hence it quickly forges an alliance with all sorts of undefined fears, compulsions, obsessions and guilts in our personal unconscious.[2] Sexuality is thus invested with a power to upset the established order that is far beyond its relative importance. On the other hand, we see that much of the ethic proposed in the New Testament stems from a concern with removing the religious response away from the level of defilement and purification into a more strictly ethical direction and beyond this into the realm of personal attitudes and dispositions.

It is important, therefore, to note that Gertrude, following the lead of the Beatitudes and monastic tradition, speaks in this text not of purity but of "purity of heart." This is such an important concept that it is worth spending some time on. The phrase is familiar, yet we do not always interpret it as richly as it deserves.

The monastic emphasis on purity of heart is generally explained in terms of singleness of purpose, inner undividedness, freedom from radical inconsistency, not having mixed motives, single-mindedness. To progress towards this goal is understood as growth in simplicity.[3]

In this case the image is seen not so much as whiteness, as a matter of being true to one's essential nature. Pure orange juice is devoid of additives and adulterants. Pure water is water and nothing else. A pure heart is a heart which is fully alive, with all its energies directed to a single end. The only object which has the capacity to hold such an intense outburst of energy is God; with anything less the energies are dissipated and concentration is lost. Purity of heart comes from being drawn toward God.

It must be obvious that the perfection of purity of heart is not effected in an instant. It is the gift of grace and the labor of a lifetime. As a result one has to go through life with the burden of being subject to another law, of seeming to possess a "double soul."[4] The more conscious one becomes of a transcendent ideal, the more one's very nature seems to rebel against it.

It is worth noting, however, that purity of heart is the result of the progressive harmonization of these very tendencies which, at first, seem so mutually opposed. This means that contrary movements of nature must remain substantially intact so that they can be included in the final state. Nothing is achieved by repressing or suppressing the "undesirable" element in the dialectic. For a synthesis to be achieved, the negative element (antithesis) must be allowed to continue its work of purifying and qualifying the positive element, adding to it what it needs to be reconstituted in a richer mode.[5] In practical terms, too much attention to the correction of faults and the elimination of vice can prevent the formation of genuine virtue, substituting for it a pallid blamelessness that is not only barren but usually temporary. Too much vigor expended in bridling the wild energies of the passions can destroy all enthusiasm leaving a residue that is bland and boring. Sin is to be excluded only so that goodness may flourish, not for its own sake.

Purity of heart is not just a matter of deciding on a pattern of life and then resolutely refusing to compromise. There is more to a pure heart than a strong will. One needs prudence and patience to space one's effort over a lifetime. One also needs to know how to endure. There is much energy within us which has the capacity to upset the balance of the heart and most of it is not amenable to willpower. One does not have to know more than a little about psychoanalysis to appreciate this. The consequence of it is that some problems go through a stage of latency. They emerge only with the passage of time, but when they do appear they are already well-established. We all know the practical utility of "nipping in the bud" destructive behavior, but this is not usually possible with regard to the deep roots from which such conduct grows. Although, theoretically, it is possible to limit the external manifestations of destructive tendencies, the tendencies themselves are intractable. If they were trivial little things which could be handled by a New Year's resolution, they could scarcely be considered real problems or threats. But those problems which derive from deep inside us cannot be easily dismissed; we will have to struggle with them in various forms throughout our life.

This being so, it is likely that the crucial factor in checking their destructiveness is remaining continually conscious of their presence so that there is less possibility of their catching us unaware. This seems to be the meaning of St. Benedict's first step of humility. Most of us are able to accept this in principle yet, as time goes by, our vigilance is relaxed until our complacency is shaken by a revival in what we had hoped was past history. When we sleep we fall, and when we fall we are awakened. So in God's providence, we are protected from all but a few bruises which quickly fade. This consciousness of our tendency to sin is not a matter of self-depreciation, discouragement or excessive guilt, but just of keeping a wary eye on an aspect of ourselves which will eventually be integrated but which, for the moment, remains unruly and potentially harmful. It is realism as opposed to wishful thinking. The process of integration will take a lifetime; meanwhile it is not very wise to think that because a tendency is not causing any trouble it has entirely lost its sting.

Purity of heart is a matter of grappling with our tendencies to vice: anger, envy, greediness, timidity, melancholy, to name a few. Lust, however has a special significance. There are a number of reasons for this: sexuality wields a powerful measure of our instinctual energies; sexuality is an area of repression for a statistically significant portion of the population; sexuality becomes especially sensitive in the case of those who dedicate themselves to celibacy and permanent continence. Whatever the relative importance of chastity to purity of heart, it must be seen that purity of heart is the absolute foundation for a chaste life. Only one who is moving toward singleness of purpose will have the courage to pursue the virtue, despite temptation and failure.

Why is chastity linked with purity of heart?

Both by nature and by nurture explicit sexuality makes a relatively late appearance in consciousness. It opposes its instinctual strength to the fragile coalition of beliefs and values of an emerging attitude to life. Ideally the result would be an instant integration of sexuality into a personal sense of identity, philosophy of life and the expression of affection. In fact, however, the ideal is never realized. Most of us, at puberty or later on, tended to one or other extreme: either we tried to carry on as normal, denying sexuality in large measure or, alternatively, we crumbled before sexuality and were overrun by it, allowing it to control us and letting go of the beliefs and values which had hitherto guided us. These are the extremes, there are many positions in between; perhaps we leapt from one side of the median strip to the other, and back again. It is probably very rare that anyone quickly achieves perfect harmony.

The point is that those who choose to allow sexuality to dominate are not, for as long as this stage of their life endures, realistic candidates for religious life. A conversion is to be hoped for. On the other hand, the sort of person who is moving toward celibacy will tend, ordinarily, to the extreme of repression. This may take the form of denying their sexuality, defining themselves and their relations with reality in asexual terms, or too easily assuming that the sexual phase of their lives has passed. If it is hard for sexually active people to integrate affectivity and sexuality, even in an enduring and creative marriage, it will probably be almost impossible for a celibate to realize his affective potential without considerable effort.

To make a decision for celibacy—especially in the climate of contemporary western society—requires a fair amount of strength in the sphere of values and a certain ability to relativize instinctual demands. Without wishing to determine cause and effect, it seems that a decision to follow a religious vocation often takes place at a time when a person experiences a comparative decline in sexual interest and a lull in the imperiousness of sexual demands. A providential plateau has been reached in which broader horizons can be viewed. The danger is that the relative calm of this transitional phase is sometimes mistaken for solid virtue and there is great alarm when the battle resumes.

Once the opening phases of religious life have been passed and spiritual growth is continuing, there tends to be a reduction in inhibition and repression as the person moves towards greater maturity and freedom. With a sense of liberation there often comes a stronger awareness of sexual needs, both physical and relational, which is sometimes fairly overt and sometimes disguised. This is often a sign of progress. The beginning is over; the process of integration is advancing. If there is a battle, one can reasonably expect to sustain some losses. This is reality, it is not Hollywood. Too many people lose their nerve at this stage, which is a tragedy because life is just starting to get interesting. Some lose heart because they don't know what is happening to them. Some are misdirected, which is not only a tragedy but a crime.

It is at this stage that we must try and determine whether a person has the gift and the call to celibacy. It seems to me that this discernment needs to concentrate less on behavior, which is often counter-indicative, and more on what a person experiences when caught in the crossfire. It is the will to follow a crucified Lord in darkness and with a sense of unworthiness that is of special relevance here. Pain, mistakes and confusion are par for the course.

It must be remembered that when we talk about "a pure heart" with regard to chastity, we are not identifying this either with the unknowing innocence of childhood or with the comfortable level of repression that was necessary to get us started along the way. We are talking about the ultimate goal of the virtue of chastity—the integration of sexuality with the rest of life. It is the same goal pursued by the married. And for both married and celibate alike the flowering of chastity demands a lifetime of vigorous endeavor coupled with generous and patient endurance.

A pure heart is not a void, featureless landscape from which all alternatives have been vigorously excluded. It is rather a rich and vibrant chorus in which disparate energies collaborate to produce a harmony which is rich and beautiful. It is fullness, not emptiness.

II. A Chaste Body

If purity of heart is a matter of the progressive integration of psychic energies, some of which may be deeper than our ordinary awareness, chastity of body is more a matter of conscious behavior, directed to ethical living according to our state in life.

Chastity is a virtue, which is to say that it is a behavioral habit, developed through the continuing repetition of virtuous action and the avoidance of their vicious opposites. As such, chastity is relatively easy to understand, even though practice is a bit trickier.

The problem is that it often seems, in the case of the celibate at least, that there are no positive actions by which the virtue can be strengthened, unless the positive effort to avoid a particular line of action is seen in this light. This means that the whole effort to practice chastity seems to be directed at omission and avoidance: not to engage in direct sexual activity, to avoid the sort of behavior which inevitably leads to it, progressively to restrict one's contact with whatever is sexually stimulating. Here, as in any other field, mere negatives make poor motivation. In marriage, chastity is clearly part of temperance, avoiding the extremes of deprivation and over-indulgence. It is a little hard to see how this can be true for the celibate. Perhaps we need a better theory.

We need a theory that is addressed specifically to celibate adults. Too often what is imparted to celibates is what is given to unmarried youth: remain continent. This means implicitly, until such time as you are married. But for the celibate it is a permanent state, lasting perhaps seventy years instead of seven. Celibate chastity is distinctive because it is permanent, it is freely dedicated to God and it is involved with the celibate's own sense of honor. A fling is more than a fling; it touches the heart.

If one does not arrive at a personal, adult appreciation of the positive aspects of consecrated chastity, life becomes impossible. Living on a diet of negatives feeds scrupulosity. The super-ego is not always a reliable guide in helping us achieve a normal, healthy sexuality without compromising the virtue. Modesty and shame can have elements in them which have nothing to do with virtue but only serve as an impedance to it. Paradoxically, the more we withdraw from potential stimulants, the more power they can have in arousing us. Celibates who have to interact with the real world cannot afford to invest situations normally considered to be neutral with a heightened sexual content. Too often the vices which crusaders condemn are in their own hearts and not in the objects of their rage.

Chastity is a virtue that requires a lot of common sense and a certain amount of patience as one tries to learn from experience and attempts to read situations as they occur. It also calls for a high degree of scepticism regarding secular ideologies of human fulfillment and the ability to follow a style of life which goes against the conventional wisdom propagated by the organs of popular culture. One needs to endure ridicule, whether we practice what we profess or not.

Nowadays we are somewhat aware of the complexity of human sexuality. There is a possible danger that because each individual's situation is so nuanced we find it hard to formulate universal norms which are both practical and realistic. The result of this is that some become entirely too passive and reactive in this area. They hope to deflect temptations as they occur, but they are not really sure about what can be done to strengthen their own defenses.

The ultimate sources of unchastity are often locked away in the unconscious. Yet there is often a connection between failures in this area and defects in personal discipline. Chastity is linked to a whole complex of values, many of which have little direct reference to sexuality. The traditional triad of poverty, chastity and obedience seem to me to support and sustain one another. The practice of prayer and humility, the relative fervor of love, service and generosity to others, the whole sense of discipleship: these are strengths which flow into chastity. But there are other more direct connections. It is a delicate question how much control is possible or desirable with regard to thoughts and fantasies, but for most of us there are pathways in the mind which lead to trouble at a more physical level. Such routes are better not taken: at best they dissipate energy which we need for other things, at worst they can lead us radically astray. This is true not only of sexual thoughts, but also of those associated with anger and envy and all the vices. Once a train of thought is initiated, its emotional and physical consequences seem inevitable. It is probably not untrue to say that a certain measure of vigilance and discipline in the matter of thoughts can save us a lot of unnecessary bother. At the same time it would be silly to expect that it were possible or useful to live without unguarded thoughts; it is more a question of watching the movement of the tides rather than being concerned with every isolated eddy.

Nobody is suggesting that chastity is only a matter of hormones and physiology, but it is delusional to think of it only in terms of relationship and intimacy, without recognizing that powerful bodily forces are involved. Sometimes I get the impression that people are too ashamed of the bodily aspects of the question to be able to discuss them comfortably or even to confront the reality of their own bodiliness. This can sometimes confuse an issue. The fact is that what is happening with regard to other bodily appetites is not irrelevant to chastity. Excessive self-indulgence in the one area tends to provide a stimulus to excess in another. This is particularly true regarding excess in food and drink. One who has lost the capacity to endure any discomfort or postpone any pleasure when reasonable circumstances demand renunciation, is unlikely to have much resistance when chastity is assailed. Sometimes, also, unchastity is a problem to be dealt with by a physician, not a psychiatrist or confessor.

Endurance is necessary in any worthwhile project. There are times when chastity will be a heavy burden, but these are to be expected since we were not designed, physically or emotionally, to live a celibate life. If we are honest, however, we will often be forced to admit that the weight of our burden is often increased by the consequences of our own half-heartedness. Sometimes this is just laziness. But sometimes we don't make an effort simply because we don't really know how our energies are best expended.

We learn from our mistakes. If we are lucky, we can also learn from someone who has fought the same battles and who has the gift not only of being encouraging, but also of seeing through the confusing tangle of events and feelings to the underlying truth. With the ongoing help of such a guide, a voluntary pattern of life can be established and maintained which is marked by genuine freedom and authentic growth, in which sexual identity works with and not against the practice of virtue.

Lust seems to be connected with what *The Cloud of Unknowing* terms "boisterous bodiliness."[6] It is often strongest at times when one is possessed by a sense of well-being: good health, comfort, esteem, material possessions, independence, success, good relationships—even a sense that one's spiritual or religious life is going well. The celibate who has just about everything will become conscious of a steady drift toward sexuality, as it were, to complete the picture. It is very hard to remain chaste if one is not obedient and poor. And the whole business is humanly impossible without loving and being loved.

III. A Love That Draws Ever Closer

When Gertrude spoke of unitive love she was thinking primarily of a love which binds the celibate to God and to Christ; to her mind this excluded the love of any created thing for its own sake. Perhaps a fuller understanding of the phrase she used is possible, respecting the hierarchy of value, but recognizing that chronologically, three loves develop simultaneously but not in a synchronized way. Each person seems to make headway through a different combination of elements. Three components of love might be singled out:

a) Love which unites us to God,
b) Love which unites us to our fellow human beings and to creation,
c) Love which unites us within ourselves.

1. God

The important element in the whole business of celibacy is not renunciation but rather attachment to God. He is the absolute who causes us to see all other good things as merely relative benefits. Once the treasure is discovered in the field, then everything is joyfully disposed of in order to acquire that treasure. This is a line of thought that has often been pursued in the West, notably by Gregory the Great. Renunciation is not a means of finding God, but its consequence. One who has the gift of being drawn to union with God finds that alternate interests are somehow less compelling. This is what is meant by the "gift" of celibacy as distinct from the "call" to celibacy. Not only does one have the attraction and the emerging capacity to live a creative celibate life, but one has the beginnings of that sort of relationship with God which alone makes it possible.

The practice of celibacy is strengthened by anything which increases our personal sense of belonging to God—prayer, desire for eternal life, solidarity with Christ. This spiritual component of celibacy has considerable practical implications. It is for the Kingdom that we remain unmarried—to lose sight of the Kingdom is to undercut our motivation for being chaste. Once we have lost the taste for spiritual realities, it is hard to persevere in a life so lacking in human comfort. On the other hand, the very comfortlessness of a life without God is often sufficient cause to regenerate our desire to be with him.

The call to celibacy is more than a functional condition which creates space in one's life so that one can devote all one's energies to working for the Kingdom. It is more than a prophetic witness to eschatological realities, although it does have a secondary function as sign of the unseen, as mystery made visible. Celibacy is essentially the experience and expression of love; it is the space in which a special outpouring of God's love is both received from God and returned to him. It is this relationship, above all else, that makes continence tolerable and even sweet.

Without losing sight of the physical and emotional aspects of the question, it remains true that it is unwise for a religious ever to dissociate celibacy from prayer, from a personal relationship to Christ and in Christ to the Father, from devotion to the mother of Christ or from a pervading sense that this life is a journey that will make perfect sense only in the hereafter. These are the realities which feed love and sustain virtue; without them even the Stoic will fall.

One of St. Gertrude's favorite texts in this regard is taken from the ancient liturgical office of the feast of St. Agnes. Speaking of Christ, one responsory continues, *quem cum amavero, casta sum*: "When I love him, then am I chaste." It is a profound thought. Self-control is not the secret of consecrated chastity; it is sustained only by a strong, personal love for Christ.

2. Others

If celibacy is to be promotive of human development and productive of human wholeness, then it must progressively lead to genuine human love. This is not the sort of love which is characterized by self-indulgence or acquisitiveness, nor serving to manipulate and do violence to the other, but a giving and receiving that looks beyond the needs of self. At the same time it is not such an ethereal reality that it is not felt deeply; on the contrary, to the extent that it is authentic it satisfies the deepest yearnings of one's being for intimacy and a sense of closeness.

Of course most relationships are less perfect than this, at least for the moment. Are they to be left aside while waiting for the real thing? It is probable that unless there is something intrinsically destructive in the shape of a particular relationship, it is better improved than abandoned, even though this can sometimes be the harder option. We instinctively sense when something is amiss in a relationship; the pain we experience as a consequence of such defects serves not only to purify our own hearts but also to improve the relationship. But this is a matter for practical discernment, since it is easy to be deluded in such matters. We can protect ourselves from being led astray by two lines of defense: firstly by striving to reduce anything in the relationship that weakens our response to our vocation, either in the short or long term; secondly, by seeking to become more selfless, in giving as much as in receiving. In such situations we should pray for clear-sightedness and for a lot of practical common sense.[7]

A genuine, mature relationship based on Christian principles does not endanger celibacy. Friendship and even a certain degree of intimacy can serve as a support to a life of continence and chastity, so long as there is no bad faith—so long as the relationship flows from freedom and virtue and is not the disguised consequence of instinct and need.

It is the experience of many that good friendships and the benefit of living in a warm, supportive community are normal conditions for perseverance in celibacy. One cannot survive without some sense of closeness and if a religious community does not provide this, it is not surprising that its members will find themselves attracted elsewhere.

There is another point that can be made about the need for love and acceptance. We are all conscious of our deficiencies with regard to this virtue, if not in deed, then in thought and desire. Perhaps we may feel that the only reason we have not made a complete mess of our lives is that we lacked the opportunity. In matters of chastity we all feel vulnerable, we all sense our liabilities. This is why the experience of forgiveness is so important for the celibate, just as it is in marriage. We need to feel that our failings are known and yet we are still loved and accepted. This is certainly true of God, but it is also true of other human beings. To receive this healing and forgiveness from a fellow mortal really is balm for our wounded souls.

On the other hand, the celibate who is cold, hard-hearted and severe is a counter-witness to the values of Christ's Kingdom. The normal outcome of a lifetime of prayer and discipleship should be a gentle and loving disposition, whatever one's initial temperament. If chastity is a virtue, then it is so only because practicing it has a beneficent effect on the whole person. One who is chaste becomes progressively warmer and more loving. Otherwise the virtue may be more apparent than real.

3. Self

In a sense that would have surprised Gertrude, unless she reflected on it, "unitive love" also means that love which brings and binds together all the energies of mind and psyche into a single and intense beam of light—a sort of laser which concentrates power instead of dissipating it. It is only when one loves God with a pure heart and one's neighbor as oneself that all human forces are integrated and moved forward. Problems disappear. Nothing else has the capacity to marshal the resources of personality and nature with such completeness that nothing is lost. Fulfillment is, of course, in heaven, but the process begins while we are yet on the way.

A love which unites us with God binds us also to one another. It integrates the disparate tendencies of our being and produces simplicity and purity of heart. To the extent that such undividedness is present, bodily instincts no longer rebel, nor are they forced underground. Instead they are summoned to make their own unique contribution to the beauty of what God has created and is so amply re-creating. After all, we do profess faith in the resurrection of the body; it is only right that its harbingers are sighted here below.

As we continue our weary earthbound journey, there is no harm in meditating on its goal, because sometimes this can illuminate the choices we have to make and give us courage to deny life in order to find life. Chastity is not merely a program of saying "No" but consent given to a specific and beautiful grace.

*   *   *

The complementary aspects of chastity—purity of heart, chastity of body and unitive love—are not merely the practice of virtue, they are an integral part of our transformation in godliness.

NOTES

[1]Gertrude of Helfta, *The Exercises*, 2.80-85; SChr 127, p. 98. The reflections following are rather undisciplined, more intended as an aid to further pondering than as a final statement. They are written from a masculine standpoint, which is inevitable, granted the sex of the author, and therefore invite a feminine complement. I am aware of many important issues not raised here; I hope that they can be treated somewhere else.

[2]Cf. Paul Ricoeur, "The Hermeneutics of Symbols and Philosophical Reflection," in *International Philosophical Quarterly*, 2.2 (1962), pp. 191-218; this study harks back to the second volume of the author's *Finitude et Culpabilité: La Symbolique du Mai*, Paris: Aubier, 1960.

[3]Thus Cassian's first Conference.

[4]The expression *dipsuchos* or "double-souled" occurs in James 1:8 and 4:8 and

the theme recurs frequently in Jewish-Christian literature. For example, *Didache* 4.4 = *Letter of Barnabas* 19.4, the two letters attributed to Clement and the *Shepherd of Hermas*. Romans 7 does not use the term, but the theme of inner division is strong there.

[5]Cf. M. Casey, " 'Balance' in Monastic Life," *Tjurunga* 9 (1975), pp. 5-11.

[6]This theme is beautifully illustrated in one of Bernard of Clairvaux's parables. Cf. "The Story of the King's Son Sitting on His Horse," in *Cistercian Studies* 18.4 (1983), pp. 283-288. In fact, several of the points made in the course of this reflection can be paralleled in this series of paranetic similitudes.

[7]Cf. M. Casey, "The Virtue of Friendship in Monastic Tradition—An Introduction," *Tjurunga* 25 (1983), pp. 21-35.

Introductory Note

"Solitariness" (*Tjurunga* 33 [1987], pp. 3-23) was written to throw light on the different species of solitude with a view to clarifying their potential contribution to a life of prayer. At about the same time I was researching a more historical piece, "The Dialectic of Solitude and Communion in Early Cistercian Communities" (CS 18 [1988], pp. 273-309). The topic continues to interest me. I have also prepared a paper on "Solitude and Community in the Thought of Bernard of Clairvaux," for the Roman Congress commemorating the ninth centenary of his birth (September 1990).

Solitariness

O beata solitudo! O sola beatitudo! "O blessed solitude! O sole blessedness!" Thus runs an ancient aphorism extolling the happiness of getting away from it all.[1] For, continues another, "one is never less alone than when alone."[2] Both sayings attest to the importance of a measure of solitude both for prayer and for ultimate contentment. One of the things which distinguishes the human species is its need not only for community but also for solitude. A certain aloneness seems to be necessary if the higher possibilities of the mind and the spirit are to be realized. "Religion is what the individual does with his own solitariness.... Thus religion is solitariness; and if you are never solitary, you are never religious."[3]

If solitude is a fundamental human need, then life will limp without it. If there is not space and time for attention to inward realities, the result will be not only increasing superficiality, but a profound feeling of alienation from one's nature. Those cultures which follow an extremely corporate form of existence develop elaborate systems of etiquette to ensure that togetherness does not become oppression. On the other hand, in prisons, the deprivation of aloneness and of everything by which a person may be individuated is far more dehumanizing than the physical brutality which often accompanies such conditions.

To say that solitude may be a value which is worth reconsidering is not to suggest that we all become hermits. It is, rather, simply a judgment that some of the malaise that persons experience in the postconciliar Church may derive from the fact that in stressing the authentic ecclesial quality of corporateness we may have taken its complement for granted. Perhaps solitude needs to be reaffirmed, not only for itself, but also for the added depth which it can bring to communion. Without the enrichment which comes from time spent alone, relationship becomes nugatory and trite.

There is so much intrusiveness in western society today that many people are developing a longing for solitude. They may find it in bushwalking, or in some quiet manual task, in walking the dog or sitting down with a book. It is not good to be seen doing nothing, so such activities are used as a disguise. Their true purpose is probably more related to a need to be alone. It can often be of great help to individuals to confront this need in purer form and to learn how to use leisure and solitariness as part of creative growth.

It is important, however, to note that being alone can serve many different purposes and cater for a wide range of different needs. It is not automatically a good thing, nor is there a single way of rendering it creative. Some attention needs to be given to the types of solitude. Otherwise we may find ourselves talking about different realities.

I. Corporate Solitude

In the sixteenth century, when the emphasis in philosophy moved from being to consciousness, a kind of individualism was born which still afflicts most western cultures. Individual consciousness isolates and so, to the extent that it is given precedence, it tends to obscure the radical corporateness of our nature. We are all unique, yet we make the same journey and have much more in common than we believe. Some of the problems which have stemmed from rationalism were less acute in the Middle Ages. Perhaps in coping with our own times we can learn by leap-frogging back eight centuries or more.

Solitudo as it appears in many monastic texts of the Middle Ages is a quality of the community, corresponding approximately to what might be called "separation from the world."[4] It was communal withdrawal from worldly involvement. By its way of life, the community provided the ambiance for spiritual growth and constant encouragement and support for the individual grappling with the inherent difficulties which such a project brings. It was not so much a question of aloneness, but of being at a distance from whatever could blunt the sharpness of spiritual living. The monasteries were built "far from human habitation" in the hallowed phrase, and where this was not possible or the monasteries were overrun, elaborate rules and structures protected the lives of their inhabitants.

> What does it mean to come into solitude? It means to consider the whole world as desert, to desire the Fatherland, to have only as much of this world as is necessary to accomplish the journey—not as much as the flesh desires.[5]

I have recently heard it said that separation from the world was especially necessary at a time when the world was predominantly Christian, since otherwise the distinctiveness of religious would be compromised by their being commingled too easily with the Church at large. On the other hand, when the world is practically non-Christian, it needs the active presence of religious to signal the existence of Gospel values and truth. The conclusion drawn was that less distinctiveness is required today, because anyone who tries to live evangelical principles is already sufficiently singular.

I do not dispute that there is some truth in this analysis, but I think that it is too simplistic to be the whole truth. Such a view seems to presuppose that members of a religious community are already well established in Gospel values. In my own case this is not so. I need a certain amount of insulation against opinions and values which would progressively erode my attachment to the Gospel. Such protection, it seems to me, is not best found merely in leaving a distance between my lifestyle and that of the society around me; it comes rather from interposing a sub-culture between me and the surrounding culture, a communal way of life which is open enough to permit mutual enrichment but sufficiently established to assert boldly the hard realities of the following of Christ.

It seems to me that religious communities have a highly significant role to play as support structures not only for their own members but for others as well, and it may be that this is where much of the action will be in the future. As Peter Berger writes, "Even religion has become largely privatized, with its plausibility structure shifting from society as a whole to much smaller groups of confirmatory individuals."[6] Theodore Roszak, in seeking an answer to the question, "Where do the little people of the world turn to when the big structures crumble or grow humanly intolerable?" examines what he calls "the monastic paradigm," according to which personal solitude and a supportive community help us to sort out what is authentic among our needs and give us the courage to pursue these, not only to our own benefit but, ultimately, for the good of all.[7] We would do well to ponder these statements from unlikely sources before dismissing too quickly the relevance of medieval *solitudo*.

Within the communal pattern of life, space was left for private living, for communion with God and for rumination. The role of silence was deemed to be important here, as a means of ensuring that one did not fritter away precious but demanding leisure through *acedia* and small talk. Another way of facilitating an inward solitariness was through the cult of anonymity. The individual blended with the crowd, modeling behavior on theirs. This meant that a lot of routine actions could be performed on automatic pilot, as it were, leaving the spirit free. This is what Arnulph of Bohéries suggests:

> However different one's interior, outwardly the set of one's countenance should leave one unnoticed amid one's fellows, that is, one should neither frown with an excess of earnestness, nor be

flushed with overmuch talk, but keep to a becoming moderation....
It is wisdom to carefully guard one's secret treasure and, like Moses,
to put a veil over a too-revealing countenance, to hide behind a kind
of restrained laughter, the splendor and seriousness of one's innermost self.[8]

It may be that such solutions seem bizarre in these days of private
rooms. It was not so in the heavily communal atmosphere of a medieval
monastery where monks did everything together, and the monasteries
were mainly composed of large communal rooms. Even light and heating had to be shared in winter and huddling together was, no doubt,
cheaper than fuel. To have anything of an inner life it had to be precisely
that—inner. The fact that provision was made for needs which were not
social can serve us as a reminder that whereas we can get great help in
finding our way to God from the community's manner of living, we also
need to grapple with life interiorly, on our own, in solitude. Communities which respect human growth probably need to make explicit
provision for solitude, otherwise a potential source of enrichment is lost.

II. The Solitude of the Introvert

One of the conclusions which life forces upon one is that all
individuals do not operate in the same way. What is experienced by one
as a stimulant can generate a mood of melancholy in another: one's meat
is another's poison. Since the time of C.G. Jung there has been a lot of
reflection on the distinctions evident between introverts and extroverts;
these are relevant and important to any discussion of solitude as a
religious value.

To the extent that one is introverted one tends to conserve energy by
withdrawing it from external objects; one thrives in solitude and perishes
without it. Being alone renews one's energies for confronting the alien
world without; one rediscovers a deep sense of identity and reintegrates
the dissipated strands of one's life. The extrovert, on the other hand,
derives energy from interaction: it is the world of objects which bestows
identity on such a person. Solitude makes some sense insofar as it enhances outgoing behavior; but it is sought without any special sense of
urgency.[9]

That introverted consciousness needs a measure of solitude in order
to function is something that needs to be taken into consideration on a
practical level as far as introverts are concerned. The danger is that
because solitude is so comfortable, introverts may shrink from the

challenge of complementing it with interaction and thus of developing the latent resources of their own personality. If they do not develop these they simply stagnate, cocooned in familiar routines and company and securely enclosed within a static world-view that has never been liberated by the impact of intrusive reality. It can become like an incipient case of agoraphobia; a preference for a private world over that which is public.

One can be a strong introvert without going any distance along this particular pathway, yet it remains a temptation, especially if native alienation is bolstered by a history of hurts. It would come as no surprise, therefore, that the introvert has to keep working very hard not to become so immersed in subjectivity that life ceases to be genuinely creative.

St. Gregory the Great wrote in his *Pastoral Rule* about how different types of people are to be admonished. His chapter on silence is remarkable for its even-handedness to both introverts and extroverts.

> The taciturn are to be admonished in one way, those given to much talking in another. It should be suggested to the taciturn that while shunning some vices *inadvertently*, they are unconsciously involved in worse. For they often bridle the tongue beyond moderation, and as a result suffer in the heart a more grievous loquacity; and so, their thoughts seethe the more in the mind, in proportion as they restrain themselves by a violent and indiscreet silence.... Often when the taciturn suffer injustice, they come to feel keener grief from not speaking about what they are suffering. For if the tongue were to speak calmly of the annoyances inflicted, grief would fade from consciousness. Wounds that are closed are the more painful.... But those who are addicted to much talking are to be admonished to observe vigilantly from how great a degree of rectitude they lapse, when they fall by using a multitude of words.... Moreover, one addicted to much speaking fails entirely to keep on the straight path of righteousness.[10]

Although the terms are different, the awareness of character distinction is clear; the taciturn are told to talk more, the talkative to be more silent. It is the same with the meek and the choleric: "The meek often grow languid in their lazy inactivity; the choleric frequently deceive themselves by what they think is their zeal for rectitude."[11] And so, in chapter after chapter, Gregory keeps making the point: we grow by cultivating the qualities which complement our nature, rather than by simply cruising along on the assets we received at birth.

There is a danger that the debate about solitude as a religious or monastic value may degenerate simply into an uncomprehending statement of personal preferences and experiences by different temperaments. The introvert can summon up a spirituality of the desert and speak with enthusiasm about silent prayer and communion with God, and it may appear to others that this is simply a "loner" speaking, someone who has never appreciated the essential Christian value of community and who, at times, gives the impression of being sociopathic and even misanthropic.

Clearly, better understanding is needed on both sides of both values: solitude and communion. As a very strong introvert, I am aware that my need for time alone is not anti-social, it is not a rejection of those who have a need for a higher degree of interaction; it is simply a condition for my survival as a person, for my continuing creativity and for my efforts to keep going out from myself. Interaction brings me more pleasure and profit than I can possibly say but my need for solitude remains. The rhythms of religious life have projected me into far more adventure, challenge and outward movement than I could ever have visualized and I am conscious of having been greatly enriched by them. But I am not sure that they would have had so much impact had I been starved for solitude.

The worst thing that can happen to an introvert, it seems to me, is to end up as a confirmed bachelor or spinster, set in familiar ways, locked into a pattern which prevents genuine growth. This is why it is important during the time of formation that introvert religious be trained to use their solitude in creative ways, and not merely to satisfy their need to be by themselves. This will be a different training to that given to extroverts, and more difficult. Introverts take readily to solitude: reflection, rumination and prayer may come relatively easily to them. Their solitude should not be allowed to develop to the point where it excludes communion, no matter how strongly the monastic ideology may propagate the merits of being alone.[12] St. Benedict is probably wiser: he recognizes that a genuine attraction to an anchoritic life follows many years living in community.[13]

Introversion is not a disability, even though it is often misunderstood in a society where it is considered virtuous to be "outgoing." Introverts need more solitude than extroverts, but probably their experience of it reaches greater depths. If we are to advance the idea of solitude as a religious value, we need to avoid the impression that everyone experiences it in the same way. I believe that solitude is too important and challenging a reality in human growth to be relegated to the status of an individual preference determined by temperament.

It is probably no accident that introverts are attracted to religious institutes which promise them an enhanced interior life. Once they arrive, it is good that they are challenged to become more sociable, more outgoing and more able to deal confidently with objective reality.[14] But if this is the only thrust in formation, spiritual direction and lifestyle, there is a real danger that violence may be done to the person. Extroverts, by nature, are more likely to impose their stamp on the style of community living. As a result, the incorporation of introverts into the community may tend to force them into an alien mold. They will be encouraged and rewarded if they conform to it; any qualifications or reservations they feel may be dismissed as individual deviation. Paradoxically it is sometimes "reformed" introverts who are the most ardent apostles of an extrovert lifestyle: perhaps it is a form of self-hatred, perhaps it is a matter of erecting their own needs for complementation into a system, or it may simply be the crusading fervor typical of a new convert. It is a fact that introverts feel good about their authentic growth, they are comforted by a newly-restated social acceptance, and perhaps delight in acquiring and demonstrating new skills. But it remains true that if such a development is purchased at the price of their own need for inwardness then there will be no real or permanent growth. In such a situation, without letting go of the positive gains which have been made, one needs to rediscover one's nature and to respect its needs. In this way one can bring to outgoing activities something of the depth and richness with which God has endowed one. The religious institute, for its part, needs to be aware that in its philosophy and lifestyle it needs a harmony of solitude and communion: either one is not enough alone.

III. The Solitude of Adulthood

I remember once lying on the beach at Cabagao, in the northern Philippines, watching a large group of ten year-old boys at play in the water. The sound was continuous and unbroken, like the roar from a busy freeway; movement was incessant, naked bodies tumbling interchangeably over one another, the individuals happily submerged in the exuberant activity of the group. It was a scene that was a delight to behold, yet I watched it with some nostalgia. Is such a fulfilling sense of total corporateness possible for a western adult today?

Solitariness is a function of consciousness. We are individuated not only by genetic factors and the events of our personal history, but especially by the residue that remains in our minds. I have experienced a unique complex of events, and experienced them from a unique standpoint; this has had a lasting impression on me. It determines so much of my present outlook on life that I myself am not fully aware of being influenced. What I see as reality is seen through my own particular rose-tinted spectacles. Nobody else sees it in the same hues. Whoever does not see the same colors as I, sees wrongly—this is my unstated assumption. "And all the world is wrong except thee and me, and sometimes I am not too sure about thee!" I go through life with my own distinctive view, never quite able to subscribe to another vision, feeling honor-bound to keep faith with what I have experienced, even though its singularity is a source of a degree of isolation.

I wonder whether we have ever confronted the essential loneliness of adult consciousness. The sense of who I am seems irretrievably tied to a sense that I am different from others. I can relate to them, build bridges to them, gain access to their hearts and give them entry to mine. Yet I remain alone. I am free, unbound, responsible for my own choices and for my own choices alone. I can never reach the point where my will can do more than decide for myself. This is why friendship is only possible in reciprocal freedom; any sort of mutual exploitation or unhealthy dependence leads away from the heart, which is where true interpersonal relationship resides. Perhaps my own freedom and identity have to be continually repurchased by my allowing others to be themselves and by being unafraid of my own aloneness.

This ultimate incommunicability of the individual is a theme which is often movingly explored in the literature of existentialism; it is seen as being related to the deep sense of dread experienced by many of our contemporaries. This passage from Albert Camus' *The Plague* illustrates the idea:

> Moreover, in this extremity of solitude, none could count on any help from his neighbor; each had to bear the load of his troubles alone. If, by some chance, one of us tried to unburden himself or to say something about his feelings, the reply he got, whatever it might be, usually wounded him. And then it dawned on him that he and the man with him weren't talking about the same thing. For while he himself spoke from the depths of long days of brooding upon his personal distress, and the image he tried to impart had been slowly shaped and proved in the fires of passion and regret, this meant nothing to the man with whom he was speaking, and who pictured a conventional emotion, a grief that is traded in the marketplace,

mass-produced. Whether friendly or hostile, the reply always misfired, and the attempt to communicate had to be given up. This was true of those at least for whom silence was unbearable, and since the others could not find the truly expressive word, they resigned themselves to using the current coin of language, the commonplaces of plain narrative, of anecdote, and of their daily paper. So, in these cases too, even the sincerest grief had to make do with the set phrases of ordinary conversation.[15]

Many of our contemporaries find the sense of aloneness intolerable; they try to drive it from their awareness through giving themselves to sex, alcohol and drugs and by immersing themselves in frivolous and meaningless pursuits, not as relaxation but as part of a determined effort to deny their own seriousness. Far be it from me to say that religious are exempt from such tensions. One would hope that they would have been given greater resources to cope with them but, alas, this is not always the case. There are many religious also who dread an encounter with aloneness; they become very adept not only in avoiding it but in rationalizing their avoidance.

Is there anything that can be done to dispel this fundamental fear of solitariness? Can such solitude become a creative means of enriching life instead of being a seemingly bottomless well of loneliness and isolation?

One way to cope with the situation is through myth. Many primitive cultures lived comfortably with a whole universe of unseen and unknown realities because each generation passed on to its succedant the tribal myths. These were more than stories meant to wile away the nights before the advent of television. They were marked by three qualities: they concerned ultimate realities; they aroused and sustained inner resonances in the hearers; they were a living bond between the generations.

Myths are about meaning: they are not primarily information or entertainment. They concern truths that are not immediate and therefore cannot be imparted simply by accompanying the young generation on its daily activities. They require time and space that is empty, sacred. Exposure to them is an initiation into the world of the unseen and the mysteries of adulthood. Once introduced into this sphere, it is expected that the youngster will become a responsible member of the group; one who progressively carries rather than is carried, one who knows the meaning of life and is thereby becoming able to make good decisions.

On the other hand, the myths are not entirely foreign. They relate also to inner realities, experiences and dreams. There is a continuity between the meaning of existence as imparted by the elders and the subjective experience of the initiate. Not only is the meaning of the universe explained, but some of the enigmas of individual consciousness are resolved.

Perhaps the key factor in myth-making is neither the content of the myth nor its mirroring of inner experience but the fact that it is the occasion for communion between generations. This is not a technical or informational exchange, it is not an exercise of tribal authority; it is, rather, deep human contact between those who have lived and experienced more of life with those on its threshold. There is much comfort here and courage. Those who live attest that survival is possible: troubles can be named, joys evoked; the future can only be what the past already is, it too can be endured.

But we must come back from Dreamtime. We have lost contact with primal symbols and there is nothing from which we can draw comfort. Perhaps we need to think about creating new myths, learning to span the generations with an evocation of ultimate truths which mirror our own experience. Maybe the reason we cannot face solitude is that we have emptied communion of its meaning. We spend time together and enjoy ourselves, but perhaps we never reach a deep enough trust to be able to share a transcendent vision. And because we have not been liberated by this sight, we fear our own aloneness, suspecting that there might be something wrong; distrusting our own eyes and going by outward norms instead.

Perhaps religious institutes and other groups need to look at the possibilities of myth-making as a means of helping individuals touch bottom, make contact with their own deepest truth and so be able to make this wonderful gift in some way accessible to others. In such a case there is a double boon: the individual comes alive and, at the same time, the human race is further enriched.

There is another way of achieving a similar result. It is not so much the work of a structured organization but of a smaller group, perhaps even of a single person, who may be called friend, confidant, spiritual director or whatever.

All persons have a basic need to tell their story, to find someone who is prepared to listen to it in depth, to hear what has been experienced and to re-experience it with them, rejoicing with those who rejoice, weeping with those who weep. Not to make judgments or discern, but simply to listen and to accept, to become more understanding. This is not an easy task nor does it consist in total passivity; one must learn the code that is being used, to penetrate behind and beneath the language games that are unconsciously played and to rebuild lost linkages, not from one's own experience, but from inside the other. To read between the lines.

It is a great gift to find someone who can act in this way; it is often the catalyst which initiates solid and creative changes, liberates energies and restores vitality and a sense of direction. To know that one is known, understood, accepted, loved is the basic stabilizing factor in life. Once this is assured, no contingency need be feared.

This looking back into the past with the aid of an understanding listener is more than a self-pitying monologue or an exercise in delusive self-glorification. The listener becomes a matrix of truth. Often there is a shedding of layers of falsity, encouraged by the other's acceptance. The burden of past accumulations is shared and thereby lightened and one approaches life with less encumbrance. It is like becoming a child again. Not irresponsible, because in owning one's past one accepts the reality of former decisions and their consequences. Not carefree, because one still has problems to deal with and difficult choices to make. Not dependent, because in the process of telling one's story the role of the listener becomes less rather than more predominant. One becomes a child in the sense that one recovers a measure of spontaneity, one learns to trust oneself and others more and, progressively, one develops an overwhelming sense of wonder at the course of one's life, and gratitude for what has accrued through many difficulties and reversals of fortune. The ground is well laid for a mysterious recovery of innocence, seemingly so definitively lost, yet now in the process of amazingly being restored.

The sense of isolation which derives from consciousness and self-consciousness can be assuaged through a more comprehensive myth making on the part of a community and by the ministry of a friend who is prepared to listen to one's story or of others who may willingly shoulder part of the burden. This sort of solitariness, although an essential concomitant of intelligence, is not something that should be developed. On the contrary, it calls out for relief; it is an insistent drive toward communion with others. It must be accepted as real, its need for deep companionship must be respected; it must never be allowed to be trivialized into an incentive to mindlessness or the romantic pursuit of an endless series of undemanding relationships. We are drawn to the other because of the dissatisfaction we feel in ourselves alone; it is only when we have entered into communion with the other that we begin to appreciate that other, not merely as wish-fulfillment for ourselves, but for inherent qualities which awake in us a response of love that goes beyond the level of mere need. This is true of other human beings. It is also true of our relationship with God, as St. Bernard clearly teaches in his tractate *On the Necessity of Loving God.*[16]

IV. The Solitude of Creativity

There are times in which the spirit sings and what one does becomes invested with a magical quality. Energy flows out from the center of one's being and transforms an activity. The work is well done, as can be plainly seen, but the reason for this special quality is that what is done is more clearly stamped with the imprint of the doer. Not in an egotistical manner, as it were labeling it and claiming credit, but mysteriously embodying the signature of the creator's very being.

In such moments of genuine creativity, one is truly alone. Not in the sense of excluding others, but in the sense of being the fine point through which a transcendent reality is expressed. One who creates feels like an instrument in the hand of a greater artisan, expressing ultimate truths even while expressing self. And while it is true that we often think of creativity especially in terms of relatively rare accomplishments, such as in the area of the fine arts, the same creative energies flow in cooking, in organization, in building, in interpersonal relations, in healing, in playing, in expressing love.

In fact, no human activity is disqualified from being creative; it all depends on the dispositions of the potential creator. A cup of cold water can be the conveyor of ultimate salvation to both the giver and receiver. As Gervase Crouchback wrote to his son, in a fine Catholic sentiment, "Quantitative judgments don't apply."[17] What determines the quality of the individual action as a carrier of personal meaning is the extent to which one is present to the deed. One who acts under compulsion, persuaded by peers, blinded by wrong meanings, driven by forces which do not yield to will, has only a minimal presence in the action or in its result. To imprint the seal of one's spirit one needs to act "knowingly and willingly." This is not to say that one acts coldly. On the contrary, because we are, by nature, feeling persons, it is likely that all creativity is accompanied by passion, but it is the fire that comes from within, not merely the heat caused by friction with one's environment.

There is such a presence to a genuinely creative action that it can often be impossible without some measure of solitude, whether emotional, intellectual or physical. Such a work demands concentration: the person is intent on what is being done; there is no scope for becoming involved in a conversation about football, except as a temporary diversion.

Often the road to creativity needs its solitude also. To become well grounded in any discipline demands application. Without going through this stage of acquiring skills, the freedom necessary for authentic creation is defective. Such solitary dedication to picking up the rudiments is hard and unrewarding; only those who have a clear vision of the goal persevere with it. It is as though there is a sense of vocation which is stronger than the clamor of their own appetites or the inducements offered in the pursuit of more mundane employments. Those who see the Holy Grail and who allow themselves to succumb to its attraction will always be apart from those who see it not.

The gauge of the genuineness of such solitude is that it is not a private exultation in a vision imparted to few, but the desire to give further expression to what is grasped, to communicate it to others. Again we see how solitude leads inevitably to communion. It seems that creation involves communication, a sharing of a transcendent reality dimly grasped but ardently loved. There is a rhythm of aloneness and togetherness which mirrors the inner composition of the soul itself.

V. The Solitude of Celibacy

The Genesis account of human creation leaves us in no doubt that man and woman were created to be together. From this we may deduce that in those cases where this union is not creatively achieved there will be great pain, deriving from the fact that a natural need is unfulfilled.

The prophet Jeremiah was called to celibacy, denied the complex of relationships which attend the position of father of a family (Jer. 16:1-2). Jeremiah was called to live a solitary life in the midst of the people, isolated not only because of his unmarried state, but also because of the nature of his message.

> Thy words were found, and I ate them
> and thy words became for me a joy
> and the delight of my heart,
> for I am called by thy name,
> O YHWH, God of hosts.
> I did not sit in the company of merrymakers,
> nor did I rejoice;
> I sat alone because thy hand was upon me,
> for thou hast filled me with indignation.

Why is my pain unceasing,
my wound incurable, refusing to be healed?
Wilt thou become to me like a deceitful brook,
like waters that fail. (Jer. 15:16-18)

The aloneness experienced by the prophet has been experienced by
many since. It seems to be part of their call that the gift which they
received from God to impart to others is nurtured and developed only in
such a state. Paradoxically they serve others and attain communion only
by a certain degree of withdrawal and being alone. Like Jeremiah they
rebel against the hardship of such a condition and think constantly of
alternatives. Finally they come to a point of decision: to submit to the
superior strength of God's word which calls and strengthens, though
without diminishing the level of suffering (Jer. 20:7-18), or to forget
the call and go another way. The resolution is by no means simple: to
accept the call and the task is an outrage to sensibility, yet to deny it is to
destroy what is, perhaps, the most beautiful part of oneself.[18]

In the unfolding of any religious vocation there will be stages when
the consequences of celibacy will seem like an impossible imposition,
when one will feel that one's solitariness is blocking the fuller development of personal resources: there will be loneliness, disgruntledness
and rebellion. There may be efforts to offset one's aloneness or unconscious compensations. In essence a choice has to be made; to experience
the rigors of a life without a family or to leave aside the dream which
had earlier inspired one. This very choice leads into a deeper and even
more demanding solitariness, which must now be discussed.

VI. The Solitude of Conscience

Each personal decision envelops us in an aura of solitude. Nobody
else can make this choice for us: others may give us guidance, support
and incentive, but the choice remains our very own. This is especially
true when we have to make a decision between strong conscious feelings
and excellent reasons, on the one hand, and the intuitive conclusions of
the heart, on the other. The reasons are pressing; the feelings are
evident, it is hard to go against them and there will be many who
applaud our "rational" resolution of the dilemma. But in cases like this,
Luther's designation of the reason as "the devil's whore" trying to woo
the will from following the promptings of the heart, seem apposite. If it
were merely a matter of making a judgment based on an analysis of the
various factors, the decision can be shared by opening up the problem to

others' appraisal. But when the contest is between overt reasons, on the one hand, and the deep, unseen movements of one's very being, on the other, then one is plunged into a profound solitude.

This time of crisis is very painful. One stands back from the placid routines of daily life for a time, and lives at a more intense level. One cannot join the crowd because the weight of thoughts, desires, needs and anxieties crowds one into a corner apart. One may try to resolve the matter prematurely, but one ends in deeper confusion and perhaps feels more isolated because of the evident disapproval of one's peers. It is a time for endurance, a time for waiting, a time for hoping for the salvation that cannot yet be seen.

Others can help. Sometimes they can ease our pain by refusing to allow us to escape it or to be distracted; they can add a measure of meaning by explaining our predicament. Sometimes they help by refusing to join the company of those who carp on our weaknesses and, instead, send us signals that all is not lost. Sometimes they pray for us and, if they are spiritual, they may desire to bear some of the burden of our suffering, communing with us at a level deeper than interaction. Others do help us, but the crisis remains very much our own, because it can begin to be resolved only by us, when we choose to follow Christ in dread and darkness rather than to seek a facile peace elsewhere.

We think of St. Thomas More struggling with the dictates of his own exacting conscience, almost alone in the world. In some senses solitary confinement in the Tower of London must have been a welcome relief after the experience of utter loneliness caused by the incomprehension of his loved ones. To decide one needs room—often at a time of crisis one ought to cater for this need by seeking also some physical aloneness—to confront the dilemma in all its enormity, to discover one's total lack of resources, to experience the hostility and emptiness of one's own inner space; it is only then that a prayer is born, a prayer that cannot be quenched. It reaches to God and one day makes contact, and after that things begin to go a little better.

VII. The Separation of Sin

Sin is separation from God; it also causes a diminution in our capacity to enter into communion with other human beings. This truth is well worth pondering.

> To the degree that the saints enter into the things of the spirit, they desire to come near to God; and in proportion to their progress in

the things of the spirit, they do in fact come close to God and to their neighbor. The closer they are to God, the closer they become to one another; and the closer they are to one another, the closer they become to God. Now consider in the same context the question of separation; for when they stand away from God and turn to external things, it is clear that the more they recede and become distant from God, the more they become distant from one another. See! This is the very nature of love. *The more we are turned away from and do not love God, the greater the distance that separates us from our neighbor.* If we were to love God more, we should be closer to God, and through love of him we should be more united in love to our neighbor; and the more we are united to our neighbor, the more we are united to God.[19]

There is a paradox about sinfulness; it is greatest when it is hidden. Most of us go through periods in which everything seems to be going well, in which there are signs of growth: our lives merit the approval of good people, there is scope for our aptitudes and our native vices are either overcome or in a state of blessed dormancy. We ourselves are active in doing good: we fast twice a week and give tithes of all we own. But sin remains and perhaps waxes strong because it is unnoticed.

> We are warned by the example of David lest anyone should become conceited when the going is good. For many fear adversity; prosperity they do not fear. But prosperity is more dangerous for the soul than adversity is for the body. The rot begins in times of prosperity, so that adversity has no trouble causing a break. My brothers, it is necessary to be very vigilant during favorable seasons.[20]

Fortunately, God does not allow our deluded complacency to perdure. Circumstances conspire against us to bring our sinfulness into awareness. Sometimes this involves actual sin, permitted by God's providence in order to accomplish greater good.[21] At other times it is the mass of accumulated malice which makes an appearance. Years of negligent living, punctuated by sinful interludes and moments in which weakness, blindness and malice predominated: suddenly these surface in the mind. Every residual trace of sin is re-experienced to the great distress of the person concerned. Nor is it merely a matter of becoming mentally aware: sin seeps from conscience to touch one's present life, swamping one's disposition and behavior in a manner more appropriate to the years of neglect than to the present. One becomes a reproach to oneself and to others. Not unfairly, but in all truth.

In fact, truth is the reality of such a phase. It is the shedding of comfortable delusions about one's own state before God and the confrontation with sin. The fact of having to admit being yet under the power of sin and still suffering its consequences is an advance. It is not a sudden decline, despite what others say, despite what one feels oneself. It is coming to a deeper perception of one's actual status before God and that is, itself, a gift.

It is already a gift of the Holy Spirit that what you have done is displeasing to you. Sins please the unclean spirit and displease the Holy Spirit. Although it is pardon that you are asking, still, on the other hand, because the evil that you have committed displeases you, you become united with God. For what displeases you also displeases him. Now two of you are contending with your fever: you and the physician. The confession and punishment of sin is not possible for a human being unaided, so when one is angry with oneself and displeases oneself, this does not take place without the gift of the Holy Spirit.[22]

What is less significant is the objective reality of sin; what matters more is the growing dissatisfaction of the sinner. Sin may continue; its consequences may still be felt, but the beginning of purgation is already underway. "Many sins are committed through pride, but not all happen in a way one can be proud of; sins are committed by the ignorant and the weak and very often by persons weeping and groaning."[23]

About the only place for one in such a condition to go is prayer. Bombarded on every side by evidence of sinfulness, one turns to God: "human frailty weeps over its shortcomings."[24] Yet relief is not always immediate. What one derives from prayer is the strength to accept the truth of one's own depravity, one's need for the help of God. One learns to live with this, to be transformed by it in thought and action. Even though it is very difficult to persevere in a prayer which yields no quarter to human comfort, yet at a deeper level one's spirit is fed. Perhaps one will eventually develop a taste for this austere diet; if one does, solid progress has been made. And there are always breathing-spaces in which the counterface of one's sin appears; progressively it is the mercy of God which is paramount.

Dimly one is aware that one is never alone in such a situation; the closer one moves to the truth, the more populated prayer becomes with the presence not only of the heavenly court, but also of the Church on earth. Again it is the reality of communion growing out of solitude: but the price to be paid is the acceptance of the dread-filled isolation that is the natural consequence of our sins. Solitude confronts us with our

sinfulness and that awareness leads us to a deeper experience of aloneness than we would have thought possible. But from this emerges, by
God's gift, the beginnings of that communion for which we were created
and which is the ultimate goal of all our striving.

Despite the attempts at romanticization, the desert is not a place
of dream fantasy, but a howling wilderness.[25] Men and women go into
the desert, according to the ancient image, to grapple with the demons
who inhabit it. It is not playtime; it is a life-and-death struggle with
powers of evil as much inside us as outside. Victory comes only from the
hand of God. Until we have been made reliant on him, peace, prayer
and progress are largely illusory and certainly impermanent.

VIII. The Solitude of Contemplation

Solitude is both the occasion for contemplation and its result. We
need time and space in order to give ourselves to God in prayer, but
somehow the motivation and energy to create such leisure is an effect of
our having found God. It is not a baleful waiting for the fulfillment of the
other side of a contract but a deeper interior drawing that attracts us
away from conscious activities and calls us to be present to God.

Solitude is an essential component in the discipline of prayer; without
it all the developments of which we have already spoken will not take
place and ultimate communion will never be realized.

> You have learned by experience that solitude is the closest friend of
> the love of God. He who is free to devote himself to the love of
> heavenly things flees the crowd, avoids noise and with Mary scorns
> the constant busyness of Martha, so that he may surely as more
> secretly hear and see Christ. Indeed, nothing contributes more to the
> exercise of love than to be solitary, that is, to be a monk. For the
> monk's religious and quiet way of life is the very solitude that holy
> love longs for.[26]

Jesus himself ordained that prayer was essentially a matter for oneself
and God; it was to take place in the inner chamber, far from the scrutiny
of potential admirers. He himself often retired to a solitary place in order
to pray and initiated his disciples into the same regimen.

This is only common sense. "It is difficult to see Christ in a crowd; a
certain solitude is necessary for our mind. God is seen by a certain solitude of gaze (*intentio*). A crowd is marked by noise and tumult; this
vision needs secrecy."[27] "It is within that this truth brings us delight; in
that place no one makes a tumult and no one hears one."[28] Prayer

demands a recession from the helter-skelter images of a busy lifestyle and an effort to penetrate to the level of the heart. One of the more effective ways of doing this is through being alone, with a heart that is undivided and a mind that seeks to minimize distraction.

From this point of view something should be said about solitude as a pedagogue of prayer. The Carthusian tradition that the cell teaches everything is another way of expressing this point. To learn how to pray one must, eventually, learn to be alone. Physically alone, certainly, but progressively one must move into a deeper aloneness so that one's resourcelessness is more amply demonstrated. We have discussed various ways in which this can take place, but it needs to be noted that their difficulty is such, even for a seasoned warrior, that they will never come to a creative resolution unless the person has been schooled to love solitude.

*   *   *

The solitariness which is part of the human condition and an integral component of the spiritual pursuit is a many-faceted reality. Perhaps it may be objected that some of the distinctions I have made are artificial since the different species of solitude tend to overlap and even merge. I do not deny this. What differs is the outcome: is solitude creative or destructive? If it is creative then the different forms are only different ports of entry into a single complex experience. It is worth distinguishing them, because sometimes one realizes the full significance of an experience only after one has traversed the whole terrain. Some lose heart and do not complete the journey. It is to aid those who wish to appropriate their own experience of aloneness, whatever its particular shape, that these reflections are offered.

NOTES

[1]Cf. Anselme Dimier, "A propos de O Beata Solitudo! O Sola Beatitudo!," *Cîteaux* 11 (1960), pp. 133-136; 13 (1962), p. 311. See also J. Leclercq, "Deux opuscules médiévales sur la vie solitaire," *Studia Monastica* 4 (1962), pp. 93-109.

[2]Cf. Ambrose of Milan, *Letter* 26, trans. Fathers of the Church Series, vol. 26, pp. 134-135. William of St Thierry, *Golden Epistle* 30, trans. Cistercian Fathers Series vol. 12, p. 19.

[3]Alfred North Whitehead, *Religion in the Making*, Cambridge University Press, 1927, pp. 6-7.

[4]I reflected on this in "Strangers to Worldly Ways: RB 4.20," *Tjurunga* 29 (1985), pp. 37-46. Articles without an author are my own; the references are included merely to contextualize what is said in the body of this article.

[5]Aelred of Rievaulx, *Sermon for the Feast of St. Benedict*, 1.19, trans. *Cistercian Studies* 4 (1969), p. 167.

[6]Peter Berger et al, *The Homeless Mind: Modernization and Consciousness*, Harmondsworth: Pelican Books, 1974, p. 167.

[7]Theodore Roszak, *Person/Planet: The Creative Disintegration of Industrial Society*, Garden City: Doubleday, 1979, pp. 288-293.

[8]Arnulph of Bohéries, *Mirror for Monks* 3.4, trans. by Hugh McCaffrey, privately circulated.

[9]Cf. C.G. Jung, *The Collected Works*: vol. 6, *Psychological Types*, London: Routledge and Kegan Paul, 1971, pp. 373-407.

[10]Gregory the Great, *Pastoral Care*, 14, trans. Ancient Christian Writers Series vol. 11, pp. 129-134.

[11]*Ibid.*, Ch. 16, p. 137.

[12]Cf. "Ascetic and Ecclesial: Reflections on RB 73.5," *Tjurunga* 28 (1985), pp. 14-23.

[13]Cf. RB 1.5. Cassian's conclusion is similar: *non deserenda praecepit fratrum consortio*: "God teaches us not to leave aside fraternal interaction," *Institutes* 9.7, *Sources Chrétiennes* vol. 109, p. 358.

[14]That this going out from self is an important aspect of introverts I have discussed in "The Pursuit of Ecstasy: Reflections on Bernard of Clairvaux's *De Diligendo Deo*," *Monastic Studies* 16 (1985), pp. 139-156.

[15]Albert Camus, *The Plague*, Harmondsworth: Penguin, 1960, p. 64. In a similar vein, David M. Foster, *The Pure Land*, South Melbourne: Macmillan, 1974, p. 98: "As long as you can talk you don't know what real suffering means. It means not being able to talk about your sufferings."

[16]Cf. "The Pursuit of Ecstasy," pp. 150-152.

[17]Evelyn Waugh, *Unconditional Surrender* in *The Sword of Honour* trilogy, Harmondsworth: Penguin, 1984, p. 400.

[18]Cf. "Consecrated Chastity: Reflections on a Text of Gertrude of Helfta," *Tjurunga* 31 (1986), pp. 3-14, see above pp. 121-134. St. Augustine, after considering how hard it is to be genuinely creative and how easy it is to destroy the hard-won fruits of such labors concludes: "The easiest things of all to do are those which serve the purpose of destruction." *In Ps.* 51.7, Corpus Christianorum (CChr) 39, p. 628.

[19]Dorotheos of Gaza, *Discourses* 6, trans. Cistercian Studies Series, vol. 33, p. 139.

[20]Augustine, *In Ps.* 50.5, CChr 38, p. 601.

[21]Cf. "The Virtue of Patience in Western Monastic Tradition," *Cistercian Studies* 21 (1986), pp. 3-23; see above pp. 95-120, see esp. note 116, p. 119.

[22]Augustine, *In Ps.* 50.16, CChr 38, pp. 611-612.

[23]Augustine, *De Natura et Gratia* 29.33, PL 44.263A. The same dynamic of

disgust is illustrated in Gregory the Great's well-known text on compunction in *Moralia* 23.43, PL 76.277-278.

[24]William of St Thierry, *Golden Epistle* 30, trans. Cistercian Fathers Series, vol. 12, p. 20.

[25]Cf. Michael de Roche, "Jeremiah 2.2-3 and Israel's Love for God during the Wilderness Wandering," *Catholic Biblical Quarterly* 45 (1983), pp. 364-376. The same negative connotation for the theme of the desert must be admitted for that much-favored monastic text, "I will lead her into the desert and speak to her heart" (Hosea 2:14).

[26]Adam of Perseigne, *Letters* 9, trans. Cistercian Fathers Series, vol. 21, pp. 134-135.

[27]Augustine, *In Ioan.* 17.11, CChr 36, p. 176.

[28]Augustine, *In Ps.* 50.13, CChr 38, p. 609.

Introductory Note

This hitherto unpublished text brings together material on the monastic approach to prayer which I had been gathering since 1983. Its immediate purpose was to accompany a course given to Tarrawarra juniors in 1988. Unsurprisingly it duplicates sentiments expressed elsewhere in this collection, but it also provides clarification and expansion on some points.

The Quality of Monastic Prayer

One practice which can greatly favor our perseverance in prayer is an annual review of our attitudes and actions in this area, to verify whether our attempts to pray really correspond to our spiritual needs at this particular season of our life. Many of our difficulties in prayer derive simply from our trying to continue with what was appropriate yesterday, ignoring the fact that a new day contains within itself a different challenge and that there are different resources available for meeting it.

> You stayed on one of the syllables of a great song; consequently you are disturbed when the all-wise singer goes on with his song. For the syllable which alone you loved is taken from you, and others follow in their proper order. For he is not singing for you alone, nor according to your will, but his own. And the syllables which follow are an obstacle to you for this reason, that they clash with the one you loved wrongfully.[1]

Part of such a review must include an attempt to diagnose the state of our soul. We can do this through introspection or through dialogue with one who knows us well. It is also possible to judge our present sensitivities by noting the manner in which we react to particular themes in the course of our reading. We will often find our attention drawn to areas which we have a tendency to overlook and which invite improvement.

If we are concerned for the vitality of our prayer it is a good idea to open ourselves each year to some general treatment of the subject and to take note of our own reactions. If we are honest with ourselves, we will often become aware of aspects of prayer which have slipped away unnoticed from our routines and which we could profitably re-embrace. It is not so much a matter of getting new information about prayer. It is letting ourselves be reminded of what we left aside while we attended to something else. "These things you should have done without neglecting the others." Prayer is such a rich reality that we cannot grasp its total potential. When one aspect of the whole ceases to be relevant for us, there are many alternatives ready to take its place. There is no need to give up prayer because it has gone stale; we simply move into another zone of prayer.

In this article I shall offer a broad survey of an understanding of prayer which emerged in Latin monasticism from about the fifth century onwards. My purpose is not primarily antiquarian. I would hope that a survey of such a distant vista may contain elements that we are culturally prone to overlook. In this hypothesis, our being reminded of them is probably worthwhile.

1. Regularity

One of the fundamental questions which most of us face is *whether* we pray. Time for prayer is not given us on a plate: we have to find the time or make the time. There is always a range of alternatives. Even if we succeed in allocating a period for prayer, we may find that we have expended a disproportionate amount of effort simply in getting started. The energies we could have used in quieting our minds and opening our hearts to God are sometimes squandered in organizing our chaotic lives.

This is one difficulty that was less rampant in ancient monasticism even before the Tridentine provision of specific time-slots. Prayer was built into the way of life. It was not a question of finding time for prayer but of making good use of the time already made available for this purpose. Somnolence and distractions were always possible—especially if a monk's heart was elsewhere—but, in general, with good will it was possible to pray with a minimum of fuss.

Perhaps we can learn from these ancient monks the importance of so incorporating prayer into our ordinary lifestyle that, without very much thought or effort, the practice of prayer becomes a constant element in our daily program.

It is such unselfconscious perseverance which gives prayer depth and even a degree of facility. Contemplation is possible only after years of fidelity, *processu longioris temporis*,[2] when "a soul not only lives for Christ but has done so for a long time."[3] It is the ordinariness of prayer which gives access to its most profound mysteries.

> The only way to pray is to pray; and the way to pray well is to pray much. If one has no time for this, then one must at least pray regularly. But the less one prays, the worse it goes.[4]

It may be that regularity is not considered exciting today, but it remains an important feature of growth in prayerfulness. One prays better when one arrives at prayer on automatic pilot. This is not to say that one is mindless or under compulsion, but rather that one has freely opted to build prayer into life in such a way that the drama of daily decision-making is avoided. The quality of prayer improves when it forms an integral element in a personal lifestyle. The principle is clearly stated by Friedrich Heiler: "The element of spontaneity does not wholly exclude fixity of expression…. Man's entire life of expression, gesture, mimicry shows the same union of emotional spontaneity and conventional fixity."[5]

Regularity in prayer is related to a willingness to give to our life what Hans Urs von Balthasar terms "form." If we are genuinely serious about prayer, we cannot avoid incorporating this priority in our manner of using time, so that our days and weeks are designed to lead to freedom and facility in prayer.

> What is a person without the form that shapes him, the form that surrounds him inexorably like a coat of armor and which nonetheless is the very thing that bestows suppleness on him and which makes him free of all uncertainty and all paralyzing fears, free for himself and his highest possibilities? What is a person without this? What is a person without a life-form, that is to say, without a form which he has chosen for his life, a form into which and through which to pour out his life, so that his life becomes the soul of the form and the form becomes the expression of his soul?[6]

Such a form is not extraneous to the person, nor is it forcibly imposed from without. It is not something giddily adopted and just as giddily abandoned. It flows from a moment in which one recognizes something pre-existent outside oneself which both expresses one's inmost qualities and invites one to live in closer concordance with them. Form gives both identity and challenge. It is the means by which a peak-experience is translated into the homelier rhythms of daily life so that the moment of grace continues to guide and animate future development.

> This precious pearl must have been espied in the first place by an eye that recognizes value, an eye which, being enthralled by the beauty of this unique form, dismisses all else as "rubbish" in order to acquire the one thing which alone is worthy of claiming our life unconditionally, the one thing which lends value to whatever we might be by allowing us to participate in its own intrinsic worth.[7]

Because prayer was an integral element in ancient monastic *conversatio*, in opting for the monastic life one opted for a life in which prayer had a guaranteed priority. The question was no longer whether to pray, but how best to make use of the opportunities provided.

Today, even in monasteries, the position of prayer is less secure.

Communities are not so regimented: monks can escape from prayer if they are so inclined. Even attendance at the Liturgy of the Hours can be sporadic. Very few would interpret strictly St. Benedict's injunction that "*Nothing* is to be preferred to the work of God." As a result, it is left to the individual monk to inject more prayer into a minimal structure. Those who do, profit from having used their freedom well. Those who fail to do so, through some form of inattention, find that the quality of their monastic life is declining faster than they would wish and without their being fully aware of the factors involved.

I do not wish to initiate a discussion on the dialectic of freedom and responsibility. The point I am moving towards is simply this: even those who live "under a rule and an abbot" may benefit by having a "rule" within the rule, according to which their life may have a form which makes possible a creative and authentic response to their own personal vocation. With counsel and in the joy of the Holy Spirit each is able to offer to God something above the assigned measure, designed as it is to avoid imposing too much on the weakest.[8] Those who are not governed by a common rule have even more need of such a structure.

If prayer has an integral part within such a personal rule of life, the presence of a dynamic principle of spiritual development is assured. Whatever difficulties, problems or faults we may have, persevering prayer will progressively equip us to handle them better. We rarely have a sense of being finally rid of such liabilities. Usually what happens is that we grow beyond them. We do not succeed in mastering them; they simply become irrelevant. It is prayer which fosters the growth that places us beyond their reach.

Our prayer will prosper if we can guarantee easy access to it in the course of our daily life. Our measure must be our own spiritual state at this time. It is not always a matter of constantly increasing the amount of prayer. What is of primary importance is that daily life corresponds to our inner ideals as far as possible. To the extent that we feel ourselves called to contemplation, our own integrity obliges us to incorporate the practice of prayer in the rhythms of daily living.

Another factor in classical monasticism needs to be mentioned. Not only was time available for prayer. The quality of life was such that potential disruptions of prayer itself were systematically minimized. Solitude, silence and the restriction of sources of stimulation can ensure a quiet mind which is able to move more easily into prayer. Such aids are not absolute. Even in the strictest monasteries monks can find plenty of diversions if their interest in prayer wanes. To pray well we need a lifestyle which not only allocates time for prayer but which also governs other times wisely. On the contrary, if our values direct us toward a lot of unnecessary chatter and excitement, then prayer will be so much more difficult. Not impossible, but certainly needing more effort. In particular, excessive exposure to the electronic media fills our minds with sounds and images which will, during times of prayer, readily invade the empty space into which we would invite the Lord. Prayer and life interact, as we shall remark later. If our prayer is genuine then, progressively, it will demand some changes in our lifestyle.

I am not trying to idealize the way the ancient monks lived since, in fact, we know relatively little about the details of their daily life. They were probably no better than we are. The point at issue is that they were not impeded as we are by some specific factors in contemporary western culture. Disjunctions between corporate prayer and personal prayer, between vocal prayer and "mental" prayer, between spontaneity and form, were largely unknown. As a result, the transition into prayer was probably smoother and less self-conscious than ours.

Structure or form is not necessarily enslaving and alienating. Nor is it the private preserve of certain obsessive personality-types. It is, as we have said above, a means by which we translate the experience of grace into semi-permanent realities of life.

> The privileged "moment" will always exist when a person falls to his knees to adore the One who says to him, "I who am speaking to you—I am He!" But the Good News cannot be reduced to such moments, since these would readily absorb all else into themselves. There are also the surfaces, time and space, and all those human factors disseminated within them and which essentially belong to what John calls "remaining": the commerce and familiarity with habits and opinions, reaching to what cannot be weighed or measured—a real life-form.[9]

We can't simply rely on peak experiences, which arrive rarely and last but a short time: *rara hora et parva mora*.[10] Our lives should be so planned that prayer is a permanent reality.

2. Received

It is theoretically possible to construct a lifestyle by a process of deduction and application of first principles. A danger exists that if the principles happen to be off-target the resulting practice will be correspondingly defective. A surer approach is to embrace a way that is already producing the desired results. In general we become spiritual by becoming part of an existing spiritual tradition. Saints attract more recruits and generate more interest and enthusiasm than the most enunciated theory. Example has more power to move than logic.

Ancient monasticism was, above all, a *praxis*. Such theory as evolved was largely a matter of grasping systematically the principles inherent in the monastic lifestyle. Knowledge of the writings of Evagrius or Cassian was not viewed as a substitute for contact with a spiritual master and integral participation in the traditional discipline: *sub regula vel abbate*. Doctrine followed practice—except, perhaps, in the case of the Rule of the Master—it was accredited by the fruits it had already produced.[11]

Monasticism did not invent prayer, nor did it set itself to formulate a specific approach to it. It received prayer as part of a tradition of God-consciousness, the origins of which trace back more than a thousand years before the Christian era. Monastic prayer is not a pure emanation from human subjectivity; it is a practice imbedded in history. It owes its essential features to a culture which evolved from the Old to the New Testament and beyond. The monks tried to pray as their ancestors had before them.[12]

Monastic prayer and the behavioral context known to nurture it are products of a developing tradition of experience. What seems to have happened is that the ancient monks' instinct to seek God led them to spend more time in the presence of God's word—reading, reflecting, responding—so that progressively their lives began to be *formed* by the scriptures, particularly by the Psalms and the Gospels. Through a growing familiarity with the biblical texts, they found models for the prayer emerging in their own spirits: lamentation, praise, confidence, thanksgiving. The scriptures were seen as a mirror of what was happening in the soul, the texts became vehicles for expressing and reinforcing a deep desire for God.

> And it seems to me that these words become like a mirror to the person singing them, so that he might perceive himself and the emotions of his soul and, thus affected, he might recite them. For in fact he who hears the one reading, receives the song as being about him....[13]

Prayer is already, as it were, prefabricated in the scriptures. The act of prayer is simply a matter of making our own those forms which have been preserved by tradition precisely because of their suitability for triggering a prayerful response.

In one sense this ancient format of prayer is both medium and message. The very content of prayer is receptivity. Passivity. Responsiveness. Submission. There is no activity of which to be conscious. No doubt this is why John Cassian quotes St. Antony as saying that "prayer is not perfect if the monk is aware either of himself or of the content of his prayer."[14] The author of *The Cloud of Unknowing* frequently returns to this point: "Travail steadfastly in this nought and in this nowhere."[15] We have to work hard in order to avoid doing anything!

> And although thy bodily wits can find there nothing to feed them on, for they think that it is nought that thou dost, yea! do on this nought, provided that thou do it for God's love.[16]

> And well is this work likened to a sleep. For as in sleep the use of the bodily wits is ceased, that the body may take its full rest in feeding and in strengthening of its bodily nature, right so in this ghostly sleep, the wanton questions of the wild ghostly wits—imaginative reasons—be fast bound and utterly voided so that the silly soul may softly sleep and rest in the lovely beholding of God as he is, in full feeding and strengthening of the ghostly nature.[17]

> And if I shall shortlier say, let that thing do with thee and lead thee whereso it list. Let it be the worker and thou but the sufferer; do but look upon it and let it alone. Meddle thee not therewith as though thou wouldst help it, for dread that thou spill all. Be thou the tree, and let it be the carpenter. Be thou the house and let it be the husband dwelling therein.[18]

It seems to me that the ancient monks did not consciously set out to give their prayer this attitude of receptivity. By the very fact of their being open to the scriptures, they were led to an ever-deeper experience of prayer. They were not so busy trying to pray well that the project of prayer was given a priority over docility to the Holy Spirit.[19] As receptivity, prayer is the opposite of self-programming.

This spirit of willingness to be formed in a tradition meant that monastic prayer was in radical continuity with the sort of prayer inculcated by Jesus himself and embedded in the New Testament. The New Testament gives us the commandment to pray. It also imparts a model for Christian prayer, so that the Lord's Prayer became the norm of all subsequent practice.[20] In addition, we find throughout the Gospels and Epistles a whole range of supporting doctrine which is progressively enriched by the faith and experience of successive generations.

A) Prayer in the New Testament is addressed to God as Father, using the familiar Aramaic name Abba. This is not simply a matter of using the "correct" form of address. It bespeaks a very distinctive relationship between the Christian and God. It is characterized by tenderness, affection, homeliness. We are to be confident about God's good will in our regard and so motivated to persevere no matter what difficulties we encounter. We are liberated from superstition and formalism. Because God is our Father we have direct access to his love.

B) New Testament prayer is strongly eschatological: full of the Spirit, it looks to the coming of God's kingdom. The use of the passive aorist imperative in the Greek text of both versions of the Lord's Prayer indicates a certain urgency: Let us have done with compromise and let the Day of the Lord appear, once and for all. Thus prayer was seen as something closely akin to hope; it is the expression of desire for God's transforming power to burst into our lives and bring us to glory.

C) Prayer in the New Testament is life-related. It is not an activity which has no relationship with the events of daily experience; it is not leaving behind the reality of who we are and what sin has made of us. It is not play-acting or putting up a barrier of words between ourselves and God. Prayer is the means by which the love of God touches not only our minds and hearts, but the totality of our lives as well. The prayer of Jesus in Gethsemane and on the Cross arose from life. The prayer of the tax collector who won acceptance reflected his real state before God. In the Lord's Prayer we pray for real needs: for daily bread, forgiveness and protection from harm. "The heart of all prayer is petition, from which indeed it takes its name."[21]

D) Prayer is corporate. It cannot co-exist with non-forgiveness. The Church prays as one to a common Father and by that fact unity is strengthened. It is impossible to turn toward God if we are at emnity with our neighbors—which is why Jesus tells us to try to bind ourselves with prayer to those from whom we are separated by hostility.

Monastic tradition took up and developed these elements of prayer. The most characteristic features of a monastic approach to prayer are, in fact, derived directly from the New Testament.[22]

3. Biblical

If monastic prayer was so marked by a scriptural character, it was because the agenda of prayer was not left to the promptings of subjectivity. Prayer was primed by constant exposure to that truth at which unaided reason cannot arrive. The monk lived in the aura of revelation: salvation history was the context of his daily life. The teachings of Christ, presaged in the Old Testament and presented in different facets by the great teachers of tradition, accompanied the monk throughout his round of activities: in the Liturgy of the Hours, at meals, at work, in conferences and in private ruminations. The word of God was a permanent feature of the monastic ambiance and a significant factor in determining the style and content of monastic customaries.

The fact that the Bible impressed itself on the communal way of life did not mean that it was a question of an executive policy, determined from on high and imposed on a passive community. One of the salient characteristics of western monasticism is that individual monks were given the opportunity and training to spend several hours each day at their individual reading. They were put in direct and personal contact with biblical sources of renewal. This is a dangerous practice in the sense that individuals reading different books may be inspired in ways which may diverge from the official policy. It is building into the institution a dynamic or prophetic element.

Not that medieval monks would be sitting in the cloister with Marx or Marcuse or reading comics! Control was still possible in the choice of books to be acquired, copied or made available. Usually the priorities in book accession were to have copies of the texts needed for the liturgy, bibles and the great commentators who built bridges between the scriptures and daily life. We see an excellent example of this in the first decade of the New Monastery at Cîteaux: the copying of the liturgical texts was finished shortly after Abbot Robert returned to Molesme; the so-called "Bible of St. Stephen Harding" followed. By 1111 the first three tomes of St. Gregory the Great's *Moral Exposition of the Book of Job* were complete.

We have medieval catalogs from which it is possible to judge what books were available; they follow these priorities as a rule. With time and with donations the scope of the libraries widened to include theological and philosophical works, even some classical history and literature, canon law and scientific texts. We cannot conclude, however, that because a monastery possessed a manuscript that it was in general circulation. But it seems safe to say that the core of the library remained relatively constant: scripture, liturgy and the patristic classics.

As a result the book selection was in profound continuity with the Liturgy of the Hours and the monastery's life of prayer. It is probable that it was reading along these lines which received the most official encouragement. Certainly we find texts which inveigh against the sort of reading which diverts the monk's attention from his goal.

Monastic reading, *lectio divina*, was conditioned by a number of factors which had nothing to do with a theory of prayer. They are simply historical accidents.

A) Because the monasteries had fewer books (a collection of two or three hundred would be considered generous), there was no prospect of rapidly engorging many different texts. As a result the monks read slowly and less widely.

B) Because books were rare they were chosen more carefully. There was relatively little pulp in the monastic *armaria*. There are examples of whimsical little works which were widely read (one presumes as light reading), but these are relatively rare.

C) The books themselves were physically cumbersome. Often bulky and heavy to hold in the hand. As a result it was usual to concentrate on one book at a time. Without chapter and verse division it was difficult to pinpoint specific texts; the tendency was to read the whole book for what one could quarry out of it.

D) The reader had to make the most of the text before him. The accuracy and clarity of the copying were not always perfect. There were few resources to provide answers to queries that arose. Some of the Fathers of the Church were regarded as knowledgeable and were consulted frequently, but for the most part it was left to the reader to puzzle things out for himself or to ask, at an appropriate time, the local expert.

E) Although most of the monks (as distinct from the lay brothers) were officially literate, levels of capability varied. *Lectio divina* was not clearly distinguished from the preparation of texts or chants for the liturgy or the memorization of the Psalms. All these activities took place in the cloister during the intervals. It could almost be said that *lectio divina* was simply working with God's word in one way or another, according to the realities of a particular situation. Despite the scarcity of books and the potential difficulties to be encountered by less educated readers, there seems to be little evidence for informal shared reading in small groups.[23] Each read his own book and took care not to disturb the others.

F) Lighting and heating were problems. More so in northern monasteries. Possibilities for reading were restricted to the cloister and to the chapter room, where lamps were lit and some refuge from the cold could be found. As a result, *lectio divina* was done in common, although the monks were always permitted to sit quietly in their place or to go to the church for prayer, if they wished. The reading itself, being a community matter, was subject to regulation, to ensure that one's lack of discipline did not hinder others.

The cumulative effect of these factors was to make of reading a slow, deliberate exercise, carried out in an atmosphere of recollection. The reading itself would have been almost audible, certainly vocal, directed towards memorization. Information systems were of the most rudimentary kind; it was only by means of memory that what was read could be progressively absorbed and become a force in the amendment of life.

One means of ensuring the continuity of moments of grace that was available to the medieval monks was the writing of *florilegia*—anthologies of quotations from what they read, sometimes classified under themes. Much depended on the availability of scraps of parchment, unless the collector were already, as in the case of St. Bede or William of St Thierry, an established author in his own right. Jerome Kodell was inspired by this ancient practice to suggest the keeping of a *lectio* journal. He distinguishes the *lectio* journal from the more subjective spiritual diary which describes spiritual states, experiences and aspirations.

> The *lectio divina* journal is more a collection of the words that God speaks to me (primarily, but not only, in a time of prayerful reading): quotations from Scripture, the Fathers, other spiritual writings, and ultimately any kind of human word (novels, poems, banners, letters) that carries the transforming word of God into my life. These are collected as privileged words of God because directed personally to my heart, with the hope that what once was a vehicle for God's sanctifying and healing touch will remain important in my life and be a source of power again later on.[24]

A few suggestions about such a journal. The book itself should, if possible, be of good quality with the possibility of permanence about it. The script should be careful and as elegant as one can manage without becoming an exercise in calligraphy. Not only should the page look attractive, the act of writing should itself become a medium of meditation, a way of dwelling on the word more fully and a means of more effectively committing it to memory. There is no need to feel a compulsion to write something every day, just for the sake of making an entry, but it is good to try to crystallize one's attentiveness to the word of God by asking, "What have I heard today?" As with so much in the spiritual life, sobriety and authenticity are more important than flamboyance. We may choose to return to what we have written for as long as we are spellbound. Then we pass on. If our instincts are right, the texts we have copied will continue to animate us many years later. They may speak more truthfully about our state of soul at a particular season than all attempts at self-diagnosis. We may also find that sharing with another what has touched us during *lectio* is to move the dialogue to a very profound point of experience.

It is clear that *lectio divina* was seen in function of prayer.[25] *Lectio* flowed from the liturgy into private reading: it filled the mind and heart so that the monk would live in mindfulness and feel drawn to prostrate himself in prayer at other times: *simpliciter intret et oret*. And so it would flow back to the liturgy. No wonder St. Benedict suggests that the ability to find prayer in the Liturgy of the Hours is one of the essential requirements in a prospective monk. If this does not happen it seems as though the integrity of monastic *conversatio* has been lost.

The dynamic relationship between reading and prayer is graphically conveyed in St. Bernard's repeated use of the image of belching. The word is eaten in reading, taken into the heart. Through meditation or rumination its content is absorbed and assimilated. This process causes a *spiritus* or wind to develop within which suddenly erupts from the depths in a belch *ructus. Eructavit cor meum verbum bonum*: My heart belches a good word (Ps. 44:2). *Memoriam abundantiae suavitatis eructabunt*: They will belch out the memory of sweetness (Ps. 144:7).

> But the words of the prophet do not apply to everyone. He said, "They will belch out the memory of your sweetness." Not everybody is nourished by such a memory. It is obvious that someone who has not tasted and those who have done no more than taste will not belch. A belch comes forth from a certain fullness and satiety. This is why those whose mind and life are secular in character, even though they honor [the feast] with celebration, cannot belch out such a memory. For them, these days will be kept out of lifeless custom, without any experience of devotion or love.[26]

The continuing practice of prayer must be nourished by sustained exposure to the scriptures. It is useless to attempt to pray unless the energy for prayer has been received through holy reading. Those who, in the words of Psalm 101:5, "forget to eat their bread" become progressively alienated from God's word and both prayer and behavior begin to decline.[27]

In our times, the breakdown of monastic life in individuals is often due to the loss of the function of *lectio divina*. Nothing else can replace it, neither more liturgy, more prayer nor more work. Daily personal contact with God's word is irreducible. When a monk stops reading well, other monastic observances lose their charm. He ceases to pursue his ideals and they progressively become unrealizable. He becomes downcast. He looks for other activities (including compensatory "good" activities) to fill the void, but the gambit does not work. Progressively his aimless heart comes under attack from sub-personal forces and, before long, his daily agenda is dictated by these and not by his grace-guided will. And so he begins a spiral of decline: *lectio divina* seems irrelevant to his felt needs and so he cuts himself off from a means by which his experience can be relocated within the totality of God's dealing with the human race. He is more tightly locked in with his own problems. The only way to interrupt the cycle is to begin afresh with daily exposure to God's word. Other aids and resources may need to be used but unless faith is fed, the specifically spiritual component of personal crisis will not be attended to.

Lectio divina is a key element in any sustained dedication to prayer. This means that it is located in a war zone. Whatever in us resists the attraction to a life of prayer will provide us with compelling reasons to abandon fidelity to holy reading.

The ancient texts speak of three potential areas in which the monk will have to struggle if he is to remain faithful to *lectio divina*. In those days a solution was sought through a communal discipline. For us, once we are aware of the dangers, we will have to devise our own countermeasures.

The first enemy is sleep. The ancient monks were not allowed to wear their hoods in a way which would obscure their faces, so that their vigilance could be verified. It is possible that we fall asleep because we are physically exhausted, but this is relatively unusual. If we turn to something else, even to a different sort of reading, then most often the tiredness vanishes and we are fully alert. If we take ordinary precautions about posture, ambiance and lifestyle and the drowsiness remains, it would seem that its roots must be psychological rather than physical.

Sometimes it is due to boredom. We have lost sight of spiritual goals and all our energies are invested in mundane affairs. Assigned work, private "obligations" or hobbies may appear more compelling. Lack of interest in *lectio divina* is not normally an indication that we should reduce it or omit it altogether.[28] It is an invitation to reassess our priorities in everyday behavior. Sleep during prayer or reading can also be one of a whole range of devices by which we escape from the insistency of God's call. It is a means of passive aggression towards God. We are too pious to rebel openly against God, but we nullify what he would do in us by unconsciously protecting ourselves against his demands. Such drowsiness, especially when it becomes habitual, can be highly significant. It can constitute massive infidelity, although it may not be recognized or owned as such.

A second threat to reading is *acedia*, that near-neurotic state of being unable to commit oneself to anything, except to non-commitment. It is thought by some that this is one of the characteristics of contemporary western culture. No correction by others is possible since most values are floating; there are no fixed points to which an appeal for change can be firmly attached. Wherever the acediac is, his heart is elsewhere; whatever he does, he would rather be doing something else; as soon as he opens one book, he remembers another that would be better.

> And when it has taken possession of some unhappy soul, it produces dislike of the place, disgust with the cell, and disdain and contempt of the brothers who dwell with him or at a little distance as if they were careless and unspiritual. It also makes him lazy and sluggish about all manner of work which has to be done within the walls of his room. It does not permit him to stay in his cell, or to make an effort to read.[29]

> Around noon, he is conscious of such a weariness of body and hunger for food that it is as though he had worn himself out by a long journey or by heavy manual work, or had gone two or three days without eating. He looks all around and grieves because none of the brothers comes to visit him [so that he may join him in a meal]. He often enters and leaves his cell, always watching the sun, as if it were slow in setting. His thinking becomes unreasonable and confused, filled with a fearsome darkness. It becomes incapable of any spiritual act, empty. He can think of no way of combating such an assault except by visiting some brother or by seeking comfort in sleep....

Having drawn the monk from his cell it makes him, little by little, forget the goal of his profession which is none other than the vision and contemplation of transcendent divine purity which can only come about through silence, permanent perseverance in the cell and meditation. In this way, the soldier of Christ becomes a fugitive and deserter from his army....

And whenever *acedia* begins in any degree to get the upper hand, either it makes the monk stay in his cell idle and lazy without making any spiritual progress or drives him out from the cell and makes him restless and a wanderer, and lazy in every kind of work. It makes him continually go round the cells of the brothers and the monasteries for no other purpose but to see where or with what excuse he can get something to eat. For the mind of the idle cannot think of anything but food and the belly, until the company of some man or woman equally tepid and indifferent is secured, and it loses itself in their affairs and business. Progressively it becomes so ensnared by these concerns, as by the coils of a snake, that it can no longer extricate itself in order to return to the goal of its first profession.[30]

The alternatives to reading which the acediac finds are well-documented: sleep, daydreaming (which would include fantasy reading), hobbies (what William of St Thierry calls, "avoiding idleness by doing idle things"[31]), meandering around, endless social chatter (often repeating the same conversation with each new person encountered), coffee and snacks, radio and television. It is not that any single item in this list is particularly harmful. The danger is when the sum total of them begins to occupy hours out of every day. An escapist lifestyle is becoming established in the context of which activities such as prayer and holy reading will become progressively more meaningless and unattractive. As will genuine fraternal interaction and all the virtues.

Acedia is self-perpetuating. Not only does it convert useful time into frivolous activity, it also invades the mind and heart when one attempts to engage in something more substantial. Distractions and fantasies so distort a potentially spiritual exercise that it serves no purpose except to produce more discouragement. Guerric of Igny describes how acediac monks appear during spiritual exercises:

Now they come to the divine office and doze, they give themselves to idle and pernicious thoughts, they sit down to read but yawn at the book, they listen to the sermon, but find it difficult to pay attention.[32]

And Aelred of Rievaulx gives this picture of a restless monk during the time of reading.

> You know, brothers, that silence is a burden for many. Quiet weighs them down. As a result everything becomes a burden when they have to stop speaking and be quiet: their head aches, their stomach rumbles, they cannot see, their kidneys weaken.... You may see a monk sitting in the cloister, looking this way and that, yawning frequently, stretching his arms and legs. Now he puts the book down, then he takes it up again. Finally, as if stung by a goad, he gets up and wanders from place to place, from one parlor to another....[33]

The third area of danger to reading appears towards the second part of the twelfth century. This was intellectualism—reading to stimulate the mind rather than to find the heart. We find warnings about philosophy and literature and the baser sorts of writing appearing in the works of Bernard of Clairvaux and Gilbert of Swineshead and this remark of Aelred's.

> I shall say a few words about that internal curiosity which consists in three things: the appetite for harmful or empty knowledge; the scrutiny of another's life, not for imitation but out of envy, if it is good, or for insult, if it is evil, or simply out of pure curiosity to know whether it is good or evil; and finally a restless curiosity to know about worldly affairs and events. When the mind is caught by these things, it gives birth to much toil, whether it makes the effort to pursue them immoderately or freely decides to resist. Those who give themselves to vain "philosophy" experience this. They join the Bucolics with the Gospels in their meditations. They read Horace together with the prophets and Paul with [Cicero]. From there they play with verse and write bawdy love songs. Without regard for the strictness of the Rule, they harangue one another, having discussions which are the seedbeds of vanity, the beginning of quarrels or occasions for lust. And so they begin to be depressed or angry.[34]

Because both study and *lectio* involve contact with books—perhaps the same books—they can become confused. Intellectual dealing with the sacred texts can also be a means of keeping God at a distance or of staving off boredom. This is why there is practical utility in making a clear distinction in our own daily program between holy reading and other bookish activities. *Lectio* is too important to allow it to slip away unnoticed.

4. Feelingful

The lifelong living out of an attraction to the practice of prayer has to cope with a range of counter-attractions. It is not always easy to continue doing the things that promote a prayerful existence because our feelings draw us in alternative directions—both the feelings which are aroused by our interaction with external reality and those passions which are governed by unconscious factors. As a result we experience a crisis in motivation when it comes to spiritual activities. We accept their theoretical importance but cannot find the energy to sustain our practice of them.

This is a phenomenon which Gregory the Great also noted: carnal appetites are assisted by antecedent feelings which carry us forward. Spiritual appetites, on the other hand, are not assisted by such a promotional drive. We are moved by them in a state of relative dryness. Our only feeling may be a strong sense of resistance. It is only when we actually embrace spiritual realities that their charm is experienced.

> There is a great difference, dear brothers, between the pleasures of the body and those of the heart. Bodily pleasures set alight a strong desire when they are not possessed, but when he who has them partakes of them, he becomes satiated and tires of them. On the other hand, spiritual pleasures are tiresome when they are not possessed; when they are possessed they cause greater desire. He who partakes of them hungers for more, and the more he eats, the hungrier he becomes. In carnal pleasure the appetite is more pleasurable than the experience, but with regard to spiritual pleasures the experience of them is more rewarding; the appetite for them is nothing. In carnal pleasures the appetite causes satiety and satiety generates disgust. In spiritual pleasures, when the appetite gives birth to satiety, satiety gives birth to even greater appetite. Spiritual delights increase the extent of delight in the mind, even while they satisfy the appetite for them.[35]

Because our feelings generally act as inhibitors of our spiritual impulses, it is important for us to appreciate how to "fight fire with fire."

If we are not to condemn ourselves to a feelingless existence, then we must learn how to find our way through to authentic spiritual feelings, the delight, *delectatio*, which Christians find in being united with God. Only this subtle spiritual satisfaction enables us to persevere through years of suffering, labor and rejection.

The cardinal role of "delight" in spiritual endeavor is a feature of the spirituality of St. Augustine, and because of his massive influence in the West, it has become widely accepted in the thousand years after him. Because monasticism belongs to the devotional current in Christianity, it has willingly welcomed this emphasis. There are many feeling words in the spiritual vocabulary of western monastic writers: *affectus cordis, compunctio, intentio* and the whole terminology of desire. In fact absence of such a positive sense of God was understood as an indication that one was not truly seeking God, but was locked in routine, in self-satisfaction, in a total absorption in one's own programs for the future. "The mind of one who does not seek the beauty of his Maker is unnaturally hard and remains frigid within itself."[36] A sort of stoic ritualism results which is disastrous—particularly for celibates who have no spouse, children or grandchildren to keep them soft, to encourage them to unselfishness and to motivate them to act.

The important thing about positive feelings of attraction to spiritual reality is that they give us the energy to be generous in breaking away from the gratifying enslavements which inhibit our freedom. Detachment is only possible on the supposition that something better has *already* moved in to take its place. "One who knows perfectly the sweetness of the heavenly life happily leaves behind everything he previously loved on earth."[37] The same priority to the positive is found in the parable about treasure hidden in a field: first comes the finding of the treasure, then, in the joy of that discovery, a willingness to give up everything in order to obtain the field that holds the treasure.

John Cassian's treatment of compunction is important in understanding the role of positive feelings, and had considerable influence in the evolution of western monastic spiritual doctrine. Firstly, compunction was more than sorrow for sin. It is, above all, a spiritual awakening. Not a paralyzing sense of guilt or inadequacy, but a compelling desire to change direction. It is a stimulant, a *punctio*, not a depressant. It can arise in various ways: the chanting of psalms, a glimpse of beauty, a moment of self-revelation, truth, the conferences of a holy man, liminal experiences.

But its effect is that it "can rouse the mind, through God's grace, from its drowsiness and half-heartedness."[38] It is a moment in which the soul/heart/spirit is lifted up and a new channel opens up into the future. Its forms can vary: it can be positive or negative. The sensibility may be flooded with joy "so that even the occupant of the next cell feels the power of the happiness of the heart."[39] Or there may be anguish and tears.[40] Sometimes there is only wordless wonder, when the soul is introduced "into a secret abyss of silence."[41] Always there is feeling.

The fact that prayer feels good does not mean that it is a real contact with God. "Look that thy stirrings...come from within, of abundance of love and devotion in spirit, and not from without, by windows of thy bodily wits."[42] It is possible to be led astray by superficial sentiment. The experience of prayer is that of "a blind feeling unto God." Its energy does not come from sense impressions but from within. We put ourselves in the way of being able to be affected by spiritual reality by being in a state of sense, imagination and intellectual deprivation: "unknowing." In such a state things become apparent which are not seen when other things absorb our attention.

The feeling involved in deep prayer is qualitatively different from the emotional impact of a sentimental film or a powerful novel. Spiritual experience demands that we begin by distancing ourselves from emotional influence by external factors and allow ourselves to move into an ever-deepening state of quiet and receptivity. In this twilight we can be touched by subtler forces and roused to feelings that are pure expressions of the heart. In the hustle of daily activities we are unaware of what is deepest. It is only in silence—of tongue, of thought, of being—that we begin to perceive what is habitually latent. Techniques of prayer or *lectio divina* do not generate this feeling, but they produce an inward quiet which enables us to experience what is, by force of circumstances, habitually repressed.

What we experience in prayer can never be at odds with objective norms: Follow the judgment of faith and not your own experiences.[43] If it leads us to live a more evangelical life with greater fervor and with more ruthless practicality, then it probably comes from God. If it leads to laxity, to complacency, to phoniness, to arrogance, to living beyond our spiritual means, to lack of prudence or to errors of judgment, then the feelings do not come from God. They need to be subject to discernment.

Feelinglessness in prayer is also something to be examined. We must recognize that there is a form of Quietism going about which mistakes the nature, confusing it with some form of pious somnolence which relaxes and interposes a buffer zone between the person and an abrasive environment. There is no content in prayer, just the chance to catch one's breath in a sort of period of emptying the consciousness. Such "prayer" is content-free: there is no relationship, there is no real challenge. As a result there is no real growth and no real spiritual experience. It is feelinglessness systematically sought.

Feelinglessness cannot be allowed to continue unchallenged. It needs to be looked at. There are different causes which endow it with significantly different meanings:

A) Feeling nothing can be an indication that the practices we use are no longer a fruitful means of bringing to the surface the prayer which is latent in our hearts. It can be seen as a call to change. Perhaps there is need for a little information or some cautious experimentation. Feelinglessness should not be mindlessly endured and rationalized by abstract theory when its causes can be recognized by ordinary common sense.

B) A loss of dedication to the life of prayer so that one's attempts to pray are only to assuage guilt, to keep up appearances or mere routine.

C) A refusal to confront negative data in our life. The only way to do this is to shut ourselves off from all feedback. As a result we also isolate ourselves from sources of potential affirmation.

D) *Specific* behavioral traits can poison our prayer; if we are firmly saying "No" to God in a particular area of daily life and refusing even to admit that this is the case, then our prayer can only be an experience of our stonewalling God. If we admit our resistance and our sin, this "confession" can fuel our prayer very successfully. Without an awareness of our expressed hostility to God, it will have the inevitable effect of locking us within our own subjectivity.

E) Feelinglessness in prayer can be a sign that prayer is in the throes of a transition from one modality to another. This diagnosis usually presupposes that the dryness cannot otherwise be explained and is not a temporary bout of disenchantment.[44]

Such are the "obscure nights" about which St. John of the Cross writes well. The first of these, especially, is not an advanced stage. It is the end of the beginning (although to those passing through it, it seems like the beginning of the end). Since these are stages in which the soul is formed in passivity, there is nothing active to be done: one may seek information, one endures, one learns to find light where, at first, none appeared. The simple task of remaining at peace under the action of God is not as easy as it sounds; it is during such stages as these that many lose heart and give up their spiritual endeavor.

Having said that prayer is always feelingful, does not mean that it always feels good. Often the feeling is bad. Prayer is a mirror which reflects the real state of our life. If, for example, our life is 45% dedicated to God and 55% directed elsewhere, the proportions are likely to be reflected in our experience of prayer. About half the time we will sense that we are distanced from God. We need to persevere with our practice of prayer, even though it seems more a matter of routine than of positive experiences. We need to stay with this anguish and separation and experience it to the full so that we may grow in a desire to change matters. The only way we improve our prayer is by upgrading our life. And this leads us to our next section.

5. Life-Related

Feelings move us: for the most part they are not under our control. We become aware of being acted upon by realities and events outside us.[45] In the previous section we emphasized the importance of recognizing that our prayer will contain a feeling component. Much of the quality of what we experience in prayer will be a direct reflection of the quality of our daily living. Our habitual way of dealing with the events of ordinary experience leaves a residue which manifests itself during the time of prayer. "Your prayer will show you in what condition you are. Theologians say that prayer is the monk's mirror."[46] It is for this reason that John Cassian counsels that if you find your prayer unsatisfactory, then it is time to upgrade your life.

> Whatever thoughts our mind conceives before the time of prayer will certainly recur in the memory during prayer. For this reason we should try to prepare ourselves before the time of prayer by being the sort of person we would wish to be when we are at prayer. The mind is shaped during its prayer by what it had been beforehand.
>
> When we prostrate ourselves in prayer, our previous actions, words, and impressions continue to play before the minds of our imagination, just as they did beforehand, making us angry or sad, or causing us to relive past lusts or foolish laughter. I am ashamed to admit that we are even entertained by comic words and deeds and our mind is diverted by recalling conversations we had previously. This is why before prayer we ought to be quick to exclude from the approaches to our heart anything that would disturb our prayer.[47]

Cassian is advocating a life lived in a progressive mindfulness of God, in which pursuits foreign to one's ultimate goal of finding God are systematically eliminated and distractions kept to a minimum. In this way the heart becomes "pure" or single, and prayer is able to flow undisturbed.

For many of us this total control over the events of daily life (and our reactions to them) is not feasible. We must keep working to diminish the level of dividedness in our days, but this is not a merely negative task, a matter of avoiding distractions. We need to give our lives a positive quality by actively seeking the will of God, through "fear of the Lord," the keeping of his commandments and the practice of evangelical virtue. This takes so much effort that we cannot help but be mindful: mindful of our own weakness so that we are motivated to call to God for help. Mindfulness is not merely a matter of enhanced awareness.[48]

It is on this understanding that the West has habitually manifested a solidly ethical stance to prayer—a trait well documented in Cuthbert Butler's *Western Mysticism*.[49] There is a causal relationship between the spiritual content of our actions and the quality of what we experience in prayer.[50] This bond is so tight that sometimes it happens that prayer exposes the phoniness of our lives. We may have convinced ourselves that we are living for God, and even had some success in selling the idea to others. It is our prayer which reveals to us the true quality of our behavior. The unconscious motivations which fill our "service" of God and others with self, will come to the surface in our prayer. Our time of quiet will be filled with the noisy clamor of self and no contact with God will be experienced. If we are sane, our prayer is a mirror which does not lie.

This does not mean that prayer is impossible to the extent that we are sinful. Sin does not prevent prayer, but it does change its quality. In prayer we experience the truth of our being: if a large measure of it is turned away from God, then this will be reflected in what we experience during the time of prayer. We do not have to wait to purge away all sin before we begin to pray, but we need to recognize that sin will often render our prayer negative.

Negative does not mean unprofitable. In fact it is usually the experience of our own weakness that brings us to prayer, breaking through the carapace of complacency and making us aware of our own fragility and vulnerability. "Because I am human, therefore I am weak. Because I am weak, therefore I pray."[51] It is precisely in the experience of our own weakness that we become aware of the Spirit animating our prayer, "interceding for our weakness" (Rom. 8:26), bridging the gap between ourselves and God. Only sin repressed, denied or rationalized upsets our prayer. Sin accepted and confessed drives us toward God. Like the publican in the Gospel (Lk. 18:9-14), we pray on the basis of our sin, and it seems that God is always willing to accept this prayer.

On a more positive note, this linkage of prayer and life can be a source of hope. Because the quality of prayer is determined by the way we live, this means that by striving to live a more evangelical life we are moving towards an ever more profound experience of God. Union with God in prayer is a matter of union of wills: our will being aligned with God's. This union is not something that can be effected quickly at the beginning of our prayer. It is accomplished through our habitual and heartfelt assent to the concrete manifestations of God's will in our nature, in our personal history, in revelation, in the duties of our way of life, and in the many avenues of challenge by which we are invited to move towards a life of greater love. This is how our wills become aligned with God's—step by toilsome step. This is the seedbed of the experience of God.

To move a notch higher. In his treatise *On the Necessity of Loving God*, St. Bernard demonstrates that ecstasy—the total experience of God which involves a total transcendence of self—begins at a very mundane level. It is not a matter of learning esoteric skills and practicing an arcane asceticism. It is learning to live in self-forgetfulness, going beyond self by reaching out to others in justice and compassion. This humble altruism is the direct way to the highest contemplative experiences. From this standpoint the necessity of displacement of self is accomplished more effectively by giving to others than by merely denying self.[52]

It is because prayer and life are inseparably married that variation in our experience of prayer is to be taken as normative. This changeableness, which St. Bernard termed *vicissitudo* or *alternatio*,[53] is something which continues throughout life, our prayer reflecting each nuance in our total relationship with God. John Cassian expresses this aspect of prayer clearly:

> I believe that it is impossible to grasp all the different forms of prayer without great purity of heart and soul. There are as many forms of prayer as there are states of soul or, rather, there are as many as the totality of states experienced by all souls together. We are not able to perceive all the various kinds of prayer due to our inner debility, nevertheless, let us try to go through those which we know from our own far from extraordinary experience.

Prayer is fashioned anew from moment to moment according to the measure in which the mind is purified and according to the sort of situation in which it finds itself, whether this be the result of external contingencies or its own doing. It is certain, moreover, that nobody is ever able to keep praying in the same way. A person prays in one manner when cheerful, in another when weighed down by sadness or a sense of hopelessness. When one is flourishing spiritually, prayer is different from when one is oppressed by the extent of one's struggles. One prays in this manner when seeking pardon for sins, and in another when asking for a particular grace or virtue or the elimination of a particular vice. Sometimes prayer is conditioned by compunction, occasioned by the thought of hell and desire for the good things to come. A person prays in one manner when in dangerous straits and in another when enjoying quiet and security. Prayer is sometimes illumined by the revelation of heavenly mysteries but, at other times, one is forced to be content with the sterile practice of virtue and the experience of aridity.[54]

In a later section Cassian describes how prayer can be invested with a wide range of different qualities, even though the same form of prayer is used.[55] It is logical, however, that our choice of prayer form would also be subject to variation, according to the seasons of our lives and the specific fluctuations of recent experience. Each day may see a different blend of the various forms of prayer, made according to the internal and external possibilities which present themselves. A passage from the *Philokalia* exposes this point:

> You should spend some of your time in psalmody, some of your time in reciting prayers (by heart), and you must allow some time to examine and guard your thoughts. Do not set limits to yourself as regards psalmody and oral prayer but do as much as the Lord gives you strength for: do not neglect reading and inner prayer. Do some of one, some of another, and so you will spend your day in a manner pleasing to God. Our fathers, who were perfect, had no cut and dried rule, but spent the whole day in following their own rule: some psalmody, some recital of prayers aloud, some examination of thoughts and some, though little, care of food. They did all this in fear of God, for it is said, "Whatsoever ye do, do all to the glory of God" (1 Cor. 10:31).[56]

The life-relatedness of prayer means that the greatest obstacles to our entering into deep prayer will be our rampant passions. These may be kept temporarily at bay by turning our attention to activities; but when we leave aside our outward pursuits and move into the emptiness of prayer, immediately our unprocessed feelings surge into consciousness. "Inasmuch as you have not renounced the passions but resist virtue and truth with your spirit, you will not find fragrant perfume in your bosom."[57] Anger, sadness, lust, vainglory will flood the awareness and subvert our attempts at prayer. According to Evagrius we must anticipate that our prayer will be an occasion for the onset of the daimonic and so come to prayer with the idea that stalwart resistance will be necessary.[58]

Cassian who continues Evagrius' emphasis on the necessity of a quiet mind,[59] sees anger and sadness as being the two chief hindrances to prayer. "The disturbance caused by anger or sadness is especially to be eliminated at its source."[60] Not denied, repressed and driven underground, but faced and sorted out. In his more extensive treatment of anger and sadness in the *Institutes*, Cassian makes it clear that he is not so much concerned about changing the external circumstances which provoked these reactions. What he advises is concentrating on our subjective part in the matter. When we discover strong feelings of anger or sadness, we should try to discover *why* we have responded to a particular situation with (perhaps) disproportionate emotion. Has there been a build-up of pressure which eventually caused an explosion (or implosion) over something minor? Have we unilaterally invested events with a symbolic significance so that our interpretation of them may not coincide with that of others involved? Have we lost sight of our ultimate goal in life, so that proximate hopes and fears assume unnecessary importance? Has the dimension of faith diminished in our daily life? This last question is of particular importance to our prayer.

Christian life and Christian prayer involve participating in the paschal mystery of Jesus. It is a question of accepting death in the hope of eternal life. Trying to avoid such death is a certain recipe for prayerlessness. As one of Camus' characters exclaims, "Who could have believed that crime consists less in making others die, than in not dying oneself?"[61] The free refusal of an invitation to die or the lack of acceptance of a death imposed by circumstances poisons prayer. It often sets up a complicated cycle of rationalization and compensation to cover its tracks, but to no avail. "The less one prays the worse it goes."[62] A minor conversion is needed if one is to continue with prayer.

In speaking of one of the clauses of the Lord's Prayer, Cassian expresses the idea that our ability to pray is concretely linked with our acceptance of God's providence in our regard.

No one can say this [Thy will be done] sincerely except one who believes that every circumstance, favorable and unfavorable, is designed by God's providence for good, and that God thinks and cares more for the good of his people and their salvation than we do ourselves.[63]

The prayer of Jesus in Gethsemane is a model for us in this regard. Do we have faith that God is acting in the events of daily life? To the extent that we do not, negative incidents will play havoc with our emotional life. We will not be like the ancient martyrs who sang Alleluia on their way to death; we will be too busy trying to avoid pain or seeking revenge. There is a time for righting wrongs and taking positive action against injustice. There is also a time to let go of our grievances and, in the unequivocal image of the Sermon on the Mount, to turn the other cheek.

Faith in God's providence is not only a means to avoiding defeat through anger and sadness, it also acts counter to another inhibitor of prayer, *acedia*. The vice of *acedia* consists in a refusal to take seriously the challenge of the moment. It is an attitude of habitually tending toward the easier and less demanding option, stretching concessions to their furthest limits and minimizing obligations. One who is defective at the level of values, who has the "confusion of thoughts" about which the Fathers wrote so often, cannot reach any depth of personal vision or commitment, and is usually content to breeze along the path of least resistance. Keeping out of serious trouble but not being creative or doing anything beneficial to others. Surviving. Perhaps practicing a little passive aggression. A life lived in subservience to this sort of escapism cannot but be superficial. It has no capacity to serve as the ground of prayer.

If we have faith in God's working through daily events and experiences, we will often feel drawn to venture something new. Our day will progressively be punctuated by calls to a more Christ-like manner of living, an act of forgiveness or service or self-effacement. To the extent that we are open to such invitations and respond positively, our prayer will remain fresh, and there will be a suppleness about our life in general that will ensure that prayer will flow freely, not only at our regular slots, but unexpectedly as well.

In fact emphasizing the continuity between prayer and life is a great enrichment. It allows us to build prayer into our ordinary conscious patterns of thought and actions. Far from being an exercise in greater and greater abstraction, it becomes simply a matter of moving closer to the person of Jesus Christ, as he is known to the ordinary Christian. It is an increasing penetration of the potential for inner richness inherent in daily life; an ability to find savor in the common expressions of doctrine and prayer current in the believing community.

This is not to deny the validity of an apophatic approach to prayer. Any searcher of the inner depths will encounter darkness, negativity and unknowing. But there is more to life than apophasis.[64] God's word is a lamp in the darkness: Christ is our light, our "Yes" to God (2 Cor. 1:20). God speaks to us in so many ways and we, in the liturgy, are given words with which to respond. Our concepts of God are imperfect approximations, but they help us to persevere in our journey toward the God who is beyond thought, and to give a word of support to others who travel the same road.

Thus the ancient monks were convinced that what happened outside prayer was the chief determinant of the quality of our experience of prayer. It was for this reason that detailed guidance about techniques of prayer is singularly lacking in this tradition. There was a recognition that to pray well one had to leave aside whatever would fill the mind. Thus austerity in lifestyle, starkness in church furnishing and sobriety of spirit ensured that inner emptiness might be fully experienced. There was a pragmatic openness to whatever fostered devotion without too much concern about the details. They were not purists or snobs, but they had an instinct for what was real—which usually guided them towards the humblest option. Authenticity and sincerity were prized in prayer; quantity was thought less important. The norm was: prayer should be kept short and made frequently. Long spells of intense prayer can become a substitute for life instead of its seasoning. Without a special grace, excessive prayer can lead to tension and, for various reasons, make life difficult. The result is a progressive cleavage between what happens during prayer and one's experience of daily life. The correct balance tends to result in a progressive overlap of prayer and life: harmony, mutual interaction.

When prayer begins to spill out of its regular sessions to punctuate work, leisure or sleep, then this is usually a healthy sign.

*   *   *

At first glance, the western monastic tradition of prayer seems not to be very substantial. So little is said and so much taken for granted. Even this lack of particularity is part of the approach. There is not much room for fanfare or self-congratulation, just continuing fidelity to the same means which are available to every Christian: the theological virtues, good living, discipline, patience, humility and commonsense. Learning to live in the context of God's love. A solid, pragmatic tradition, if we look closely, but nothing about *mantras* or *sutras, asanas,* or *pranayamas,* no theory of *shakras.* It does have its particular disciplines, but their names are not exotic. Its attitudes and practices are familiar to us. Fundamentally, it envisages a way of life and a way of prayer which are characterized by being ordinary, obscure and laborious. It seems very close to the way of the Gospels. The challenge is not in its novelty but in the demands of persevering in it.

NOTES

[1]Guigo, *Meditations* (trans. John J. Jolin), Milwaukee: Marquette University Press, 1951, #149, p. 24.

[2]Bernard of Clairvaux, SC 57.11; SBO, 2.126.12.

[3]Bernard of Clairvaux, SC 69.1; SBO 2.202.11-12. "Knowledge, labor, and patience are everything in art: what can occur in an instant has been in process for years." Translated from Fernand Pouillon, *Les Pierres Sauvages,* Paris: Editions du Seuil, 1964, p. 22.

[4]Dom Roger Huddleston (ed.), *The Spiritual Letters of Dom John Chapman, OSB,* London: Sheed and Ward, 1935, Letter 12, p. 53.

[5]Friedrich Heiler, *Prayer: A Study in the History and Psychology of Religion,* New York: Oxford University Press, 1958, pp. 10-11. He is speaking about the external shape of prayer, but what he says about the interaction between spontaneity and fixity applies also to the decision to pray: whether it be a spur of the moment choice or an option habitually built into the day.

[6]Hans Urs von Balthasar, *The Glory of the Lord: A Theological Aesthetics,* Volume One, *Seeing the Form,* San Francisco: Ignatius Press, 1982, pp. 23-24.

[7]Balthasar, *The Glory of the Lord,* pp. 26-27.

[8]See RB 49.

[9]Balthasar, *The Glory of the Lord,* p. 30.

[10]Bernard of Clairvaux, SC 23.15; SBO 1.148.20. The same phrase is used by John of Fécamp, *Letter to a Nun,* line 78; Jean Leclercq and J.-P. Bonnes, *Un Maître de la vie spirituelle: Jean de Fécamp,* Paris: Vrin, 1946, p. 308.

[11]Holiness is often understood as legitimating a lifestyle. Thus Peter of St John wrote to Hato of Troyes, "If the Order of Cluny were not pleasing to God, then these holy Fathers would hardly have attained heavenly glory." Giles Constable and J. Kritzeck (eds.), *Petrus Venerabilis: 1156-1956,* Rome: Studia Anselmiana 40, 1956, p. 50, line 37.

[12]It is for this reason that the study of the phenomenology of prayer is illuminating. The classical work is that of Friedrich Heiler, cited above. More recent is Maurice Nédoncelle, *The Nature and Use of Prayer,* London: Burns and Oates,

1964. This somewhat banal title is less revealing than the French original: *Prière Humaine, Prière divine.*

[13]Athansius of Alexandria, *Letter to Marcellinus*, (trans. R. Gregg), New York: Paulist Press, 1980, p. 111.

[14]Quoted in John Cassian, *Conferences*, 9.31; SChr 54, p. 66.

[15]*The Cloud of Unknowing*, ch. 70. In the edition of Phyllis Hodgson published for the Early English Text Society, *The Cloud of Unknowing and the Book of Privy Counselling*, Oxford University Press, 1944, p. 124.

[16]*The Cloud of Unknowing*, ch. 68, ed. Hodgson, pp. 121-122.

[17]*The Book of Privy Counselling*, ed. Hodgson, p. 152.

[18]*The Cloud of Unknowing*, ch. 34, ed. Hodgson, p. 70.

[19]In SC 47.8; SBO 2.66.17-26, Bernard argues that our concentration on the inspired text must be such that even useful spiritual thoughts should be left aside for the time being in order to give full attention to the meaning embedded in the text by the Holy Spirit.

[20]A useful pointer to the seriousness with which the Lord's Prayer was approached in primitive Christianity is Robert L. Simpson, *The Interpretation of Prayer in the Early Church*, Philadelphia: The Westminster Press, 1965. A listing of patristic commentaries on the Our Father is given on pp. 176-177.

[21]Heiler, *Prayer*, p. 17.

[22]A glance at Cassian's commentary on the first four phrases of the Lord's Prayer in *Conferences* 9.18, demonstrates that the elements listed above were clearly regarded as significant in the ambiance from which he wrote.

[23]Apart from RM 50.9-15 and 62-63. In the Rule of Fructuosus 1.64, it is envisaged for juniors.

[24]Jerome Kodell, OSB, "*Lectio Divina* and the Prayer Journal," *Review for Religious* 39 (1980), p. 587.

[25]Texts are given in Adalbert de Vogüé, "*Lectiones sanctas libenter audire*: Silence, Lecture et prières chez saint Benoît," *Benedictina* 27 (1980), pp. 12-16.

[26]Bernard of Clairvaux, Adv. 3.2; SBO 4.176.7-13.

[27]Cf. Bernard of Clairvaux, Adv. 5.2; SBO 4.189.12-20.

[28]Except in the comparatively rare case of those who habitually over-indulge in *lectio*. In this case the physical organism has more sense than they do. If they try to stay in the bath too long, it pulls out the plug.

[29]The section continues: "He often grumbles that he has stayed such a long time in the same place and yet has made no progress. He sighs and complains that he will reap no spiritual fruit so long as he is joined to such a group. He laments that there will be no spiritual fruit so long as he remains in this place. He is well able to govern others and be helpful to them, but here he cannot be a source of growth to anyone and no one profits from his direction or teaching. He sings the praises of far-distant monasteries and describes locations which make progress easier and are more conducive to health. He paints a picture of the pleasant community of the brothers there and the high spiritual quality of the way of life. Meanwhile everything nearby is rough. Not only is there no good example among the brothers who live in this place, it is impossible to find food

for the body without a great deal of labor. He comes to the conclusion that he cannot be sure of salvation if he remains in this place, and since he would die if he remained in his cell, he goes forth from it at the first available opportunity."

[30]John Cassian, *Institutes*, 10.2-6; SChr 109, pp. 384-392.

[31]"It is ridiculous to concern oneself with idle matters in order to avoid idleness." William of St Thierry, *Golden Epistle*, #82; SChr 223, p. 206.

[32]Guerric of Igny, *Sermons*, 38.4; SChr 202, p. 292. Translated by monks of Mount Saint Bernard Abbey, *Liturgical Sermons*, Volume Two (Cistercian Fathers Series 32), Spencer: Cistercian Publications, 1971, p. 114.

[33]Aelred of Rievaulx, *Sermo in Adventu Domini*, #11, PL 184.823a-b. This is regarded as the first of Aelred's series of sermons *De Oneribus*.

[34]Aelred of Rievaulx, *Speculum Caritatis* 2.72 (Ch. 24); CChrM1. p. 100.

[35]Gregory the Great, *Gospel Homilies*, 36.1, PL 76.1266.

[36]Gregory the Great, *Gospel Homilies*, 25.2, PL 76.1191a.

[37]*Ibid.*

[38]John Cassian, *Conferences*, 9.26; SChr 54, p. 63.

[39]John Cassian, *Conferences*, 9.27; SChr 54, p. 63.

[40]John Cassian, *Conferences*, 9.30; SChr 54, p. 65.

[41]John Cassian, *Conferences*, 9.27; SChr 54, p. 63.

[42]The author of *The Cloud of Unknowing, A Pistle of Discrecioun of Stirrings*, in Phyllis Hodgson (ed.), *Deonise Hid Divinite and Other Treatises on Contemplative Prayer Related to The Cloud of Unknowing* published for The Early English Text Society by Oxford University Press, London, 1958, p. 69.

[43]Bernard of Clairvaux, Quad. 5.5; SBO 4.374.20-21.

[44]Bernard's phrase describes one of these routine modulations of spiritual experience: "In all these things it is a matter of custom rather than delight.... I keep the commandments, I suppose, but, in doing so, my soul is like a waterless land," SC 9.3; SBO 1.43.22.

[45]This includes the effects of outward realities which (knowingly or not) we have internalized and which may have a delayed reaction, causing their effects long after the initial exposure. Thomas Merton excluded from his concept of the "inner self" these components of the unconscious mind. "Those recesses of the unconscious in which neurotic and psychotic derangements have their center, belong in reality to man's exterior self; because the exterior self is not limited to consciousness." See "Inner Experience: Some Notes on Contemplation," *Cistercian Studies* 18 (1983), p. 126.

[46]St. John Climacus, *The Ladder of Divine Ascent*, London: Faber, 1959, Step 28, #34, p. 255.

[47]John Cassian, *Conferences*, 9.3; SChr 54, pp. 42-43.

[48]See "Mindfulness of God in the Monastic Tradition," Cistercian Studies 17, (1982), pp. 111-126. See above, pp. 61-77.

[49]See also "Saint Benedict's Approach to Prayer," Cistercian Studies 15 (1980), pp. 327-343, above, pp. 17-34.

[50]See John Cassian, *Conferences*, 9.2; SChr 54, p. 41: "It is for this reason that it is not correct immediately to treat of the experience of prayer, since prayer comes

to its perfection only with the practice of all the virtues. It is necessary, on the contrary, to make a list of all those things which must be eliminated or acquired as a means to prayer, and to discuss them first."

[51]St Augustine, *On the Psalms*, 29/2.1; CChr 38, p. 174.

[52]See "In Pursuit of Ecstasy: Reflections on Bernard of Clairvaux's *De Diligendo Deo*," *Monastic Studies* 16 (1985), pp. 139-156.

[53]For a more complete treatment of the theme of *alternatio*, see *Athirst for God, Spiritual Desire in Bernard of Clairvaux's Sermons on the Song of Songs*, Cistercian Studies Series 77, Kalamazoo: Cistercian Publications, 1988, pp. 251-280.

[54]John Cassian, *Conferences*, 9.8; SChr 54, pp. 48-49.

[55]John Cassian, *Conferences*, 10.10; SChr 54, pp. 85-90.

[56]E. Kadloubovsky and G.E.H. Palmer, *Writings from the Philokalia on Prayer of the Heart*, London: Faber and Faber, 1951, p. 357. The quotation is #45 in the section entitled, "Holy Fathers Barsanuphius and John: Directions in Spiritual Work."

[57]Evagrius Ponticus, *Chapters on Prayer*, (trans. J.-E. Bamberger), Cistercian Studies Series 4, Spencer: Cistercian Publications, 1970, #141, p. 78.

[58]This is manifest throughout the *Chapters on Prayer*. As an alternative source of harassment and distraction he nominates mosquitoes: #100 and #105, (p. 72).

[59]John Cassian, *Conferences*, 9.2; SChr 54, p. 40: *Ad immobilem tranquillitatem mentis ac perpetuam nititur puritatem*. This seems to be based on Evagrius' idea of *katastasis*: the stability and freedom which possesses the mind as the result of the sustained practice of virtue. The term is synonymous with the more familiar *apatheia*.

[60]John Cassian, *Conferences*, 9.3; SChr 54, p. 42.

[61]Albert Camus, *The Fall*, Harmondsworth: Penguin Books, 1963, p. 83.

[62]See note 4, above.

[63]John Cassian, *Conferences*, 9.20; SChr 54, pp. 57-58.

[64]Fully apophatic prayer is especially ill-advised in the context of community life. One who has a taste only for dark, solitary contemplation will come to feel progressively alienated from the community, whose concerns will be dismissed as trivial, and its prayer. In this way one grows away from community interaction, from the liturgy and even from the Scriptures. "Objectless" meditation can sometimes serve a useful purpose at certain phases of life, and sometimes nothing else is possible. It is rarely prudent to pursue it exclusively.

Introductory Note

Ten years after the death of Thomas Merton I wrote "Thomas Merton Within a Tradition of Prayer." This was published in two parts in *Cistercian Studies* (13.4 [1978], pp. 372-378 and 14.1 [1979], pp. 81-92). It was subsequently reprinted in *The Legacy of Thomas Merton* (ed. Patrick Hart, Kalamazoo: Cistercian Publications [CS 92], 1986, pp. 25-47). After the elapse of another ten years I returned to the topic with another study of Merton's teaching on prayer, this time centered on his "Notes on Inner Experience." The material was assembled for a day organized by the Institute for Spiritual Studies to commemorate the twentieth anniversary of Merton's death.

In the article I have tried to provide some commentary on *Inner Experience*, especially by relating it to his other writings, notably *The Climate of Monastic Prayer* written about the same time.

Merton's Notes on "Inner Experience"
Twenty Years Afterwards

Michael Mott begins his biography of Thomas Merton by remarking on the diverse perceptions of Merton among those who had been his friends and associates.[1] A similar range of opinion is probably found also in those who know him more distantly through his writings. Merton's particular gift seems to have been that he was able to express with clarity and passion what his readers were feeling in a vague, unformulated way. For many of them, contact with Thomas Merton's writings was the channel by which they came to experience themselves and their aspirations more intensely. He was a catalyst of some deep enlightenment. As a result, Merton became forever bonded with their inmost spiritual feelings to the extent that he became a living symbol of spiritual awakening. Not a red-blooded individual but a hologram or projection of a deeply-felt spiritual ideal, providentially inaccessible behind enclosure walls amid distant Kentucky knolls.

Many people in different situations found themselves initiated into spirituality through random contact with Merton. Listen to the actor Richard Moir being interviewed by Caroline Jones:

> I was looking in a novel called *Real Presence* by American author Richard Bush.... There was a quote from this man called Thomas Merton in the front of the book which was, I thought, terrific, beautiful.... It caused me to look into Thomas Merton and contemplation, which is where I'm at. Nothing inspires me or interests me more except perhaps pieces of the Bible and so on. I find this good —contemplation. I'd like to be a contemplative, I think.... I read a piece of Merton every day and I write it down and I just attempt to allow it to sink in....[2]

The sense of close spiritual kinship with Merton probably explains why so many reacted strongly when the uncensored details of his life began to be published in the decade after his death. Although there were harbingers in the 1960s, such as Merton's involvement with the peace movement and his increasing interest in eremitism and in non-Christian religions,[3] the process really began with the breathless recital of the juicier revelations of *The Man in the Sycamore Tree* by *Time Magazine*. As if his pre-monastic past were not enough, the rumor machine continued to propagate a lengthening list of anecdotes about hermitage parties, outings, picnics, beer-drinking, vocational doubts, eastern religions, difficulties with the institutional Church, profanity and the subversion of authority, finally triumphing in the story of a romantic involvement. No one was interested in hearing any more edifying stories about Merton.[4]

For many people these stories were more than human interest items about the private life of a public figure. They touched very deep levels. Some were scandalized and felt betrayed as if their trust in him had been misplaced. It seems, however, that many more of his admirers were greatly encouraged to learn of the patchiness of Merton's virtue. It gave them hope. The message they gleaned from the untouched portrait was that their own continuing deviations from the ideal were not an inseparable barrier to their continuing spiritual quest.[5]

Many readers identify with Merton—and not only those who (in fact or in fantasy) flocked to Trappist monasteries in his train. This bonding certainly does no harm to Merton Industries, Inc., but it does make it a little difficult to find objective analyses of Merton's thought. Many persons who begin to write about Merton end up propagating themselves.[6]

There are other difficulties as well. Merton, at various stages in his literary career, generated far more ideas than he had the capacity (or the opportunity) to synthesize. This means that there are internal tensions, if not outright contradictions, in his writings. Who can tell what he really thinks?[7] Moreover, the different contexts which triggered particular lines of thought have been largely lost, so that there is always the possibility of mistaking an ephemeral aside for the solemn proclamation of an eternal verity. It may simply be an idea gleaned from a random conversation that he wears for a couple of days before finally discarding it.[8]

There are always hidden factors to be considered about anything Merton wrote: his own attitude towards his writings, his later reservations and even disgust in regard to some of them.[9] Those unfamiliar with the monastic sub-culture may be unaware of the extent to which Merton was influenced by it, sometimes without himself being aware of the extent to which he had been formed.[10] Finally there are values which he embodied in living which seemed so self-evident to him that they did not find literary expression.[11]

There is a considerable body of *Mertonia* published: biographies, collections, monographs, academic theses, articles and impressions. Most of them deal with issues that genuinely interested Thomas Merton in his lifetime and many of them contribute to our better understanding of these matters. I am less sure that much progress has been made toward isolating Merton's characteristically complex stance in such areas of interest. To some extent he remained a very private person even behind the barrage of material published about him.

It would seem worthwhile to formulate some sort of methodology before tackling a theme in Merton. In dealing with a pervasive theme such as contemplation, it is even more important to go to the trouble of trying to determine what Merton actually believed, what was his own experience and how he changed or developed.

In writing this, I cannot pretend that I have achieved this point of understanding, nor even that I shall attempt to do so in the course of this article. I begin by stating the difficulty as a means of underlining the tentative nature of the remarks which follow.

1. "Inner Experience"

If there is any single work which has a claim to representing Merton's mature thought on a particular subject, it must be his unpublished manuscript, *Inner Experience: Some Notes on Contemplation*.[12] As its title indicates, it is not a scientific treatise. It is a sustained discourse about contemplation and related matters. It seems not to have been governed by inner logic but by free association. A thought is triggered and developed. It is pushed to the limits of Merton's experience of it, perhaps developed in alternate colors and then, abruptly, left aside. Almost immediately its antithesis emerges from the wings and occupies the stage. No true synthesis is reached. There is just an eclectic juxtaposition of overlapping but not synonymous propositions. Because of this sense of incompleteness, the total effect is dynamic. It is like stepping into a rehearsal, a workshop or a busy kitchen. The elements are assembled in an atmosphere of deliberate disarray. While one waits the product begins to take shape. One is surrounded by energy and although only a spectator one feels involved in the process of creation. Reading *Inner Experience* had this impact on me. So many elements; so much energy![13]

Merton's plan to write a comprehensive treatise on contemplation remained unfulfilled, though it absorbed his attention spasmodically during the last years of his life and its elements fed into other schemes during these years.[14] From 1961 he produced no less than four drafts. It seems that he intended to review the material once more after his return from Asia. This means that *Inner Experience* took shape during Merton's most interesting decade. During that time he evolved considerably both on a personal level and in his attitudes. A significant aid to interpreting the text is another book which he wrote on the subject; as it happens, his last.[15] From a methodological point of view it would be interesting to work with a synopsis, comparing the four drafts and watching the material evolve. Add in its relationship with contemporary events and other writings of the period and there would be some hope of appreciating the book's particular dynamic.

Inner Experience draws from all Merton's assets. It brings together the Scriptures, the writings of the mystics and of the Fathers of the Church (some of whom were not available in translation at the time Merton wrote), various non-Christian traditions, philosophers and philosophies. All these are piled on top of one another within the framework of his own experience, interpreted by decades of study and enhanced by the understanding he gained from dialogue with others. No matter that he wrote easily, Merton was no light weight.

The end of the product is exciting, but not as smooth as he probably would have liked. Some readers have found it less than totally persuasive. Because of their own expertise they are more aware of the holes in Merton's presentation. To anyone who reads the text closely, his leaps from one tradition to another can seem facile. No doubt he has serious and solid reasons for the opinions he expresses, but he does not always enlighten his reader as to what those reasons are. What does it mean to say that there is pseudo-gnosticism in Marxist thought?[16] Will every reader concur in the view that there is in Philoxenus of Mabbug "a striking affinity with the epistemological bases of Zen Buddhism"?[17] Is it helpful to assert that "the verses [from the *Bhagavad-Gita*] can easily be harmonized with St. Augustine, due allowance being made for divergences in ontological theory"?[18] In such arcane matters, many readers will have difficulty understanding what Merton is saying, yet somehow or other will feel themselves carried along to his conclusions by his irresistible authority. Is it lèse-majesté to suggest that, since Merton is no longer around to nuance his views, we read what he has written with a cautiously critical eye?

If this is true about scholarly topics, it is also true about Merton's observations about contemporary society, the Church and monastic life. The value of the practical recommendations he makes[19] depends on the accuracy of his perceptions and the absence of substantial change since the mid-1960s. It was paradoxical that Merton, a profoundly contemporary man, should be so out of sympathy with so much that was contemporary—and with those persons whose lives were inextricably bound up with the things he despised. Readers must ask themselves whether Merton's "anti-modernism" is a necessary component of a prayerful life.[20] The fact of the matter is that his view of western society was simplistic and, as a consequence, his solutions often verged on the romantic. His strong feelings occasionally led him to make extravagant statements, such as:

> The conscious life of modern man is completely lost in intellectual abstractions, sensual fantasies, political, social and economic clichés, and in the animal cunning of the detective or the salesman.... The tragedy of modern man is that his creativity, his spirituality and his contemplative independence are inexorably throttled by a superego that has sold itself without question or compromise to the devil of technology.[21]

In many such outbursts there seems to be more heat than his argument warrants. One is left with the distinct impression that Merton is veering toward autobiography again. He is reacting against those elements of his personal history which had brought him pain, projecting them onto a social and even cosmic scale.

Inner Experience is to be read intelligently because there is much in it that is excellent, some of which does not find expression elsewhere. To appreciate its quality it is necessary first to identify and leave aside some of its infelicities.

In this project Merton aimed to demonstrate that there is a universality in spiritual experience which transcends the various attempts by religions (and anti-religions) to provide theoretical explanations. The way to achieve unity of the human family is not through a reconciliation of doctrines and the elaboration of a theoretical synthesis. It is to look to the unity of human experience of the spiritual. Because there is but one human nature, human experience of transcendent reality is cross-cultural. Merton's concern in this work is with the *subject* of contemplation, the *person* who has the experience.

Merton aims to show this by drawing on his wide reading in different traditions to illustrate the fact that descriptions of the contemplative experience display a marked degree of convergence. Interpretations vary, but the experiences seem compatible.

If this is so, then, according to Merton, those who are contemplatives can serve as bridges between different traditions. "A contemplative is one who has transcended divisions to reach a unity beyond division.... His mission is to be a complete and whole man, with an instinctive and generous need to further the same wholeness in others, and in all mankind."[22] Far from being Catholic mystics or Hindu mystics, their experience belongs to the human family as a whole, even though it is interpreted differently in different traditions. Merton thinks that genuine contemplatives owe it to themselves and to others to become familiar with other traditions, since such exposure can progressively throw light on our particular blind spots. "Up to the present, our judgments have been too vague and undocumented, and have borne witness chiefly to our own ignorance."[23] This begins, perhaps, at a practical level but progressively it will involve the acceptance of some elements of theory: the theory of meditation, to begin with, but perhaps aspects of alternative cosmologies and theologies as well.

All of which could lead to a charge of "relativism" and the fear of this would have been sufficient to have induced Merton to have insisted that the work not be published. In fact, the text as it stands is reasonably "safe." It was certainly adventurous in the early 1960s, but nowadays its content is less singular. It could have begun to appear heterodox if the project had continued to evolve, but perhaps Merton was more timid in such matters than is generally appreciated. He was an intelligent man, well-educated and widely read; as such he must have been aware that his strictly theological expertise was less developed than other skills. As a result he tended to be cautious in his published opinions on borderline questions. He may have been bold as a social critic but there is an element of defensiveness in many of his theological treatments. This is true of *Inner Experience*; it seems that the author was unwilling to express himself openly on the topic that was at the heart of his book. Instead he skirts around the margins, throwing up all sorts of hints, seemingly hoping that the reader will arrive at the conclusions he wished to convey.

For all its limitations and incompleteness, *Inner Experience* is a key text and is likely to remain a significant element in understanding Merton's thought and, on a more global level, a key text for appreciating the unity of contemplative experience throughout different cultures and traditions. As such, it is worth examining some of its essential concepts more closely.

2. The Person Who Contemplates

Twenty years after his death Merton's books are still current. They are being read by many who never experienced much of the preconciliar Church and know little of its luminaries. Such readers need to be reminded that Merton lived in a different world. When Merton was converted to Catholicism, he came under the intellectual influence of Neo-Thomism, the Church-approved restatement of the philosophy and theology of St. Thomas Aquinas and Scholasticism. His friendship with Dan Walsh brought him under the sway of such figures as Jacques Maritain and Etienne Gilson.[24] Merton, like so many of his contemporaries, was so formed by the compelling rationality of this school of thought that, even though he did not follow its method or use much of its vocabulary, his thinking was irretrievably sharpened by having been exposed to its categories.

There is one important distinction which Merton drew from Neo-Thomism which is of fundamental importance to his view of contemplation. This is the distinction between individuality and personality —two words which are often used synonymously.[25]

In Scholastic thought, and in Merton, *individuality* is not such a good thing. It derives from the material component of human being. It is what separates one from others and is equally the source of fragmentation or compartmentalization within oneself. As such it is the enemy both of personal integration and of spiritual union with other persons. Individuality can be acted upon by forces external to oneself and is shaped by them. As a result its authenticity is dependent on the integrity and humanity of the formative ambiance. It is not completely subject to the personal will. An individuality molded according to the likeness of a crass and unspiritual society thus becomes a fifth column, secretly working against the genuine freedom and growth of the person.

Personality, on the other hand, is the human being's participation in the sphere of spirit. It derives from our being created in the image and likeness of God. It signifies interiority to self, the capacity for knowledge and love. Thus it is the source both of one's own functioning as a spiritual person and of one's union with other persons and with God. Personality confers freedom, since it ensures that no one need be fully defined by extrinsic factors. Each is able to know and to will and, ultimately, to choose a destiny. The endowment of personality means that we can become recipients of grace and so begin to operate at a level far beyond human excellence.

An essay by Jacques Maritain entitled "Individuality and Personality" is almost essential reading at this point. Two paragraphs may serve to delineate the approach he takes:

It should be noted here that man must realize through his will that of which his nature is but the sketch. In terms of a commonplace—and a very profound one—which goes back to Pindar, man must become what he is. And this he must do at a sorrowful cost and with formidable risks. He himself, in the moral order, must win his liberty and his personality. In other words, as observed above, his action can follow the bent either of personality or of material individuality.... If the development occurs in the direction of material individuality, it will be oriented towards the detestable ego whose law is to *grasp* or absorb for itself. At the same time personality, as such, will tend to be adulterated and to dissolve. But if the development occurs in the direction of spiritual personality, man will be oriented towards the generous self of the heroes and saints. Thus, man will be truly a person only insofar as the life of the spirit and of liberty reigns over that of the sense and passions.

Here we are confronted with the crucial problem of the education of man. There are some who confound the person with the freedom of expansion to which it aspires, they reject all asceticism: these would have the tree bear fruit without having been pruned. Instead of self-fulfillment, the man, thus educated, becomes atrophied and the sense exacerbated, or else all that is most human in man recoils into a vacuum veiled in frivolity.[26]

Maritain's was not simply a casual philosophical opinion which Merton happened to encounter in his years of studying theology. It was an expression of much that was best in the thinking of Catholics in the 1940s and 1950s. There is an emphasis on the innate spiritual aspects of the human person with the consequent relegation of the material to a merely relative position. There is a conviction that the search for God is in profound harmony with the deepest strands of human reality. There is at least an implicit assumption that one who wishes to live a spiritual life must seek protection against the malign influences of a materialist world. That Merton was thoroughly formed in such a philosophy is not irrelevant to his subsequent doctrine on contemplative prayer.

It is interesting that Merton, as a student at Columbia, denied much interest in Thomism, preferring Eastern thought.[27] Perhaps even at that stage Merton was aware that Neo-Thomism—especially when parroted at several removes from genuine philosophical insight—contained some dangerous possibilities. In particular, there were those who did not understand Aquinas' subtle terminology and thus inflated the distinction between body and spirit into a full-blown separation, with many disastrous consequences. To compensate for this latent tendency to dualism, Merton later returned to the East. Not all who follow him on this latter part of his journey appreciate the complementary principles he had absorbed in his youth.

Contemplation involves personality. One whose life is dominated by individuality will be so fragmented that no access is possible to the point of "togetherness" at which the ego disappears and God is all. Such a one is disqualified from contemplation. Only an interior cataclysm can remove the obstacle or, failing that, years of labor in the pursuit of wholeness and undividedness. This is the point at which Merton begins his exposition:

> The first thing you have to do, before you start thinking about such a thing as contemplation, is to try to recover your basic natural unity, to reintegrate your compartmentalized being into a coordinated and simple whole, and learn to live as a unified human person. This means that you have to bring back together the fragments of your distracted existence so that when you say "I" there is really someone present to support the pronoun you have uttered.[28]

If we feel called to contemplation, the first thing to do is to allow ourselves to be unlayered of all the inauthentic accretions that have hitherto constituted our persona.

✓ All sin starts from the assumption that my false self, the self that exists only in my egocentric desires, is the fundamental reality of life to which everything else in the universe is ordered. Thus I use up my life in the desire for pleasures and the thirst for experiences, for power, honor, knowledge and love, to clothe this false self and construct its nothingness into something objectively real. And I wind experiences round myself and cover myself with pleasures and glory like bandages in order to make myself perceptible to myself and to the world, as if I were an invisible body that could only become visible when something visible covered its surface.

But there is no substance under the things with which I am clothed. I am hollow, and my structure of pleasures and ambitions has no foundation. I am objectified in them. But they are all destined by their very contingency to be destroyed. And when they are gone there will be nothing left of me but my own nakedness and emptiness and hollowness, to tell me that I am my own mistake.[29]

We are called to be rid of the "exterior self" and to allow the "inner self" to emerge.[30] This inner self is a mystery. We do not yet know its full stature because it is still in a state of becoming. It is unique. It cannot be isolated and cultivated systematically. It is awakened in spiritual experience. Each appearance reveals a new facet of its beauty; its totality is never grasped, at least in this life.

> Unless we discover this deep self, which is hidden with Christ in God, we will never really know ourselves as persons. Nor will we know God. For it is by the doors of this deep self that we enter into the spiritual knowledge of God. (And indeed, if we seek our true selves it is not in order to contemplate ourselves, but to pass beyond ourselves and find him.) The "self" to which grace is opposed is not merely the passionate, disordered, confused self—the rambling and disheveled "ego"—but much more the tyrannical "super-egos," the rigid and deformed conscience which is our secret god and which with an infinitely jealous resourcefulness defends its throne against the coming of Christ.[31]

Merton compares this awakening of the inner self to the Zen experience of *Satori*: "a kind of inner explosion that blasts away the false exterior self and leaves nothing but his 'original face,' his 'original self before you were born.' "[32] And there is another surprise. The result appears externally as something very ordinary and unglamorous. Superficially there is no sudden change: the action has taken place at a very deep level of the personality; it will be years before any outward effect is discernible.

> The inner self is not an *ideal* self, especially not an imaginary, perfect creature fabricated to measure up to our compulsive need for greatness, heroism and infallibility. On the contrary, the real "I" is just simply ourself and nothing more. Nothing more, nothing less. Ourself in all our uniqueness, dignity, littleness and ineffable greatness ...[our] real and "homely" self, and nothing more, without glory, without self-aggrandizement, without self-righteousness, and without self-concern.[33]

Having once formulated this notion of the "inner self," Merton seeks to demonstrate its presence in the Christian mystical tradition, evoking the theme of the *imago Dei* and citing texts from Augustine, Tauler and John of the Cross. His conclusion is incisive:

> Since our inmost "I" is the perfect image of God, then when that "I" awakens, he finds within himself the Presence of Him Whose image he is. And, by a paradox beyond all human expression, God and his soul seem to have but one single "I."[34]

Immediately Merton nuances what he has written by countering the view that the inner self is unrelated to the external world: a theme that occupies many pages in *New Seeds of Contemplation*. The inner self remains linked to the outside world, but its relationship is one of spiritual freedom. It is not enslaved, but freely reaches out in charity. Love is indivisible: love for God cannot coexist with an absence of love for others. It was the sense of being loved which led us to the discovery of the inner self, the effect of that experience is to make us want to communicate to others the love we ourselves have received. The vigor of our contemplative life is dependent on the quality of our relationship with others:

> Here [the text from St Augustine he had just quoted] it is quite clear that charity, which is the life and awakening of the inner self, is in fact to a great extent awakened by the presence and the spiritual influence of other "selves" that are in Christ.[35]

Contemplation cannot occur in the context of a loveless life: instead a false mysticism results with excessive interest in "religious experiences" on the one hand, and a consuming passion for visions and miracles on the other.

> True Christian charity is stifled in such an atmosphere and contemplation has no place in it. All is heavy, thick, biased and dark with obsession, even though it lays claim to blinding and supernatural lights. It is a realm of dangerous appetites for command, of false visions and apocalyptic threats, of spiritual sensuality and of a mysticism charged with undertones of sex-perversion.[36]

In such a case Merton understands that the desire for spiritual life is authentic: it derives from God-given humanity. Because of ignorance, misinstruction, the "modern barbarism" of a technological society or other darker forces, this élan toward God has been twisted out of shape. It has degenerated into what Merton vigorously condemned as an "appetite for experiences—or, more crudely, for kicks—[which] is the greatest danger to the development of an authentic mystical life."[37]In fact, the contemplative life demands such sustained labor, it is no wonder that a consumer society, once it has glimpsed a desirable product, seeks to obtain it at a discount. "Hence the use of alcohol and drugs to obtain a spiritual release."[38] There are other substitutes: "emotional, sentimental, erotic and even bacchanalian."[39] The message is clear: to discover the inner self and so to begin leading a contemplative life it is first necessary to put a distance between ourselves and the "collective barbarism" of modern western society.

The reason for rejecting the ideology of the world around us is anthropological. Society imposes on us an image of human reality which works counter to the development of spiritual potential. The goals it offers as worthy of pursuit are incompatible with the contemplative life. So we need to be liberated from it. "The secular world is a world that pretends to exalt man's liberty, but in which man is in fact enslaved by the things on which he depends."[40] Instead we need to look more deeply into the wisdom of our Christian tradition, learning from other cultural strands where the acuity of our vision has been blunted. Human nature is one. Spiritual reality is one. The human experience of the spiritual, although it is interpreted and explained through the prism of different traditions is, likewise, ultimately one. To understand contemplation we need to deepen our grasp of the nature of the person who contemplates.

3. Preliminaries of Contemplation

Merton was interested in dialogue with other traditions. That is not to say that he was moving "beyond" Christianity. This becomes clear when we examine one of his definitions of contemplation: "At the moment, it is sufficient to say categorically that this contemplation is a deep participation in the Christ-life, a spiritual sharing in the union of God and man which is the hypostatic union."[41] Orthodoxy is essential, "because dogmatic error would in fact imply disastrous practical consequences in the spiritual life of each Christian."[42]

It is only in the light of Christ's total acceptance of all that is human that we can be reconciled to our humanity *in its totality*. "The basic and most fundamental problem of the spiritual life is the acceptance of our dark and hidden self...."[43] Spurious spirituality promises comfort and peace—but at the price of truth. A genuine attraction to contemplation is not an invitation to a life of restful contentment. It is more a matter of a continuing challenge to be free from complacency and comfortable delusions and to find one's only security in God.

> The important thing in contemplation is not enjoyment, not pleasure, not happiness, not peace but the transcendent experience of reality and truth in the act of a supreme and liberated spiritual love. The important thing in contemplation is not gratification and rest, but awareness, life, creativity and freedom.[44]

This is why one of the most common difficulties which people encounter and with which they often cannot deal is the sense of *dread* which confronts all who would walk this way. It was the theme of dread, no doubt borrowed from European existentialism, which formed an important focus in *The Climate of Monastic Prayer*—much to the surprise and confusion of many of his admirers.

> The monk who is truly a man of prayer and seriously faces the challenge of his vocation in all its depth is by that very fact exposed to existential dread. He experiences in himself the emptiness, the lack of authenticity, the quest for fidelity, the "lostness" of modern man, but he experiences all this in an altogether different and deeper way than does man in the modern world, to whom this disconcerting experience comes rather as an experience of boredom and of spiritual disorientation. The monk confronts his own humanity and that of his world at the deepest and most central point where the void seems to open out into black despair…. The monk faces the worst and discovers in it the hope of the best.[45]

Merton does not suggest surmounting dread by attaining a level of impassivity which enables the monk to burst through the pain barrier into the bliss of the other side. It is only a sense of solidarity with the paschal mystery of Christ's death and resurrection which renders the unavoidable experience of dread somewhat supportable. The only alternative is what Merton termed elsewhere, "Promethean mysticism."

> The Promethean instinct is as deep as man's weakness. This is to say, it is almost infinite. It has its roots in the bottomless abyss of man's own nothingness. It is the despairing cry that rises out of the darkness of man's metaphysical solitude—the inarticulate expression of a terror man will not admit to himself: his terror at having to be a person. For the fire Prometheus steals from the gods is his own incommunicable reality, his own spirit. It is the affirmation and vindication of his own being. Yet this being is a gift of God and it does not have to be stolen. It can only be had by a free gift—the very hope of gaining it by theft is pure illusion.[46]

It is not that the attempt to lead a spiritual life generates a dark mass of negativity. That burden is always ours, given by our humanity and fostered by forces in our culture. The ascent to truth means that progressively we become aware of the liabilities under which we labor. But there is more. A faith introduces a positive element to counter the source of such dread, which enables us to pass through it and so to attain a measure of spiritual freedom. It is only at this point that contemplation becomes possible.[47] The bottom line is simple: whatever deepens the reality of our belonging to Christ leads us directly (though not immediately) to contemplation. Whenever we deny our lower instincts and give assent to the grace of God, we move in that direction. "Union with the will of God in action is the necessary step to contemplate awareness of God."[48]

Merton speaks of three areas of "the active life" which have a role in leading toward contemplation: the liturgy, "union with God in action," and the efforts made to deepen prayer through asceticism, the ordering of life and application to spiritual exercises.[49] These are important and necessary concerns, but they are only preliminaries. They can help us develop the twin attitudes which make us responsive to grace offered: the desire of contemplation[50] and the sense of sin.[51] "No one can give himself completely and seriously to contemplation unless he is mentally and spiritually prepared."[52] It remains true, however, that the deepest experience of purification and contemplation is not the result of conscious actions on our part. We are recipients of God's action. The nexus between cause and effect is ruptured. What results is pure gift. The time of the giving, the form of the gift and the state of the recipient cannot be predicated. Contemplation comes from God: we are merely receivers.[53]

4. Experience of Contemplation

It is easier to say what contemplation is *not* than to offer a good description of it. Inevitably authors resort to superlatives in order to convey something of its reality. The result of this is to make it appear as something so exalted that it is beyond the capacity of ordinary people even to know the meaning of the word, much less to experience the reality itself. Merton was aware of this possibility and tried to offset it.

> Contemplation should not be exaggerated, distorted and made to seem great. It is essentially simple and humble. No one can enter into it except by the path of obscurity and self-forgetfulness. It implies justice to one's state in life, obedience, charity, self-sacrifice. No one should delude himself with contemplative aspirations if he is not willing to undertake first of all the ordinary labors and obligations of moral life.[54]

While it is true that "the contemplative life requires special mental and spiritual aptitudes, and one who does not have the necessary gifts should not presume to push his way into affairs that are beyond his capacity,"[55] if any are excluded permanently it is usually because they refuse to be humbled and become "little ones": they will not take seriously the challenges inherent in ordinary goodness. Far from being a pursuer of spiritual "highs,"

> the true contemplative is a lover of sobriety and obscurity. He prefers all that is quiet, humble, unassuming. He has no taste for spiritual excitements. They easily weary him. His inclination is to that which seemed to be nothing, which tells him little or nothing, which promises him nothing.[56]

"Genuine contemplation involves no tension."[57] It is not a high-powered, high-browed activity reserved for a self-styled intellectual elite. "Contemplation is not to be confused with abstraction. A contemplative life is not to be lived by permanent withdrawal within one's own mind."[58] Contemplation is simply an awareness of being united in love with the God of the Gospels: it is as open to the underprivileged as all the other gifts of grace.

Although contemplation adapts itself to the personality and circumstances of different people, it is possible to say something in general about what the experience is like. The utility of doing this is that it can enable us to identify its presence more deftly and so be capable of giving ourselves to it more fully and of allowing it to shape our lives.

Merton gives a list of eleven "essential elements of mystical contemplation,"[59] followed by five texts from the western mystical tradition which illustrate some of the points he has made.[60] As a summary its form is imperfect, with many repetitions and overlaps. As often happens when Merton does a list, the later items become longer and more diffuse. The first two are of two lines each, the last one rambles over more than two pages. It is an astringent diatribe against both authoritarian monasticism and the liturgical changes which scarcely belongs among "the essential elements of mystical contemplation."

In fact, the eleven points could probably be reduced to four fundamental propositions:

a. Contemplation transcends the conscious self. (#1, #2, #3)
b. Contemplation is to be identified with divine charity. (#4, #5, #6, #7)
c. Contemplation demands passivity of the subject. (#8)
d. Contemplation is marked by negativity. (#9, #10, #11)

It is worth reflecting briefly on each of these topics.

a. Contemplation transcends the conscious self

Mystical contemplation is not a work of the senses or imagination and it goes beyond the feelings generated at that level. Similarly, it is not simply the operation of the intellect or the will. "It is not the work of one faculty or another uniting the soul with an object outside itself."[61] If the "organ" of mystical experience is sought, then the heart must be nominated, "the deepest psychological ground of one's personality, the inner sanctuary where self-awareness goes beyond analytical reflection and opens out into metaphysical and theological confrontation with the Abyss of the unknown yet present—one who is 'more intimate to us than we are to ourselves.' "[62] To reach beyond the realm of consciousness and so arrive at the heart requires a generous measure of active detachment. Asceticism produces nothing; its task is to push into the background those alternative activities and preoccupations which could prevent the heart from being lifted up. "Contemplation presupposes a generous and total effort of self-control."[63] Only by such means can prayer be an expression of pure and disinterested love and not merely a subtle cloak disguising the pursuit of self-gratification.

b. Contemplation is to be identified with divine charity

Contemplative prayer is a gift of God; it cannot be achieved by any species of human effort. "The deciding factor in contemplation is the free and unpredictable action of God. He alone can grant the gift of mystical grace and make Himself known by the secret, ineffable contact that reveals his presence in the depths of the soul."[64] "Mystical contemplation...is a gift of God that absolutely transcends all the natural capacities of the soul and which no man can acquire by any effort of his own."[65] The fact that contemplation depends on the initiative of God relativizes the human contribution, so that it necessarily is a surprising development. "True contemplation is not a psychological trick but a theological grace. It can come to us only as a gift, and not as a result of our own clever use of spiritual techniques."[66]

Furthermore, it is not something confined to an imagined elite.[67] Contemplation is an awareness that is co-extensive with grace. As such it begins with that state of union with God which is initiated with baptism which "brings not only faith but the power to taste the fullness of faith in contemplation."[68] This new life of grace is nourished by the sacraments and by the whole sanctifying impact of the liturgy:

The mere existence of the Church's liturgy is then a call to active contemplation. To remain withdrawn from the liturgy and outside it is to exclude oneself from possibilities of active contemplation that the Church offers to all, with many graces and lights that she alone can contribute to her children.... The Blessed Sacrament is not a sign or figure of contemplation. It should not be surprising then that one of the most normal ways of entering into infused prayer is through the graces given in Holy Communion.[69]

Another term for the fundamental state of union with God from which stems the "super-sensory intuition of the divine"[70] is charity. "Contemplation is itself a development and a perfection of pure charity."[71]

> *Theologia*, or pure contemplation, ("mystical theology" in the language of Pseudo-Denis) is a direct quasi-experiential contact with God beyond all thought, that is to say without the medium of passions. This excludes not only concepts tinged with passion, or sentimentality, or imagination, but even the simplest intellectual intuitions that require some sort of medium between God and the spirit. Theology in this sense is a direct contact with God. Now this supreme Christian contemplation, according to the Greek Fathers, is a quasi-experiential knowledge of God as He is in Himself, that is to say of God as Three Persons in One Nature: for this is the highest mystery in which He has revealed Himself to us. Entrance into this supreme mystery is not a matter of spiritual effort, of intellectual subtlety, still less of learning. It is a matter of identification by charity, for charity is the likeness of the soul to God.[72]

Towards the end of *The Climate of Monastic Prayer* Merton expressed his convictions in a pithy sentence: "The whole mystery of simple contemplative prayer is a mystery of divine love, of personal vocation and of free gift."[73]

c. Contemplation demands passivity of the subject

If contemplation is God's work, our task is to be still, to receive, to be passive under the divine activity. There are two ways in which this is experienced: in the first, one is conscious of what God is doing and how one is being carried along at a rate beyond one's own energies; in the second, one is aware rather of one's own incapacity to do anything. In many of his earlier writings Merton waxes poetic about this state of darkness, unknowing and undoing. Here he is more brutally frank: remaining faithful to the call to passive prayer is a demanding task.

> The "depths" of dereliction and bitterness that surround us when we are out of our natural sphere, do not lend themselves to accurate observation. At such times, reflection on ourselves too easily becomes morbid or hypochondriacal. Faith, patience and obedience are the guides which must help us advance quietly in darkness without looking at ourselves.
>
> As for the consolations of contemplative quietude: too intent a reflection on them quickly turns into a kind of narcissistic complacency and should be avoided. Even supposing that one is genuinely passive under the action of God (and some people are adept at imagining that they are when this is not the case), still reflection on ourselves would be just the kind of activity that would prove an obstacle to the action of grace.[74]

The test of the authenticity of contemplative inaction is that it is neither somnolence nor the experience of blank neutrality.[75] Perhaps "the word 'contemplation' is too pale, too vague and too inactive to convey the full spiritual strength of a genuinely religious experience of God."[76] This is no benign, boozy awareness but an overwhelmingly powerful and sharply focused encounter with spiritual reality that causes one's whole being to come alive. Although one's separate faculties are disengaged, each detached from its proper object, yet each becomes part of a responsive whole that is touched, animated and fulfilled in the experience. At one level there is passivity; at another supreme activity is taking place.

Contemplative passivity can be difficult to understand if one has not identified it in one's own experience. Merton is also aware of the prevalence of a neo-quietist trend in contemporary spirituality:[77]

> There is a temptation to a kind of pseudo-quietism which afflicts those who have read books about mysticism without quite understanding them. And this leads them to a deliberately negative spiritual life which is nothing but a cessation of prayer, for no other reason than that one imagines that by ceasing to be active one automatically enters into contemplation.[78]

> Would-be contemplatives must be on their guard against a kind of heavy, inert stupor in which the mind becomes swallowed up in itself. To remain immersed in one's own darkness is not contempla-

tion, and no one should attempt to "stop" the functioning of his mind and remain fixed on his own nothingness.[79]

The passivity of contemplation is, to a large extent, a passivity that is imposed—it is not generated by techniques. Perhaps it would be better termed "responsiveness." It is an effect of the action of God in the soul. It is born in the soul especially during those periods of transition in which one discovers that one has reached the limits of one's capacity to act.[80] These are the "obscure nights" about which St. John of the Cross speaks.

> At such a time, the interior senses and feelings dissociate themselves from our spiritual effort and hinder us instead of helping us. The conscious mind begins to realize its lack of full autonomy and the unconscious makes its hidden power felt in obscure disturbances. All this is necessary to detach us from an immature way of prayer and lead us to mature spiritual contemplation.
>
> During the "dark night" of the feelings and senses, anxiety is felt in prayer, often acutely. This is necessary because the spiritual night marks the transfer of full, free control of our inner life into the hands of a superior power.[81]

This already anticipates the final proposition.

d. Contemplation is marked by negativity

Merton outlines three areas in which contemplative prayer is accompanied by negative experience. First there is the pain of exposure to too much light. "The soul, impure and diseased, weakened by its own selfishness, is shocked and repelled by the very purity of God."[82] This is that initial shock which comes to the conventionally religious when confronted by the holy God: a sense of awe and of being undone—what is traditionally called "fear of the Lord" which is the beginning of wisdom. Secondly, there is the experience of "a terrible interior revolution,"[83] the obscure nights about which we have spoken above. Finally there is an area in which everyone suffers somewhat and Merton more than most, that of alienation from the external environment in which one lives.

Merton writes as though it were the institution (or "contemplative machine")[84] which is entirely at fault because it does not appreciate contemplative aspirations:

> The life of a contemplative is apt to be one of constant tension and conflict between what he feels to be the interior movements of grace

and the objective, exterior demands made upon him by the society to whose laws he is subject....

Even where the contemplative is not expressly forbidden to follow what he believes to be the inspiration of God (and this not rarely happens) he may feel himself completely at odds with the accepted ideals of those around him. Their spiritual exercises may seem to him to be a bore and a waste of time. Their sermons and conversations may leave him exhausted with a sense of futility, as if he had been pelted with words without meaning. Their choral offices, their excitement over liturgical ceremony and chant may rob him of the delicate taste of an interior manna that is not found in formulas of prayer and exterior rites.[85]

Most persons drawn to the interior life will experience a certain degree of alienation from the busy concerns of the community in which they live. Few will be as outraged by it as Merton was. There is a deep ambivalence here. On the one hand he insists that contemplation is not withdrawal into a private world,[86] on the other, it seems that he has ceased to dialogue with those about him. He has become defeatist:

Wherever there is conflict between the interior and the exterior, the exterior must always win. One must always, and above all, conform to the collective idea. Now it is true that this can be a very meritorious sacrifice, but it is equally true that short-sighted minds have turned the religious life, by this means, into a procrustean bed on which potential saints and contemplatives have been so pulled apart and crippled that they have ended their lives as freaks. And this is why, in so many contemplative monasteries, there are few or no contemplatives. That is why, very often, men of character and interior delicacy are repelled by the atmosphere of these monasteries, once they have spent a few months inside them, and leave in great discouragement, renouncing the interior life altogether.[87]

Merton dreams of a "small monastic community, where a superior with broad views and deep understanding of human problems can adjust the tempo of life for the best interests of all his monks,"[88] yet he seems not always to have been aware that at least some of his disenchantment came from his own false idealizations and projections, and that even in such a community he would probably have been equally angry. The solution he offers is mild compared with the intensity of his condemnations. "If one finds himself in a cramped or rigid institution, he [sic] should not give in to anguish and despair."[89] One should be humble, docile and obedient, etc. Perhaps he never arrived at a creative solution of his own conflicts with Gethsemani and has no basis on which to write for others.

Negativity is an essential concomitant of contemplation, although not all contemplatives will be so powerfully alienated from the community in which they live as Merton himself was. Contemplation is not a life sentence to negativity: this is only a subsidiary aspect of it. Quite the contrary is true: "Infused contemplation has a definitely positive element, dynamic, living, creative, transforming."[90] It temporarily dismantles only that which impedes the ultimate welfare of the person. "As our inner spiritual consciousness awakens, our exterior and worldly consciousness is befuddled and hampered in its action."[91]

Having thus described the contemplative experience Merton gives three "signs" by which one can know that one is moving into a deeper contemplative life.

> The first sign of infused prayer is then this inexplicable and un-daunted seeking, this quest that is not put off by aridity, or darkness, or frustration. On the contrary, in the deepest darkness it finds peace, and in suffering it does not lack joy. Pure faith and blind hope are enough. Pure knowledge is not necessary.... The mere fact of seeking Him blindly, undauntedly, in spite of dryness, in spite of the apparent hopelessness and irrationality of the quest, is then the first sign that this pre-experiential contemplation may be infused.
>
> Another sign would be the forgetfulness of ordinary cares and of the routine level of life, in the darkness of prayer. Though the contemplative seeking of God may seem in a way quite senseless, yet in the depths of our soul it makes a great deal of sense, while on the other hand the seemingly rational preoccupations and projects of normal life now appear to be quite meaningless.
>
> Finally, a third sign that pre-experiential contemplation may have an infused character is the very definite and powerful sense of attraction which holds the soul prisoner in mystery. Although the soul is filled with a sense of affliction and defeat, *it has no desire to escape from this aridity*.[92] Far from being attracted by legitimate pleasures and lights and relaxations of the natural order, it finds them repellent. All created goods make it restless. They cannot satisfy it. Even spiritual consolations have lost their appeal and become tedious. But at the same time there is a growing conviction that joy and peace and fulfillment are only to be found somewhere in this lonely night of aridity and faith.[93]

Merton does not much treat of the higher reaches of spiritual attainment. He is mostly concerned with the important transition into contemplation, which is a stage at which many persons are confused and sometimes misdirected.

> In the present work we are concerned almost entirely with the beginnings of infused contemplation and therefore we can concentrate on the night of the senses, which brings us into the illuminative way of contemplation. And the first thing to do is to realize and appreciate the fact that for all the suffering and bewilderment of this night, and all its apparent frustrations, it is a very great gift of God, a grace to which we should try to correspond with all the power of our hearts.[94]

This "correspondence" does not necessarily entail entering a contemplative monastery. After giving some indication about the shape which formation should take in such monasteries, firing off some familiar artillery, Merton turns his attention to lay people, particularly those who are married. The general lack of structures which would guide them towards a deeper prayer is not to be taken as a license for doing nothing.

> If you are waiting for someone to come along and feed you the contemplative life with a spoon, you are going to wait a long time, especially in America. You had better renounce your inertia, pray for a little imagination, ask the Lord to awaken your creative freedom, and consider some of the following possibilities.[95]

Merton then proposes five avenues of action for the lay person: moving out of the city into a rural environment, making use of the quiet times of the day, especially early in the morning, making Sunday a holy day in fact, committing oneself to a spiritual discipline, building spirituality on the foundation of married love.[96] They are suggestions. For most people they will prove difficult to put into practice in their entirety, but many will find aspects of them helpful—at least to reflect on.

The book was never finished, and so its status is difficult to assess. There are plenty of imperfections in it, but this makes it all the more interesting, closer to the man who wrote it. Even in its incompleteness it is a work of quality. Read in combination with *The Climate of Monastic Prayer*, it makes an original, provocative and pastorally useful contribution to contemporary literature on contemplation—even twenty years after.

NOTES

[1]Michael Mott, *The Seven Mountains of Thomas Merton*, Boston: Houghton Mifflin Co., 1984, pp. xxi-xxii. The same impression is gleaned from Paul Wilkes (ed.) *Merton: By Those who Knew him Best*, San Francisco: Harper and Row, 1984.

[2]A transcript of the program aired by the Australian Broadcasting Commission on 26 May 1987 is printed in *The Merton Seasonal of Bellarmine College* 12.4 (Autumn 1987), pp. 3-8.

[3]Merton himself was aware of the complaints and malicious rumors that his activities caused. "They demand that I remain forever the superficially pious, rather rigid and somewhat narrow-minded young monk I was twenty years ago...." *Raids on the Unspeakable*, New York: New Directions, 1966, p. 12. In this article, works without an author are Merton's.

[4]Amid all the speculations about whether Merton intended returning to his monastery, there are few references to an interesting letter written to John Howard Griffin two days before his death. "I have not found what I came to find. I have not found any place of hermitage that is any better than the hermitage I have, or had, at Gethsemani, which is after all places, a great place." John Howard Griffin, *Follow the Ecstasy: Thomas Merton, the Hermitage Years, 1965-1968*, Fort Worth: Latitudes Press, 1983, p. 206.

[5]There is a kind of parable in the history surrounding the photographs of St. Therese of Lisieux. For many decades only retouched images which seemed to accord with pious expectations were permitted. When, eventually, the saint's actual likeness was published, many were delighted by the plump, smiling face with its refreshing candor and evident humanity. It would seem that truthfulness has more power to attract and edify than fabricated images, tailored according to perceived demand.

[6]I do not excuse myself from this stricture.

[7]After blasting away merrily at institutional monasticism as the "procrustean bed on which potential saints and contemplatives have been so pulled apart and crippled that they have ended their lives as freaks," he blithely continues in the next paragraph: "He should not give in to anguish and despair. Nor should he waste time in futile acts of rebellion.... One must avoid eccentricity, self-will, and vain show.... Wherever there is a real conflict with obedience, he who gives in and obeys will never lose...." *Inner Experience*, p. 68. We note that this change of direction occurs in the space of a single page; even more radical shifts are discernible across the decades.

[8]From a methodological point of view I am uneasy about the practice of stringing together chains of quotes from different Merton epochs and presenting them either as synthesis or as sequential argument. There are changes in his use of words. As Mott notes, "When Merton speaks of solitude in the 1940s, he often means privacy. When he speaks of contemplation, he often means concentration" (*Seven Mountains*, p. 216). It seems to me that Merton was not one of those people who eternally grind out new applications and conclusions from a few

basic premises. He seems to have been constantly engaged in querying and qualifying even his most fundamental tenets. His thought was as turbulent as the events of his life . No matter how much he craved the calm haven of consistency, there was always the tendency to look further afield and to want to keep moving.

[9]Of course, this did not prevent the publishers bringing out new editions of them.

[10]I have written about some aspects of this in "Thomas Merton Within a Tradition of Prayer," in *Cistercian Studies* 13 (1978), pp. 372-378 and 14 (1979), pp. 81-92.

[11]Although Merton nowhere wrote about the theory of relics, it was found when his personal effects were returned to Gethsemani that he had taken a selection of his favorites on his tour of the East.

[12]Merton made provision that the notes would not be published as a book. See Robert E. Daggy (ed.), *The Road to Joy: Letters to New and Old Friends*, New York: Farrar, Strauss, Giroux, 1989, p. 301. The greater part of the text, edited by Patrick Hart, was printed as a series of eight articles in *Cistercian Studies* 18 (1983), pp. 3-15, 121-134, 201-216, 289-300; 19 (1984), pp. 62-78, 139-150, 267-282, 336-345. Since none of the page numbers overlap, reference will be made simply to the page. The reader will need to bear in mind that the blocks are not sequentially numbered.

[13]The fact that the text was never to be published immobilizes it eternally in the act of becoming. The reader is a privileged voyeur, permitted to glimpse what goes on behind the scenes. At the same time, one is not permitted to criticize what one witnesses, because the product is unfinished. The embargo on publishing proved to be a remarkably effective marketing device.

[14]One sees the same dynamic in Sibelius' ambition to write the perfect symphony.

[15]*The Climate of Monastic Prayer*, Cistercian Studies Series 1, Spencer: Cistercian Publications, 1969. This volume was republished under the title *Contemplative Prayer*.

[16]*Inner Experience*, p. 341.

[17]*Inner Experience*, p. 122.

[18]*Inner Experience*, p. 132.

[19]See especially *Inner Experience*, pp. 276-282.

[20]See Dennis Q. McInirney, *Thomas Merton: The Man and His Work*, Cistercian Studies Series 27, Washington: Cistercian Publications, 1974, p. 30: "A third important theme in Merton's poetry is anti-modernism. This is the most comprehensive term I could think of to embrace the other 'antis' which his poetry reflects: anti-urbanism, anti-technology and anti-Americanism. All of these are interconnected and often overlap. The most characteristic aspect of the modern age, its identifying soul, was technology, which he abhorred because of its dehumanizing attributes. The city was the focal point for technology and hence to be avoided...the central system for all which was evil in modern society." For all that Merton seems not to have been adverse to a day on the town!

[21]*Inner Experience*, pp. 271-272.

[22]*Inner Experience*, pp. 304-305. See *The Asian Journal of Thomas Merton*, New York: New Directions, 1971, p. 313. Merton would surely have appreciated *Mystical Union and Monotheistic Faith: An Ecumenical Dialogue*, (Moshe Idel and Bernard McGinn, eds.), New York: Macmillan Publishing Co., 1989.

[23]*Inner Experience*, p. 133.

[24]See Robert Imperato, *Merton & Walsh on the Person*, Lake Worth, FL: Sunday Publications, 1988. This is a reprint of the author's 1984 thesis on the subject. A brief note by him appears in *The Merton Seasonal of Bellarmine College*, 13.1 (Winter 1988), under the title "Thomas Merton and Daniel Clark Walsh," pp. 2-5.

[25]Merton sometimes uses the terms loosely, but it is clear that not only is he aware of the distinction, it is an important element in his own synthesis. Thus he writes in *New Seeds of Contemplation*, London: Burns and Oates, 1962, p. 37: "The man who lives in division is not a person, but only an 'individual.' "

[26]In *The Person and the Common Good*, London: Geoffrey Bles, 1958, pp. 31-32. The whole essay (pp. 13-33) may profitably be read. See also Jean Leclercq, "Maritain and Merton: The Coincidence of Opposites," in *Cistercian Studies* 19 (1984), pp. 362-370.

[27]Mott, *Seven Mountains*, p. 115.

[28]*Inner Experience*, p. 3.

[29]*New Seeds of Contemplation*, pp. 27-28.

[30]See *Inner Experience*, p. 126: "I mean to make clear the fact that those recesses of the unconscious in which the neurotic and psychotic derangements have their center, belong in reality to man's exterior self; because the exterior self is not limited to consciousness."

[31]*The New Man*, London: Burns and Oates, 1962, p. 30.

[32]*Inner Experience*, p. 7.

[33]*Inner Experience*, p. 9.

[34]*Inner Experience*, p. 15.

[35]*Inner Experience*, p. 125.

[36]*Inner Experience*, p. 126.

[37]Foreword to William Johnston's *The Mysticism of the Cloud of Unknowing*, New York: Desclée Company, 1967, p. xiii.

[38]*Inner Experience*, p. 129.

[39]*Inner Experience*, p. 127.

[40]*Inner Experience*, p. 212.

[41]*Inner Experience*, p. 207.

[42]*Inner Experience*, p. 203.

[43]*Inner Experience*, p. 215.

[44]*Inner Experience*, p. 134.

[45]*The Climate of Monastic Prayer*, pp. 36-37.

[46]*The New Man*, pp. 15-16.

[47]It follows that where spiritual freedom is spasmodic, contemplation will come and go; it becomes somewhat habitual only when a substantial level of spiritual freedom characterizes the whole of life.

[48]*Inner Experience*, p. 216.

[49]*Inner Experience*, pp. 289-297. See *The Climate of Monastic Prayer*, p. 40: "It is understood that the personal prayer of the monk is embedded in a life of psalmody, liturgical celebration and the meditative reading of scripture (*lectio divina*). All this has both a personal and communal dimension."

[50]*Inner Experience*, p. 146: "Let anyone desire it, provided only he is sincere and prudent and remains open to the truth."

[51]*Inner Experience*, pp. 147-149: "The first step toward spiritual liberation is not so much the awareness of what lies at the end of the road—the experience of God—as a clear view of the great obstacle that blocks its very beginning. That obstacle is called sin.... To have a sense of sin is to realize myself to be not only morally but spiritually dead.... Part of the mission of the contemplative is to keep alive in the world the sense of sin."

[52]*Inner Experience*, p. 142.

[53]Merton affirms this repeatedly. Sometimes, however, he seems to forget it. In his section on "Preparation for the Contemplative Life" (*Inner Experience*, pp. 273-276), a reader may infer that following the author's recommendations will automatically make monasticism more effective in producing contemplatives. Likewise, although he is quite dogmatic in stating that contemplation is incompatible with urban living (p. 279), he retains his enthusiasm for the urban-living Little Brothers of Jesus (pp. 336-337). It is important to be clear: if contemplation is gratuitous, strict conditions do not apply.

[54]*Inner Experience*, p. 146.

[55]*Inner Experience*, p. 142.

[56]*Inner Experience*, p. 141.

[57]*Inner Experience*, p. 144.

[58]*Inner Experience*, p. 340.

[59]*Inner Experience*, pp. 63-68.

[60]He quotes from John of the Cross, Jan Ruysbroeck, *The Cloud of Unknowing*, Meister Eckhart and Bernard of Clairvaux: *Inner Experience*, pp. 68-72.

[61]*Inner Experience*, p. 63.

[62]*The Climate of Monastic Prayer*, p. 48.

[63]*Inner Experience*, p. 63.

[64]*Inner Experience*, p. 63.

[65]*Inner Experience*, p. 64.

[66]*The Climate of Monastic Prayer*, p. 125.

[67]Merton deliberately excluded himself from the debate which had raged in the preceding decades about the nature of contemplation and the conditions for eligibility; *Inner Experience*, p. 297.

[68]*Inner Experience*, p. 293.

[69]*Inner Experience*, p. 294.

[70]*Inner Experience*, p. 297.

[71]*Inner Experience*, p. 64.

[72]*Inner Experience*, p. 298.

[73]*The Climate of Monastic Prayer*, p. 127.

[74]*Inner Experience*, pp. 64-65.

[75]Merton writes trenchantly of the television addict as demonstrating such bogus passivity, *Inner Experience*, pp. 269-270: "The life of the television-watcher is a kind of caricature of contemplation. Passivity, uncritical absorption, receptivity, inertia. Not only that, but a gradual, progressive yielding to the mystic attraction until one is spellbound in a state of complete union. The trouble with this caricature is that it is really the exact opposite of contemplation: for true contemplation is precisely the fruit of a most active and intransigent rupture with all that captivates the senses, the emotions, and the will on a material or temporal level. The contemplative reaches his passivity only after terrific struggle with everything that appeals to his appetites as a half-animal member of the human herd. He is receptive and still only because the stillness he has reached is lucid, spiritual and full of liberty. It is the summit of a life of spiritual freedom. The other, the ersatz, is the nadir of intellectual and emotional slavery."

[76]*Inner Experience*, p. 292.

[77]The section on quietism has been omitted from the text published in *Cistercian Studies* on the grounds that it already appears in *What is Contemplation?*, Springfield, IL: Templegate Publications, 1981, pp. 68-73. Another contemporary aberration mentioned by Merton from time to time in *Inner Experience* is illuminism: "Taking one's subjective experience so seriously that it becomes more important than truth, more important than God" (p. 139).

[78]He continues: "Actually this leads one into a mere void without any interior, spiritual life, in which distractions and emotional drives gradually assert themselves at the expense of all mature, balanced activity of the mind and heart. To persist in this blank state could be very harmful spiritually, morally and mentally." *The Climate of Monastic Prayer*, p. 124.

[79]*Inner Experience*, p. 296.

[80]"The urgency of the problem comes from the fact that when we begin to be frequently absorbed in the passivity of pre-experiential contemplation...we feel that we are losing our ability to meditate and pray." *Inner Experience*, p. 76.

[81]*The Climate of Monastic Prayer*, pp. 105-106.

[82]*Inner Experience*, p. 65.

[83]*Ibid.*

[84]*Inner Experience*, p. 274.

[85]*Inner Experience*, pp. 66-67.

[86]*Inner Experience*, p. 340: "Contemplation must not be confused with abstraction. A contemplative life is not to be lived by permanent withdrawal within one's own mind. The diminished and limited existence of a small, isolated, specialized group is not enough for 'contemplation.' The true contemplative is not less interested in others in normal life, not less concerned with what goes on in the world, but more interested, more concerned. The fact that he is a contemplative makes him capable of a greater interest and a deeper concern."

[87]*Inner Experience*, p. 68.

[88]*Inner Experience*, p. 275. As I read these words, and others like them, I ask myself whether Merton did not secretly feel frustrated at not being in a leader-

ship position in the monastery. He had been disappointed that he was not considered a likely candidate for a Superior of a proposed foundation, in Ohio, but when Dom James Fox hinted that in the future he might be considered, he became alarmed saying that there was a serious reason debarring him. He then made a private vow on October 8, 1952: "As long as I live, I will never accept any election to the office of Abbot or Titular Prior either in this monastery or any other monastery of the Cistercian Order." Mott, *Seven Mountains*, p. 283. Previously Merton had been shocked to find that his past constituted a "legal impediment" to his entering the Franciscans (Mott, *Seven Mountains*, pp. 155-156). If he had thought that the sins of his youth excluded him from becoming abbot and acted accordingly, it is natural that later he would become resentful of the effects of the vow. Such a feeling would, no doubt, color his whole attitude to abbots and to authority, especially in moments of reduced realism when he inwardly felt qualified to assume the governance of a community. Excluded by his own hand from the direct exercise of political power, it is not surprising that he appeared cynical and sarcastic about authority and those who enjoyed it.

[89] *Inner Experience*, p. 68.

[90] *Inner Experience*, p. 72.

[91] *Inner Experience*, p. 75.

[92] Cf. *The Climate of Monastic Prayer*, p. 121: "Contemplative prayer is, in a way, simply the preference for the desert, for emptiness, for poverty. One has begun to know the meaning of contemplation when he [sic] intuitively and spontaneously seeks the dark and unknown path of aridity in preference to every other way. The contemplative is one who would rather not know than know. Rather not enjoy than enjoy. Rather not have *proof* that God loves him."

[93] *Inner Experience*, pp. 73-74.

[94] *Inner Experience*, p. 78.

[95] *Inner Experience*, p. 278.

[96] *Inner Experience*, pp. 279-282.